Doing Your
Education
Research Project

Doing Your Education Research Project

Neil Burton, Mark Brundrett and **Marion Jones**

Second Edition

Los Angeles | London | New Delhi
Singapore | Washington DC

Los Angeles | London | New Delhi
Singapore | Washington DC

SAGE Publications Ltd
1 Oliver's Yard
55 City Road
London EC1Y 1SP

SAGE Publications Inc.
2455 Teller Road
Thousand Oaks, California 91320

SAGE Publications India Pvt Ltd
B 1/I 1 Mohan Cooperative Industrial Area
Mathura Road
New Delhi 110 044

SAGE Publications Asia-Pacific Pte Ltd
3 Church Street
#10-04 Samsung Hub
Singapore 049483

Editor: Marianne Lagrange
Assistant editor: Kathryn Bromwich
Production editor: Nicola Marshall
Copyeditor: Peter Williams
Proofreader: Caroline Stock
Indexer: Judith Menes
Marketing manager: Catherine Slinn
Cover design: Naomi Robinson
Typeset by: C&M Digitals (P) Ltd, Chennai, India
Printed in India at Replika Press Pvt Ltd.

© Neil Burton, Mark Brundrett and Marion Jones, 2014

The first edition was published in 2008, reprinted in 2008, 200
and 2011.

Library of Congress Control Number: 2013947842

British Library Cataloguing in Publication data

A catalogue record for this book is available from
the British Library

ISBN 978-1-4462-6676-2
ISBN 978-1-4462-6677-9 (pbk)

CONTENTS

LIST OF FIGURES AND TABLES

Figures

Tables

LIST OF ABBREVIATIONS

AfL	assessment for learning
BERA	British Educational Research Association
CAQDAS	computer-assisted/aided qualitative data analysis software
CPD	continuing professional development
CRB	Criminal Records Bureau
DENI	Department of Education Northern Ireland
DfE	Department for Education
DfEE	Department for Education and Employment
DfES	Department for Education and Skills
ECM	Every Child Matters
EPPI	Evidence for Policy and Practice Information
G&T	gifted and talented
GCSE	General Certificate of Secondary Education
GNVQ	General National Vocational Qualification
GTC	General Teaching Council (for England)
HEA	higher education academy
HEI	higher education institution
HTDF	History Teachers Discussion Forum

ITE	initial teacher education
ITT	initial teacher training
IWB	interactive whiteboard
KS	Key Stage
LA	local authority
LEA	local education authority
LftM	Leading from the Middle
Niace	National Institute of Adult Continuing Education
NPQH	National Professional Qualification for Headship
NQT	newly qualified teacher
Ofsted	Office for Standards in Education, Children's Services and Skills
PAR	participatory action research
PGCE	Postgraduate Certificate of Education
PPD	postgraduate professional development
QDAS	Qualitative Data Analysis Software
QTS	qualified teacher status
SEF	self-evaluation forms
SIP	school improvement plan; school improvement partner
SMART	specific, measurable, achievable, realistic, timescale
TA	teaching assistant
TDA	Training and Development Agency (for schools); Teacher Development Agency (England)
TLA	Teacher Learning Academy
TS	teaching school

ABOUT THE AUTHORS

Neil Burton is the Partnership Manager and an Associate Tutor of education masters courses with the University of Leicester, having worked in teacher education for several universities for the past 20 years. He is a member of the editorial board of *Education 3–13* and is a recent past Chair of the Association for the Study of Primary Education. In addition to working with several school-based initial teacher training providers, he also teaches children (6–18 years old) in schools on a regular basis for the joy of it.

Mark Brundrett taught in secondary, middle and primary schools and was a head teacher for five years before he entered higher education. He has subsequently held posts as Senior Lecturer in Education at Leicester University, Professor of Educational Leadership at the University of Hull and Senior Research Consultant at the University of Manchester. He is currently Professor of Educational Research and Head of the Centre for Research and Evaluation at Liverpool John Moores University. He has written over one hundred published items and edits the journal *Education 3–13*.

Marion Jones is Professor of Teacher Education at Liverpool John Moores University. Her area of investigation is related to the professional training and development of the educational workforce. She has extensive experience in leading projects which have involved teams comprising a diverse range of education professionals. She has disseminated her findings on mentoring and teachers' continuing professional development at national and international conferences and has published widely in academic journals.

SECTION 1

THINK BEFORE YOU DO – PLANNING

Effective, meaningful, manageable, achievable, useful research doesn't just happen. It is the result of the careful consideration of the context which you are working in – *and with* – linked to your own inspirations and aspirations. In addition to the careful identification and clarification of your research focus, your success will be based upon your reading around the subject to select from existing ideas and findings in order to be able to confidently determine what should be asked, of whom and how the evidence might be collected. If you allow yourself to stand back from the process, it should be possible to perceive parallels between planning for research and planning for teaching.

This section of the book explores the initial research planning processes, taking you from the identification of the initial ideas through to the point where your have clarified the purpose of your research and have assimilated the lessons from existing theories and findings from published research.

CHAPTER 1

THE PLACE OF RESEARCH WITHIN THE CLASSROOM AND SCHOOL

By the conclusion of this chapter it is anticipated that you will have considered and be able to:

- understand the role of research to inform and improve practice;
- understand the importance of exploring potential options before acting and evaluating the impact of initiatives;
- appreciate the value of educational research to the school/college practitioner.

This chapter provides an examination of the need, for those working in schools and colleges, to develop and utilise research skills for their own personal professional development and organisational improvement. While this chapter will not tell you *what to do* or *how to do it* (later chapters will do that), it will provide you with an appreciation, hopefully an understanding, of *why*. Developing an understanding of why you are doing something (indeed why there is a need for you to do something) will allow you to gain much more from the activity and give you much more control and understanding over the decisions that you will face with regard to how you will carry out your research.

By engaging with new ideas and research findings to develop new practices and evaluate curriculum change, educational practitioners (such as yourself) will be better placed to formalise and enhance personal and organisational reflective practice. Excellent teachers improve their effectiveness, that is how well the learners are learning, by asking the right questions and reflecting on the responses, in light of what they have previously experienced and read, before deciding upon a specific course of action. In many learning environments (classrooms) you may only have a fraction of a second to cycle through these processes. In order to become 'effective', in this sense, it is appropriate to deconstruct these processes, slow them down so that the different elements can be appreciated and valued and practised. In order to be able to scale down to the micro-decisions made constantly during a working day, it is appropriate to examine the processes on a much grander scale, to ask 'bigger' questions and formally gather evidence to analyse in order to draw robust conclusions – and make the 'right' decisions.

There is an increasing number of pressures on those working in the education profession (and those in training to join!) to become more 'research active' in order to inform and develop their own practice. Teaching schools (TSs), as one of their key responsibilities (DfE, 2012) are required to lead 'research and development' within the profession. Consequently it must be seen as highly desirable that new entrants to the profession begin their careers with the skills and abilities to be capable and confident of using research skills to improve their own performance and also be able, with experience, to add to the body of knowledge within their profession.

The move toward a 'masters-level' profession

It would be reasonable to suggest that in England from the perspective of early 2013 the qualifications expected of those entering the teaching profession are a little 'confused'. In the state-funded sector, pre-service qualifications are increasingly being delivered and assessed at postgraduate (that is to say masters) level, with post-degree level qualifications for entry to the teaching profession changing to accommodate this. However, certain sections of the state-funded provision, specifically 'free schools' and, potentially, academies, are allowed to employ as teachers individuals who have not demonstrated that they have met the professional standards required as a prerequisite for employment in local authority (LA) maintained schools.

In the early years of the twenty-first century, the bodies in England responsible for funding and supporting the quality of continuing professional development (CPD) provision for teachers, the Training and Development Agency *for schools* (TDA) and the General Teaching Council *for England* (GTC), both led the profession towards masters level in service professional development. The TDA, through its subsidisation of masters-level study as part of the PPD (postgraduate professional development) initiative, attempted to ensure that school teachers develop the skills to enable them to become more rigorous in the way that they perceive, reflect upon and analyse the impact of educational initiatives that they are involved in. Although significant funding was made available (TDA, 2007) and tangible professional and financial benefits were shown to accrue to participants, the uptake was relatively small. The GTC approach, through the Teacher Learning Academy (TLA) took a rather more direct approach. In order to progress up the pay spine teachers had to demonstrate their impact within (and beyond!) their school. Level 3 within the TLA criteria (Lord et al., 2009) equated to masters-level study in which teachers were expected to apply appropriately rigorous approaches to gathering and analysing evidence of their 'impact'. Within current proposals (Coates, 2011) the ability to self-critique and robustly analyse learning and the learning environment are implicit within the expectations for 'Master Teacher Standard'.

The National College has well a established professional qualification for school leaders, NPQH (National Professional Qualification for Headship), which has now reached such blanket coverage for prospective school leaders that additional qualifications (such as educational masters) are required to enable employers to distinguish more effectively between the candidates. The qualification for departmental or subject leaders, Leading from the Middle (LftM), has also reached a point where holders of the award are expected to convert it into 'academic currency' through gaining accreditation within a masters qualification. Pay and professional progression are increasingly being employed to encourage teachers to develop additional reflective and analytical skills. Within the maintained sector, teaching is increasingly moving away from being a graduate profession to becoming a *masters* profession.

With the loss of funding due to the economic turndown and change of government policy since 2010, coupled with the political drive to transfer the responsibility for initial and continuing training and development of the teaching profession from higher education to schools there is a change in the underlying nature of the provision available.

In higher education institutions (HEIs) the role of research activity is complicated by the academic expectations of the sector. While it is acknowledged, as Hattie and Marsh suggest:

> *Universities need to set as a mission goal the improvement of the nexus between research and teaching . . . The aim is to increase the circumstances in which teaching and research have occasion to meet.* (1996: 533)

The precise nature and focus of this research is less clear. Academics are expected to possess subject expertise within a field of study and to develop this expertise through further study and research, in doing so extending the boundaries of the field and enhancing knowledge within the subject. This 'new' knowledge will then be used to inform the content of their teaching. However, to be an effective teacher of their subject they also need to be aware of, and be able to develop further, the effectiveness of their knowledge/skills transfer to their students. University academics are expected to both be effective researchers within their subject and effective teachers of their subject. Until the establishment of the Institute for Learning and Teaching in Higher Education the focus for training in higher education was strongly biased towards the research requirements. Currently the Higher Education Academy (HEA) offers accreditation for courses (HEA, 2012) which support the development of the student learning experience – a pedagogic rather than subject focus. This distinction is crucial when focusing upon the precise nature of research which underpins personal professional development as a teacher (in any phase of education).

Outstanding schools (as defined by Ofsted inspection outcomes), since 2012 have had the option to apply to become 'teaching schools', either individually or in clusters, to support and develop the quality of the profession through the provision of Initial Teacher Training (ITT) and CPD courses, coaching and consultancy. While many TSs have long established links with HEIs for both provision of professional training and research activity, others are still in various stages of development. Through the National College there are some opportunities for sharing practice and research activity within TSs, but other professional routes for dissemination, such as subject associations, also need to be acknowledged.

Towards research informed practice

Over the past few decades 'research evidence' has increasingly been used by policy-makers, nationally and locally, to encourage particular ways of working within education. The educational agenda, from the nature and construction of the curriculum through approaches to pedagogy to the training and deployment of professionals working in education, is justified and driven by 'best practice' as defined by local, national and international research. Systematic inquiry is designed to unveil the 'best' ways of achieving desired outcomes. Research methodology (as opposed to the approach) focuses upon the identification of sources of evidence and how such evidence might be gathered and is explored in detail in Section 2 of this book, where issues of *qualitative* and *quantitative* evidence will also be addressed.

The literature on forms of education research is rich in terminology (jargon) which attempts to explain the perspective from which the research is performed (*paradigms* – the research model). In an attempt to obtain clarity and establish lines of demarcation, approaches which would otherwise be seen as complementary are treated almost as incompatible. *Positivism*, which takes an objective perspective of evidence, focusing on the measurement of outcomes in order to predict and identify patterns (Cohen et al., 2007), is made distinct from *interpretive* approaches, which concentrate on the interpretation of evidence and bringing meaning. On the whole, research evidence only becomes 'useful' (to individual schools, departments or teachers) when findings are explained, interpreted and contextualised. At a 'research-aware' level, this interpretation may be overlaid by the political perspectives of the researcher and the way that they view society and social interaction (e.g. feminist and Marxist research). This 'political perspective' often provides a guide as to how the researcher views and constructs 'knowledge' and is referred to as the *epistemology.*

This book is firmly constructed to meet the needs of the educational professional who is employing research processes and skills as a basis for 'improvement', rather than for researchers working in the field of education. For this reason it is at this early stage three basic models of research activity will be presented and 'visualised' as a means of providing 'anchors' by which you can make connections between the research activity you need to perform and the research processes which will be revealed and explored within this book.

The first is about taking a 'snapshot' of reality. In practical terms this could be the act of constructing a case study of an individual child's (or teacher's or class's or school's) needs; examining the range of options available prior to making an intervention; and reviewing the current state of resource availability or perceptions of a particular issue – the key element being that it is focused on a particular point or period in time. Generally the evidence is gathered and analysed in preparation for a decision upon a course of action to take. Visually it might be useful to present it as shown in Figure 1.1.

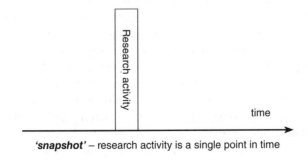

'*snapshot*' – research activity is a single point in time

Figure 1.1   Snapshot

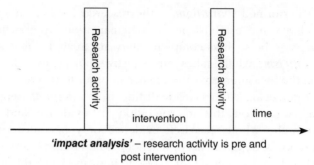

'*impact analysis*' – research activity is pre and
post intervention

Figure 1.2   Single-cycle research

Alternatively, the research activity could be used to evaluate or judge the
effectiveness of an intervention – an *impact analysis*: where evidence is
gathered pre- and post-intervention in order to consider the effect (impact)
that the intervention has had. Clearly such a research activity takes place
over time, but the timescale may vary considerably from intervention to
intervention. It may be as short as part of a lesson or as long as a year or
beyond. This model is designed around the need to establish how effective
a particular resource, pedagogic approach, policy, strategy, etc. has been as
applied to an individual situation, child, group/class/cohort of children or
teachers/classroom staff or even whole school (for example in attempting
to evaluate the effect of a new whole-school behaviour management
policy). It can be pictured as in Figure 1.2.

The final model to keep in mind is a multi-cycle approach where the
research and the intervention almost constantly inform one another. Here
the researcher will be working with a particular outcome in mind using the
analysis of the evidence being gathered to inform and flex the intervention
towards achieving the goal. For example, the outcome might be for a group
of children to learn a particular skill. If the 'impact analysis' model were to
be used, a strategy would be chosen and followed through – the focus
being on the intervention rather than the outcome (which is just the means
of measuring the effectiveness of the intervention). Using the 'multi-cycle'
model, each cycle is designed to get progressively closer to the desired
outcome, which is achieved through changes to the intervention informed
by the research process – the focus is the outcome, the intervention(s) is
the means of achieving it. This is more difficult to present visually – it could
be seen as the research activity and intervention being entwined or an
open-ended ongoing process (although it should be noted that the number
of cycles might be fixed – but not four) determined purely in terms of
achievement of the 'goals'.

Although this final model, action research, will be explored in full detail
in Chapter 10, it is worth pausing over it at this point so that its similarities
to and differences from the 'normal teaching processes' can be considered.

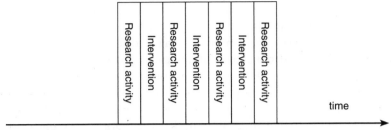

'*multi-cycle*' – research activity continuously informs and shapes the intervention towards a (usually) pre-determined goal or outcome

Figure 1.3　Multi-cycle research

It is all too easy for the experienced teacher to perceive action research with an unwarranted over-familiarity due to misplaced connections made to reflective practice.

Reflective practice, which can lead into an action research approach, may be described as *phenomenological*, in that it values the importance of the study of phenomena through direct experience, which is then interpreted and used as the basis for future understanding or modified actions. Smyth (1989) succinctly presents it as a four-stage model:

1. *Description* – an evidenced commentary of the current situation
2. *Information* – interpreting the evidence for meaning
3. *Confrontation* – explaining the evidence and the progression to this point
4. *Reconstruction* – suggesting possible ways of progressing from this point

For the teacher, there are clear parallels between this model and the reflective teacher model inherent in current school-based education. As a paradigm, it is worthy of further consideration. It does not preclude the adoption of positivist or interpretive approaches – indeed it is enriched by the inclusion, and it also offers some degree of connectivity to approaches which teachers have some familiarity with.

If we accept that research *does* inform practice in the field of education, a focus on the technologies underpinning effective learning and teaching might lead to the reasonable assumption that there will be an emphasis on action research, the implication being that research will inform practice through an iterative process based upon a developing synthesis of theory and practice. In the longer term this may well be an appropriate position to take, but it does imply that all research activity concerning change or improvement must be dynamic in nature and implementation. As teachers we can appreciate that assessment can be for different purposes, but the same is equally valid of research. Assessment *for* learning (formative, diagnostic) can immediately be seen as being part of a continuous process whereas assessment *of* learning (summative) relates to a specific point within the learning process (and not necessarily an end point). Equally, it would be entirely valid to perform a research activity at any given point within a 'learning' or 'development cycle' in order to, perhaps, determine the most appropriate course of action from a range of alternatives or to evaluate the impact of an initiative against an appropriate set of success criteria. In each case the research activity is being used at some level to inform a potential future course of action.

From teacher to researcher

While teacher qualification relies upon meeting government determined professional standards, Taber's (2007) 'weak' model of the teaching profession, research proficiency provides it with depth, robustness and a sense of potential future progress. To support this, research should be viewed very much as a process-driven activity. While the outcomes of individual research studies are important and can have a significant impact on future actions, the process provides a tool that can become an essential element of a teacher's long-term development aspirations. It is perhaps helpful to consider a very simplistic comparison of the teaching and researching processes (Table 1.1). When contemplating a change it is always worth identifying the similarities and differences between what you are already doing and what you need to be doing – a concept which lies at the heart of formative assessment (assessment for learning – AFL).

Because 'research' is a very diverse collection of approaches and frameworks, it is important to offer a restricted perspective of the nature of research to achieve some level of 'manageability', particularly with the novice researcher in mind.

While the model in Table 1.1 does not provide exact parallels between the teaching and research processes, there is sufficient connectivity to see it as a starting point for development. Equally, it must be acknowledged that there is not an exact link to Smyth, as Smyth's model relates to a specific point in an otherwise dynamic process – the reflective interlude between periods of activity. Indeed, the teaching column is open to question in that it suggests a single learning cycle, but perhaps this is realistic if it is assumed that a 'lesson' is made up of a series of learning cycles, some focusing on individuals, some on groups and others on the class as a whole, which is perhaps more representative of the complexities of a lesson format.

Phase 1 holds the key to success: if the lesson (or the research) is ill-founded, the remainder of the process will either be inefficient or flawed. The social constructivist view of teaching holds that we first establish the existing understanding and skills levels of the learners before constructing

Table 1.1   A simplistic comparison of the teaching and researching processes

Phase	Teaching	Researching
1	Pre-assess the children to ensure that the 'starting point' for learning is revealed and review the National Curriculum documents to clarify expected learning. Establish learning objectives.	Perform a contextual analysis to clarify the issues that the study will focus on and review any relevant national documentation to reveal the wider background and influential factors. Establish key research questions. *What am I trying to find out?*
2	Read subject material (schemes, subject association journals, ...) to collect ideas on how the concepts and skills might be taught and the possible approaches to teaching and learning.	Read the literature on relevant theories to establish a wider conceptual perspective for the study and published empirical research to review potential outcomes and possible methodologies. *What do I already know?*
3	Use contextual knowledge of the group to be taught along with reading of pedagogic texts to establish and clarify the teaching and learning strategies to be employed to meet the learning objectives. Construct the means of assessing learning and record the assessment outcomes.	Use knowledge of the context and research population along with reading from the research methodology literature to establish and clarify the research methodologies to be employed to gather evidence to address the research questions. Construct the research tools. *How can I find out what I need to know?*
4	Evaluate the outcomes of the learning against the expectations of the learning objectives and evaluate the pedagogic qualities of the teaching.	Analyse the outcomes of the research against the key research questions using the theoretical/empirical expectations from the literature. *What have I found out and what does it mean?*
5	Draw conclusions as to the learning that has taken place and the effectiveness of the teaching. Make recommendations for future teaching and learning.	Draw conclusions from the analysis of the research findings. Make recommendations for future action. *So what and what should I do about it?*

the learning opportunity. If the learning is based upon the teacher's assumptions of the learners there is likely to be a degree of mismatch, but as time and resources are clearly a factor in this equation, there needs to be an appropriate balance between assumption and assessment. Similarly, while the research needs to establish a clear focus for the research effort it should not attempt to pre-empt the research outcomes. In both cases, reading around the likely issues will enable the teacher/researcher to identify the key factors that need to be addressed – either in terms of the learning or research – so that clear learning or research objectives can be established.

While the wider reading indicated in phase 2 may frequently be sidelined by the experienced teacher, it should be regarded as an essential requirement for both the novice teacher and the novice researcher. For the novice the learning inherent in the process is just as important, in the long term, as any outcomes that may arise.

The third phase focuses on the question 'how will I gather evidence?' – the teacher's question of 'how will I know what they have learnt?' which translates as 'how will I know that I've answered my research questions?' for the researcher. In both cases, phase 4 represents a matching of expectations against outcomes using the evidence that is available and the final phase uses this as a basis for future action.

Although it is helpful and possibly reassuring to realise that there are similarities in the process which allow for the possibility of a more successful transfer of skills from one context to the other, it is also important to recognise the differences. It would be all too easy for the experienced educator to fall into the trap of treating research activity with the contempt of perceived familiarity. Because all teachers are individualist in their approaches to teaching and learning (no two lessons, however close the planning, will ever be taught identically) these differences need to be acknowledged and highlighted within the learning processes.

Individualised learning

While learning frequently takes place within a group experience (a class) for reasons of economic as well as educational efficiency, this form of collaboration, in addition to the motivational impact, also provides important opportunities to share, trial, test and demonstrate individual learning. It is important to note that this shared learning experience does not need to mean a shared content – indeed there is often more to be learnt from the experience when the group does have slightly different learning needs and interests.

A strength of personal professional development, as an issues-driven research focus, is that it allows for (if not encourages) a collaborative approach to discussing and sharing understanding of the underlying factors. If, for example, 'poor classroom behaviour' is perceived as being a generic issue for the organisation or the group of teachers who are working together which needs to be addressed, the views of teachers should be aired to consider the extent and possible factors impacting on the unwanted behaviour. It then allows different teachers to explore the possible impact of these various factors and contribute to a more informed debate with a view to approaching this through more detailed and differentiated (by context or precise focus) research. As the research activity should be based upon individual and contextual needs, duplication of effort can be avoided with the potential to learn from each other. Even in cases where the conceptual focus (for example, the use of the same behaviour strategy) is the same, the uniqueness of each learning situation (age of class, learning environment or subject area) will individualise the learning experience.

Even without a clear 'personal need', organisational and departmental development plans offer opportunities to identify issues which can used to stimulate both personal and organisational growth. It is also worth noting that this also offers a wider audience from which to receive feedback and

support. It is always worth mapping personal development plans and aspirations against the needs of the organisation in order to find areas of joint
interest and compatibility which should lead to greater opportunity and
access to valuable resources (such as time!).

Base-lining and evaluating impact

Education, due in no small part to the wealth of research evidence driving
developments, is rich in new initiatives. All too frequently the 'new' simply
overlays existing structures, systems and approaches with only passing
regard to the overall compatibility and coherence to those impacted upon.
The adoption of new ideas is most effective when a clear 'starting point' is
identified to allow a more harmonious coexistence of the current with the
new – a meshing rather than a grating. To be confident about accurately
identifying the current disposition of the situation (a classroom, subject,
department, school, …), self-evaluation is an essential first step. If you have
a destination in mind (the 'new initiative') the journey will be much more
successful if you have a clear idea of where you are starting from (again,
the parallels with the learning/teaching process should be immediately
apparent).

Most incidences of 'change' in educational settings have three distinct
opportunities for research activity:

- Where are we? (static base-line assessment – *snapshot*)
- Are we getting there? (dynamic tracking against clear success criteria –
  multi-cycle)
- Are we there yet? (dynamic – completion of tracking or static re-
  establishing of a 'set' position – *impact analysis*)

For a number of years, schools in England have been driven by school
improvement plans (SIPs) policed by centralised inspection regimes
(Ofsted) which call on schools to clarify their strengths, weaknesses and
goals through self-evaluation forms (SEFs), which are then checked through
direct observation. Increasingly the process is driven by a greater reliance
on evidence generated within the school with comparisons to wider colla-
tions of 'comparative data'. It is the nature of this evidence base and the
interpretations that can be placed upon it that offer significant opportunities
for personal and organisational development.

For all those operating as teachers within educational settings, all initial
training processes are constructed around the concept of self-reflection and
personal responsibility for professional development through some form of
mentoring or coaching process. But whether the focus for development is
on the organisation of the individual, research activity is at the heart of the

process. For this reason alone it can be appreciated that the value of developing educators in the skills of researchers is not a purely academic exercise to give credibility to training programmes, but rather an essential skill necessary for the future development of the education sector and the professionalism of those working in it. While it is acknowledged that the delivery of effective learning may be placed into the competent hands of education technicians such as high-level teaching assistants, coaches or trainers, teachers are increasingly being required to rely upon skills developed through contextually focused research activity in order to accurately assess a situation, choose an appropriate course of action and evaluate the impact. These skills, which can be honed in the learning environment, are becoming an essential for those in and aspiring to educational leadership.

Essentially making changes to the learning environment or the wider organisation requires a significant investment in resources, time in particular. So before doing anything particularly drastic it is worthwhile establishing a precise need to ensure that any initiative that may be implemented is appropriate to the need, addresses perceived weaknesses and builds upon strengths and areas of confidence. A well directed research activity should establish that what is thought to be the problem does not, in reality, turn out to be simply a symptom of a bigger issue.

Frequently organisations have little control over the initiatives that they are required to adopt and fail to invest time in gaining an understanding. This lack of knowledge can lead to a superficiality in the approach and result in poorly constructed implementation. By engaging with the research underpinning the initiative, ownership can be taken leading to greater personal and organisational investment. This can be further supported by constructing research-informed tools for tracking the implementation process.

Learning teacher, learning school, learning organisation

The concept of the learning organisation is not new but is quite fitting for the education sector, being, as it is, in the 'business' of education. All those working in the education sector should be focused on the learning of their students (admittedly, there may be a dual focus in the case of universities) and to best achieve and maintain this emphasis, everybody within those organisations must continuously focus on their own learning. The successful adaptation to change and uncertainty, which schools and colleges strive for, is most likely to occur when sufficient and appropriate learning takes place throughout the organisation.

Although research activity can only ever claim to be part of a range of learning opportunities, its impact can be significant. It can be used not only to identify specific needs in the self and others but also to explore deficiencies and untapped potentials. Professionally focused inputs (such as 'tricks for teachers' forms of CPD) can be embedded and their longer-term impact on educational quality evaluated. Links between processes, skills and strategies applied to the learning environment and the wider organisational needs can be identified and developed (e.g. linking strategies for motivating staff and students) to offer a more coherent approach.

Above all else, research activity makes you think more deeply about what you are doing, to evaluate impact and applicability and to consider alternative options. By encouraging a more healthily sceptical view of innovation it is possible to develop within the professional staff a more enduring and robust capability for change.

Learning check

An important question to ask is – 'what is your motivation for developing your educational research skills?'. As we see with our own learners, the more that they can perceive a purpose for the learning and can appreciate its applicability to their wider needs, the more highly motivated they will be. While there will always be some element of 'learn it for the test' within education, the superficiality of this approach and the transitory nature of that learning in our memory is often a woeful waste of effort in the longer term. Those who learn and apply research skills as part of their initial professional development for the education profession will perhaps need to focus on embedding and developing the core technical skills in the early part of their career and may not perceive research activity as a crucial aspect of their own early progression.

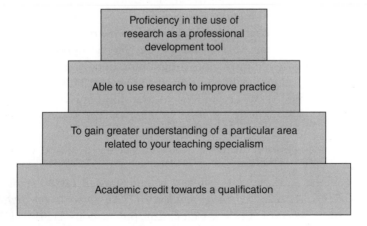

Figure 1.4   Level of engagement with research activity

Figure 1.4 offers a hierarchal means of viewing your own engagement with the importance and applicability of the research process. There is likely to be a base line in terms of the completion of academic credit, but this really needs to be perceived more as a reward or acknowledgement of competence than a goal in itself. At the lowest level of effective engagement it may simply be considered as a tool to access a more secure understanding of a particular aspect of teaching or learning (or educational management) which is relevant and specific to your individual needs at this point in time.

Using research to improve practice can be viewed in two ways: firstly in terms of being able to engage constructively with published research through having sufficient understanding of the process to be able to critically review findings; secondly in terms of being research active and being competent in the use of a narrow range of skills which enable you to track your own progress and development and challenge yourself through the incorporation of a wider range of ideas gained through reading. In effect, you become a fully committed reflective practitioner through the use of action research methodologies.

Ideally the value of research as a tool for learning will be such that you will consider it as a primary choice and a means of driving and supporting your own personal development and the development of your organisation.

References

Coates, S. (2011) *Second Report of the Independent Review of Teachers' Standards*. At: http://media.education.gov.uk/assets/files/pdf/s/independent %20review%20of%20teachers%20standards%20%20%20second%20report.pdf (accessed 15 October 2012).

Cohen, L., Manion, L. and Morrison, K. (2007) *Research Methods in Education*, 6th edn. Abingdon: Routledge.

DfE (2012) *The Role of Teaching School Alliances – Research and Development*. At: www.education.gov.uk/nationalcollege/index/support-for-schools/ teachingschools/teachingschools-programme-details/teachingschools-research-and-development.htm (accessed 15 October 2012).

Hattie, J. and Marsh, H. W. (1996) 'The relationship between teaching and research: a meta-analysis', *Review of Educational Research*, 66 (4): 507–42.

HEA (2012) *Accreditation*. At: www.heacademy.ac.uk (accessed 15 October 2012).

Lord, P., Lamont, E., Harland, J., Mitchell, H. and Straw, S. (2009) *Evaluation of the GTC's Teacher Learning Academy (TLA): Impacts on Teachers, Pupils and Schools*. At: www.nfer.ac.uk/publications/TLI01/TLI01.pdf (accessed 15 October 2012).

Smyth, J. (1989) 'Developing and sustaining critical reflection in teacher education', *Journal of Teacher Education*, 40 (2): 2–9.

Taber, K. (2007) *Classroom-Based Research and Evidence-Based Practice.* London: Sage.

TDA (2007) *Postgraduate Professional Development.* At: www.tda.gov.uk/partners/ppd.aspx (accessed 21 May 2007).

CHAPTER 2

ANALYSING SITUATIONS – IDENTIFYING ISSUES

This chapter will explain the importance of clarifying the context of the external and internal environments faced by the researcher in order to identify the key issues that are worthy of research. Specifically, by the completion of this chapter, you should:

- be able to identify and clarify an explicit focus for research;
- have considered the local and national factors which impact upon classroom, departmental or organisational practice;
- be able to compose the key questions that will give you answers which will help you (and/or your school) progress forwards.

Having addressed some of the issues surrounding why research activity is so important for the individual's professional development and the health of educational organisations, here we focus on making a secure start to your endeavours by identifying an issue to research. All too frequently, novice researchers, particularly those completing a research task in order to obtain an academic award, approach the process with a set of preconceptions which act as constraints on the research design process. A starting point will often be the adoption of a 'research design' (Hitchcock and Hughes, 1995: 79), such as action research or survey, rather than the purpose or focus of the research. It is rather like a teacher deciding to use 'small-group discussions' and then thinking about what the students need to learn. Section 2 of this book will show the importance of matching the research methodology to the focus and context of the research. The processes by which evidence might be collected will be subject to both real and perceived constraints – and before deciding on a particular approach it is important to identify what those constraints might be! However, research activity should not be considered as simply being driven by constraints, so the researcher should be aware of potential opportunities, from both national and local imperatives. By aligning research activity with a current national initiative (there are usually so many to choose from!) or to an issue identified within an organisational or departmental development plan, the research is likely to receive more support and encounter less resistance.

This chapter will explore how you can achieve the difficult balance of identifying an opportunity for research activity which has the potential to reveal important and meaningful outcomes, while at the same time being manageable and achievable. Hold on to these key questions while searching for a focus:

- What interests me?
- What is important to me (my department or school)?
- What do I know already?
- What is achievable (in the time/access to resources that I have)?

Research with a purpose

As far as this book is concerned, the purpose of research is to gather and analyse appropriate evidence on which to base decisions to bring about change – preferably improvement. In order to successfully achieve that outcome it is important to analyse the situation in which you find yourself in order to identify the 'right' questions to ask. This is a crucial stage of the research process as it is frequently all too easy to allow personal prejudice or misperception, or a superficial understanding of the situation, to bias a study to make it invalid and unreliable. Given the effort that you will be putting into the study, it is vitally important to start from a secure foundation. In effect, you will be carrying out research to clarify what you need to focus your research on. Partially this requires 'reading around' the issues in order to appreciate the current perceptions and to familiarise yourself with the terminology and the key conceptual constructions and theoretical perspectives (read on to Chapter 3 for more on how to achieve this). But most importantly it is the context in which you will be performing the research that will most directly provide the opportunities and stimulus. In effect, this is an 'eighth question' to add to Denscombe's 'sequence of seven basic questions' (2012: 6).

While there are several texts on research methodology, such as Denscombe (2010), which identify the purpose as being the major driving force behind the construction of the research activity, they tend to focus on the various means of collecting evidence. Even where planning frameworks for research activities are offered (Cohen et al., 2007), which acknowledge the crucial importance of 'a clear statement of the problem' (p. 79) or purpose and go on to suggest links between overarching purposes and research methodologies (pp. 84–6), the primacy of the methodology is apparent. But how do you arrive at the purpose? All too often, the asking of the 'right question' is the hardest part of getting to the answer.

In an environment which is often driven by 'targets', actual goals are frequently difficult to define or measure so that 'indicators' are identified as a more measurable alternative – examples being exam grades as an indicator of learning, and attendance figures an indication of learner engagement. This can lead to an overemphasis on short-term measurable gains against indicators rather than concentrating on the core factors which these indicators indicate. For example, educational organisations have been known to offer financial bribes to encourage learners to attend rather than explore the potential underlying factors which result in non-attendance (fear, inappropriate curriculum, financial loss of possible earnings are only some of many), so there is a concentration on the symptoms rather than causes. When faced with a concern such as 'low attendance', a researcher may ask the question 'why?' and gather evidence to identify a possible root cause, or be presented with a preferred solution (a financial bribe to the learner) and asked to provide evidence to determine 'will it work?' Getting to the 'root' of the issue should also provide insights as to where the evidence might be sourced and how it might be obtained.

It is likely that you will be set some artificial constraints as a consequence of a qualification or an award – the issue that is to be at the heart of the research may be restricted to specific aspects of education, such as 'assessment', 'special educational needs' or 'behaviour management', or by subject area or age/phase or location within an organisational hierarchy.

Whatever the imposed focus, it is important to examine how this might relate to the context in which you will be working and researching. By making the research specific to your own development needs as well as those of your host organisation, you immediately widen the audience for your research outcomes and give it a purpose beyond the qualification alone.

Locating the focus – identifying the key influential factors

Regardless of whether the study aims to underpin change for yourself (as the teaching professional), your class (or individuals within a class), your department or school, it is essential to be able to dispassionately identify and note the impact of internal and external factors on the study. Teachers do not operate in isolation. The intention to focus on the 'challenge' of accurately and consistently recording pupil progress needs to take into account the 'environmental factors'. The 'local' factors need to be identified and acknowledged – class size, ability range, adult support, school policy – to determine what is important and what is not. Likewise the external influences must be taken into account – national policies and priorities (and the balance between these and local factors). In this particular example the focus of the study might come down to the balance of influence – is progress primarily recorded for purposes of external accountability or individual pupil improvement? Clearly these ends are not mutually exclusive, but the balance between them might significantly influence the implementation of the process. Through a thorough consideration of these factors a greater awareness of the 'true' focus of the intended study might be achieved.

The process is one of funnelling to get from the possible to the probably to arrive at a clear and specific focus which your research will be related back to at all stages of the research activity. The first of these is to explore the wider influences on the specific area of educational activity, particularly those determined and driven by government policy. If you are in a complete quandary it might be helpful to start with a review of the key issues that are present in the educational press. Key British sources to explore would be:

- *The Times Educational Supplement* (www.tes.co.uk)
- BBC education news (www.bbc.co.uk/news/education/)
- *The Times Higher Educational Supplement* (www.thes.co.uk)
- *The Guardian* (www.guardian.co.uk/education)
- Department for Education (England) (www.education.gov.uk/inthenews)

> **Case Study 2.1   Investigating the factors behind the failure of A/B grade passes at A level to rise in line with overall passes at the school**
>
> Secondary Head of Faculty (MA student) 'Jon'
>
> *Constraint:* Study must focus on 'curriculum management'
>
> The 13–18 age range school had experienced a trend of rising rates of A level passes in line with the national averages, but passes at A/B grades were well below this average. Government documentation pointed towards a more inclusive approach to 16+ education, but also the need to address attainment of the most able students. School data suggested that the more able were underachieving, particularly the boys, but why? Jon wanted to explore the possible causes to the discrepancies:
>
> * What opportunities are provided within the school for students to achieve the higher grades?
> * What are the key motivators for the staff and students and how is this translated into learning habits?
> * Does the nature of the curriculum meet the learning needs of the students?

External influences

One of the key benefits of having an interventionist government, in respect of educational policy, is that it offers a literature-rich starting point for almost any aspect of educational research that you could imagine, whatever phase of education might be the focus. While the general list of recent government proposals, papers and proclamations (and reports of funded research projects) is to be found at the Department for Education (DfE, 2012a) website, more specialised documents can be found on the Internet sites of other quasi-governmental organisations. There are similar repositories for national strategies and policy initiatives for Wales (Welsh Government, 2012), Scotland (Education Scotland, 2012) and Northern Ireland (DENI, 2012). As a result of the schools inspection process, Ofsted has become an excellent source of data on performance trends through a collation and aggregation of individual school inspection reports, but it also offers tools for school self-evaluation and tracking pupil achievement (Ofsted 2012a) which might be of use for education-based research later in the planning and preparation process. Ofsted

(2012b) also publish reports which offer an overview of education practice within the different phases.

There are a considerable number of different sources for information in respect of the curriculum that schools are required to deliver and assess, which provide a setting for research into the nature, structure and assessment of the curriculum and the associated learning and teaching. In addition to the official government sources, professional subject and educational phase associations also hold a considerable quantity of information, not just the published national policies and government-sponsored research reports within their area of interest but frequently also their commentary and response to it.

While various associated sources, which provide guidance and direction on aspects of pedagogy and resources for learning and teaching, are provided to support the implementation and assessment of the curriculum, much of this has now been devolved to semi-autonomous free schools and academies and also to teaching schools (DfE, 2012b). Over the coming few years these are very likely to have a major influence on the nature of learning and teaching in schools and subsequent phases of education.

The sheer scale of this guidance, which determines the environment in which teachers operate, suggests, according to Taber an '*implicit* mistrust of teachers using their professional judgement' (2007: 5) – which takes us into the 'guidance' for training and development of teaching professionals. As indicated in the previous chapter, each major phase of education has its own entry requirements and 'gatekeepers' which are quasi-governmental organisations. In teacher education, this role is fragmented between:

- the Teaching Agency for schools (DfE, 2012c) which focuses on the recruitment and development of the workforce in schools and controls the professional assessment criteria for award-bearing training;
- the National College (NC, 2012) which commissions and provides training for leadership roles within schools.

However, with the Every Child Matters (ECM) agenda continuing to influence educational policy and provision (DfES, 2003), there is a much broader spectrum of identifiable influence impacting, in definable ways, on the operation of classrooms and schools which will, perhaps, need to be taken into account. It is only once we begin to place the actions of the school, department, teacher or learner into this wider context that we can begin to appreciate and understand why things happen the way they do. Issues which are regarded as 'important' on the national scale, such as meeting the individual needs of learners and communities of learners in the PCE sector (Niace, 2012), can then, at the very least, be justified much more successfully at the local level. The perspective offered by the national source will often provide an overview of the key factors and so offer a rationale for the closer examination of the local context. On the whole, national initiatives are usually supported by robust justification which can be used to provide meaning to small-scale, localised research activities.

It is particularly useful, if the research activity needs to be sanctioned by senior leaders within an organisation, if only to pay the fees, if the focus can be linked to a national initiative that the organisation is committed to working towards. It is when the leadership within the organisation can see the wider application of the outcomes of any research that they will be more inclined to support the activity through some material means or by providing access to information.

These national issues often provide a very great influence on the direction that research activity will take. For example, 75 per cent of a cohort of primary-phase undergraduate trainee teachers recently chose AfL (assessment for learning) as the focus for their dissertations – but there was not one duplication, because each was uniquely located within its own context: age group, subject area, aspect of assessment, assessment tool, breadth of evidence base and so on.

Internal issues

While a general search though the national perspective will identify the potential big issues that education is currently being required to address, it is only an examination of the context in which the research is likely to be carried out will that determine whether the research themes are possible. In many respects, the review of 'internal' and 'external' issues needs to be performed concurrently – top-down and bottom-up to meet somewhere in the middle. It is the balancing act that most teachers have to master every time they enter the classroom – the set requirements of the curriculum against the needs of the individual learners. Here it is an awareness of the importance of relative wider issues mapped against the priorities of the class, teacher, department or school. One can be used to validate and enhance the importance of the other when agreement to perform the research is being sought.

To a very large extent, the approach that you can take to identify potential research topics depends upon your *positionality* in respect of the research context, positionality being your relationship to the context and the potential research population. For example, being a newly qualified teacher (NQT), your relationship to the research population, access to information and personal biases will be very different if you decide to gather evidence of your senior leadership team's ability to perform effective self-assessment rather than the ability of the students in your Year 8 tutor group. Similarly, if you are already working in the organisation, you are likely to have a greater awareness of the issues which are deemed to be important or priorities than if you are simply using it as a source of research evidence. This variation throws up different strategies that the prospective researcher may need to adopt in order to gain access to potential sources of evidence. Whichever of the strategies you employ, it is important that the research topic holds a real interest for you and that it offers the possibility of meaningful gains for you not just in terms of the qualification (if any is on offer!) but also in terms of your personal and professional growth.

In order to identify potential research topics, it is helpful to explore possibilities – informally seeking the views of colleagues and peers about issues that appear important to you and perhaps in the national perspective as well. These anecdotal responses will hopefully give you some sense of direction and help you to select a more precise focus to examine the possibilities in greater depth. You do need to take care that you don't take it too far – in effect, you are looking for questions, not the answers at this stage.

But what actually is *the* issue that you should be focusing upon? Sometimes it is difficult because you will be given a focus – either because it is an issue that the organisation wants you to research (making *their* priority *your* priority) or because it is given in the form of an assignment focus. In the first instance it is at least likely that you will receive appropriate support and resources from the organisation; in the second, it might take a little more effort to convince your host that your priority becomes one of theirs!

Researching in your own organisation

Depending on your length of service and your position within the organisation, it is likely that you will be aware of organisational or departmental priorities which you might be able to embed your research activity within. It is also possible to use your own performance management targets as a focus for your research activity. If you can demonstrate to your line manager the connections between the priorities and your research goals then there is a much greater likelihood of being supported and being given access to appropriate sources of evidence. However, in most circumstances it is likely that you will be faced with a number of competing, seemingly equal priorities. Even taking account of the views of peers and colleagues may not take you much further towards your research focus. At this point you should consult with your line manager, mentor or research supervisor to try to obtain a more objective perspective of the options that you have open to you. Ideally, this will continue to include a balance of the organisation's and your own personal priorities.

Researching in a host organisation

This is more likely the case if you are performing the research as part of an initial teacher training/education programme which is not wholly school- or college-based. Here it is best to approach the organisation with potential research projects which are seen as being based on 'important' issues from the national perspective. If the research is to be tied into a period of classroom/teaching experience, the greater the 'self-focus' and the more contained around your own teaching, the more acceptable it is likely to be. If it is to be completed by taking on the role of 'researcher', then it is important to confirm that the host is sympathetic to the aims at the very least, but ideally it will focus on something that the hosts themselves see the benefit of. Where both the research and the host are likely to benefit from the activity, there is a greater likelihood of the research being given wider access to evidence and resources by the host.

 Case Study 2.2   Design technology and as a model of assessment for learning

Primary BEd student 'Jenny'

Constraint: Study must focus on your 'specialist subject' (design technology)

The 4–9 age range school that Jenny had been placed in for her final teaching experience were grappling with the problem of getting Key Stage 1 children to successfully self- and peer-assess. Jenny had noticed the similarities between the AfL (assessment for learning) and design processes. Trawling government reports and curriculum documentation made the connections more apparent and also reinforced the importance of pupil involvement in AfL. School documentation also highlighted the priority of the issue. With this as justification, Jenny identified two key questions:

- Can KS1 children be taught how to self- and peer-assess using the design process as a model?
- Can they successfully transfer this skill to other areas of the curriculum?

Questions to define the focus

There is an art and a science to asking questions. The best teachers are very expert in this – they have to be in order to get to the heart of any misconceptions, misunderstandings or 'blocks' to learning that a student is having. By deconstructing the 'problem' they are adept at getting down to a firm foundation in order to help a learner reconstruct a more successful understanding. At the beginning of a research activity it is important for research to progress through a similar process. It is all too easy for a teacher to 'assume' that they know the problem that a learner is having and choose a starting point which fits their ready-made solution – a researcher is capable of doing something very similar. They begin the research with an outcome in mind and tend to collect evidence which supports their idea. Asking questions should help to keep the research 'honest' by focusing down to the key or fundamental issues.

Questioning should be seen as the process by which you get from the important general (but probably amorphous) theme to the manageable specific research focus. Sometimes it is possible to achieve this simply by self-analysis but to avoid missteps due to unacknowledged internal bias, lack of objectivity or positionality (the location of the researcher in respect of the focus of the research), it is often helpful (if not explicitly required!) to discuss the broad focus of the research with a mentor, coach, tutor or line manager in order to obtain a different perspective.

Is it just me or do we have a problem here? As well asking 'those with power over your research' it is also helpful to informally/anecdotally seek the views of peers and colleagues as to the appropriateness of your study:

- What do you think about …?
- Do you find … a problem/helpful/challenging/too time-consuming/…?
- What do you think we should do about …? (which does have the bias of assuming that there is some inherent/acknowledged pre-existing problem)

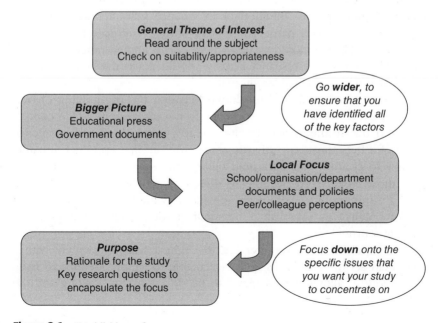

Figure 2.1 Establishing a focus

Obtaining a wider range of views prior to fully formulating an approach or even finalising the focus does allow the study to settle towards a position of 'least resistance' or even greatest support, which should have a significantly positive impact on the research processes, particularly in the willingness of colleagues to contribute and participate in any evidence gathering (see Figure 2.1).

While some sources, such as Hitchcock and Hughes (1995: 81) offer a simplified framework for establishing a focus for the research, others (Cohen et al., 2011; Denscombe, 2010) rather bypass this stage of the process. It is left to more recent publications, including Fox et al. (2007) and Taber (2007) to adopt a more holistic approach and consider the need to filter down to the key focus. Walliman (2011) adopts the pragmatic approach of identifying the focus (the 'what') before moving onto the justification (the 'why'), although there is an undeniable element of 'chicken and egg' here.

Starting points and open minds

In the role of a tutor, coach or mentor my biggest concern at the initial planning stage is not for the researcher who comes in saying 'I don't know what to do', but the one who says 'our school/class needs to do ...' – and then state the outcome of the research. Performing research to gather evidence to justify a decision already made might be appropriate in some circumstances, but it does immediately close down the possibilities of what could be 'better' options. 'Intuition' or 'experience' will often lead a teacher to seek (and expect) a particular 'answer' which reinforces their view of reality. This reflects a closed system where only a limited range of options is possible, whereas a research activity should grasp the opportunity to explore the new and consider alternatives.

A clear distinction should be drawn between the pre-judging of outcomes, reinforced by a biased approach to the research in which conclusions and the resultant actions are already decided, and an objective testing of a hypothesis (positivistic research). The first approach innately attempts to confirm currently held beliefs; the second attempts to challenge those beliefs. To be able to effectively challenge currently held views it is important to acknowledge what they are (a further component of positionality) to establish a personal starting point for a potential 'learning journey'.

However, there is no requirement to begin a research activity with a firmly held set of views! It is quite acceptable to simply identify an issue and explore it, allowing your views to be driven by the reading and the evidence.

Case Study 2.3   Evaluating the effectiveness of the mentoring for a graduate primary, employment-based, initial teacher training programme

Training manager, primary teacher and MA Education student 'Jo'

Constraint: Study must focus on 'performance management'

Jo manages a school-based teacher training programme which relies exclusively on the mentoring of the trainees to support their development towards qualified teacher status (QTS). All the mentors are primary teachers and have been trained to support the trainee teachers using specific structures and strategies. While all trainees who have completed the programme in the past three years have been successful it is not clear which particular elements have contributed most.

In discussions with the tutor, the difficulty in defining 'effective' became apparent, particularly in considering the perceptions of the different interested parties. The decision rested upon the purpose to which the outcomes might be put – to be incorporated within a self-assessment for public consumption a purposive (quantitative) approach would be preferable, but to inform future practice, especially the recruitment and training of mentors, a phenomenological (qualitative) approach would be more useful. Choosing a developmental purpose gave the research a specific focus, perspective and direction.

Clarifying purpose

Reading around the subject and exploring the context (national and local background) increases your awareness of the range of factors that impact on your study (see Figure 2.1). From this wider understanding of the issues a precise focus and purpose for the study can then be more confidently established. The purpose is of crucial importance to the success of your study as it should require you to convince yourself why you are doing it before you have to convince any one else to help you collect evidence. It is the opportunity to make explicit the focus you have chosen and to distil this focus into a select number of key research questions that can then be used to establish and maintain the direction of the study throughout the subsequent stages – keep checking your progress and focus against them.

There is an important 'reality check' that needs to be considered as the purpose of the study begins to form based around the achievability of the proposal.

- Ethics (addressed in greater detail in Chapter 5) – can any potential risks, in terms of the physical, emotional, financial or general well-being of the potential participants or stakeholders, be prevented or minimised?
- Resources – do you have the time, skills, financial means (travel, phone calls, photocopying, …) to successfully complete the research?
- Access – are you likely to be able to gain access to the key sources of information and evidence necessary to address the key research questions?
- Scope – is the depth, range and scale of the research appropriate for your expected level of activity and engagement?
- Benefit – are the outcomes of this research likely to be of professional benefit to you or your institution?

If you are able to give a confidently positive response to each of these, it is time to explore the conceptual literature and published research underpinning the study in greater depth.

References

Cohen, L., Manion, L. and Morrison, K. (2007) *Research Methods in Education*, 6th edn. Abingdon: Routledge.

Cohen, L., Manion, L. and Morrison, K. (2011) *Research Methods in Education*, 7th edn. Abingdon: Routledge.

DENI (2012) *Department of Education*. At: www.deni.gov.uk/ (accessed 21 November 2012).

Denscombe, M. (2010) *The Good Research Guide*, 4th edn. Maidenhead: Open University Press.

Denscombe, M. (2012) *Research Proposals: A Practical Guide*. Maidenhead: Open University Press.

DfE (2012a) *Publications*. At: www.education.gov.uk/publications (accessed 21 November 2012).

DfE (2012b) *What's Involved in Being a Teaching School?* At: www.education. gov.uk/nationalcollege/index/support-for-schools/teachingschools/ teachingschools-programme-details.htm (accessed 21 November 2012).

DfE (2012c) *QTS Standards and ITT Requirements*. At: www.education.gov. uk/schools/careers/traininganddevelopment/initial/b00205422/qtsanditt (accessed 21 November 2012).

DfES (2003) *Every Child Matters: Change for Children*. At: www.education. gov.uk/publications/standard/publicationDetail/Page1/CM5860 (accessed 21 November 2012).

Education Scotland (2012) *Transforming Lives Through Learning*. At: www. educationscotland.gov.uk/ (accessed 21 November 2012).

Fox, M., Martin, P. and Green, G. (2007) *Doing Practitioner Research*. London: Sage.

Hitchcock, G. and Hughes, D. (1995) *Research and the Teacher*, 2nd edn. London: Routledge.

NC (2012) *Be Who You Want to Be*. At: www.nationalcollege.org.uk/signin? indexidol=no&url=http%3A//www.nationalcollege.org.uk/index (accessed 21 November 2012).

Niace (2012) *Annual Review 2011/12*. At: www.niace.org.uk/annual-review/2011-12 (accessed 21 November 2012).

Ofsted (2012a) *Surveys*. At: www.ofsted.gov.uk/resources/surveys (accessed 21 November 2012).

Ofsted (2012b) *Our Expert Knowledge*. At: www.ofsted.gov.uk/inspection-reports/our-expert-knowledge-0 (accessed 21 November 2012).

Taber, K. (2007) *Classroom-Based Research and Evidence-Based Practice*. London: Sage.

Walliman, N. (2011) *Your Research Project*, 3rd edn. London: Sage.

Welsh Government (2012) *Education and Skills*. At: http://wales.gov.uk/topics/educationandskills/?lang=en (accessed 21 November 2012).

CHAPTER 3

SEARCHING THE LITERATURE FOR IDEAS

This chapter will discuss some of the key issues in conducting literature searches, outline the increasingly popular, and linked, research approach embodied in the systematic study, and then go on to suggest ways of making all studies more systematic in order to construct a clear conceptual framework for research. Specifically, you should be able to:

- identify a conceptual focus for the study;
- accurately record and reference the sources used for the study;
- consider the ideas, concepts and strategies suggested by previous authors;
- appreciate the applicability of the findings of published research in the field;
- justify the key issues that need to be explored and addressed.

Conducting a high-quality review of existing ideas is probably the most important element of any successful research study in the social sciences. This is not universally the case because, occasionally, researchers will undertake 'blue skies' research that is at the cutting-edge of development and, by inference, there will be very little material available on the topic under scrutiny. However, such circumstances are very rare since it is unusual to find a topic that has been completely unexplored in the past. Even issues that may seem to be very new indeed are unlikely to be entirely without antecedents and a determined and thorough review of the literature will almost always reveal a wealth of relevant material that the researcher can draw on in carrying out their study.

The process of conducting literature reviews has been revolutionised by the increasing, and now ubiquitous, use of electronic database searches that enable the researcher to interrogate vast amounts of literature with speed and with ease. However, even the best and most user-friendly of databases pose certain challenges to the researcher. The very size of the database is often problematic since the insertion of a keyword may produce thousands of responses that place the researcher in no better a position than if they still relied on manual examination of card indexes and published summaries of research material according to topic. The researcher still needs to acquire a series of key skills that will enable any search to be carried out successfully and in a way that will refine the amount of material to a manageable level. The first of these to be focused upon here is the accurate identification and recording of the location of the sources – referencing.

Scholarly skills – referencing

Any formal research report should reveal that the researcher has high levels of skill and understanding in scholarship and scholarly conventions. One of the most important sets of skills to demonstrate is that associated with appropriate referencing of material in the text of the report. It is of crucial importance that you are able to accurately and consistently identify the sources of the information that you have gathered from literature or archived sources. This is not something that you do at the end of the writing process but needs to be completed as you access the material that you *might* refer to in the text of your assignment or report. For this reason it is of the upmost importance that you record your sources as you access them, as attempting to do this in retrospect will be considerably more difficult and time-consuming.

Most research reports in the social sciences employ the Harvard referencing system as outlined in Box 3.1 below. However, there are a number of other systems of referencing; requirements may vary from institution to institution and researchers are always well advised to check on the particular expectations that may be placed upon them.

Box 3.1   The Harvard referencing system

Collecting material for referencing

For *books*, record:

- The author's or editor's name (or names)
- The year the book was published (bracketed)
- The title of the book (italicised)
- If it is an edition other than the first
- The city the book was published in
- The name of the publisher

For *journal articles*, record:

- The author's name or names
- The year in which the journal was published
- The title of the article
- The title of the journal (italicised)
- The page number/s of the article in the journal
- As much other information as you can find about the journal, for example the volume and issue numbers

For *electronic resources*, try to collect the information as above if it is available, but also record:

- The date you accessed the source
- The electronic address or email
- The type of electronic resource (email, discussion forum, www page, etc.)

In addition to these details, when you are taking notes, if you copy direct quotations or if you put the author's ideas in your own words, write down the page numbers you got the information from.

References or bibliography

When you use the Harvard system, you are only usually required to produce a reference list – all the sources you have referred to in the text. However, you may also want to produce a bibliography where you list *all* sources you have consulted but not referred to in the text.

How to list references in a reference list

Book with one author:

Brundrett, M. (2000) *Beyond Competence: The Challenge for Educational Management*. King's Lynn: Peter Francis Publishing.

Book with two authors:

Burton, N. and Brundrett, M. (2005) *Leading the Curriculum in the Primary School*. London: Sage.

Book with three or more authors:

Brundrett, M., Burton, N. and Smith, R. (eds) (2002) *Leadership in Education*. London: Sage.

Book with an editor:

Brundrett, M. and Terrell, I. (eds) (2003) *Learning to Lead in the Secondary School*. London: RoutledgeFalmer.

Chapter in a book written by someone other than the editor:

Silcock, P. and Brundrett, M. (2006) 'Co-constructing learning in primary schools: new perspectives on pedagogy', in R. Webb (ed.), *Changing Teaching and Learning in the Primary School*. Maidenhead: Open University Press.

Books with an anonymous or unknown author:

The University Encyclopedia (1985) London: Roydon.

Journal articles:

Brundrett, M., Rhodes, C. and Gkolia, C. (2006) 'Planning for leadership succession: creating a talent pool in primary schools', *Education 3–13*, 34 (3): 259–68.

World Wide Web page/image/audio or video file:

DfEE (2001) *Supporting the Target Setting Process*. London: DfEE. Accessed at: www.standards.dfes.gov.uk/ts/pdf/DfES_065_2001.pdf [online], on 20 August 2007.

Currently there are a number of software packages (an example being EndNote) that are able to store, organise and import references directly into word-processing software. However, if you intend to use such systems it is important to remember that they are only as accurate as the information that has been loaded in to them (by you!) and that it is always your responsibility to ensure that the correct referencing format is used.

Conducting a literature review

A literature review is an account of what has been published on a topic by other researchers. All forms of publication outlet may be used in such a review but special weight is placed on research-based text, sometimes termed research monographs, and articles published in peer-reviewed journals. At their simplest, a review of the literature on a topic may consist of little more than the collation of evidence based on a few minutes spent exploring one particular database or an electronic catalogue search using only one or two key words. Such an approach is perfectly acceptable if the aim is to find some initial material on an issue of interest. This may be invaluable in the initial stages of a research study since it can serve a number of key functions including:

- providing information as to whether the topic is one that has been explored in detail already or whether there is a paucity of research on the topic and thereby assisting in the decision whether or not to pursue that line of inquiry;
- gathering initial material that will form the basis for further exploration;
- acting as a 'framing exercise' to set up the parameters of a study by discovering the range of literature and the current state of research and thinking on a topic.

However, one must differentiate between a search and a review. The search is the process of accessing and retrieving data whereas the review is the product of the analytical process that is undertaken consequent on one or more searches. As such the review must be defined by a guiding concept such as the main research problems, aims or questions. Birley and Moreland (1998: 90) suggest that the researcher must always keep in mind their original aims when conducting a review and provide the helpful mnemonic: *AIM – Author's Intended Message*, as a way of ensuring that original goals are never lost from sight throughout the process. Such a review must not be just a descriptive list or summary of the material available. It should:

- synthesise;
- analyse; and
- present a clear line of argument.

This latter is probably the most difficult to accomplish, especially for the emerging or new researcher since such argument should never be solely the unsupported views of the researcher but should rather be a consistent line of argument consonant with the researcher's views *but based on the evidence*. In order to ensure this is accomplished a number of key questions need to be asked by the researcher, such as:

- What is the specific thesis, problem, or research question that my literature review helps to define?
- What type of literature review am I conducting? Am I looking at issues of theory? methodology? or policy?
- Am I interested in outputs-based quantitative research, qualitative research or the development of theory?

- What is the scope of my literature review? What types of publications am I using (e.g. journals, books, government documents, popular media)?
- What discipline am I working in (e.g. nursing, education, psychology, sociology, medicine) and which databases (and increasingly websites) will be most relevant?
- Have I critically analysed the literature I used? Do I follow through a set of concepts and questions, comparing items to each other in the ways they deal with them? Instead of just listing and summarising items, do I assess them, discussing strengths and weaknesses?
- Have I cited and discussed studies contrary to my perspective?
- Will the reader find my literature review relevant, appropriate and useful?
- How does this book or article relate to the specific thesis or question I am developing?

(University of Melbourne, 2007a)

The resultant literature review should be a piece of discursive prose, not a list describing or summarising one piece of literature after another. Instead, organise the literature review into sections that present a thematic overview or identify trends in relevant theory (Taylor and Proctor, 2007). A good review will have a clear rationale for structure and presentation that can be traced back to the nature of the study. One of the simplest ways to provide logical structure is by examining the key research questions, aims or issues and attempting to define a theme that can be pursued in the literature. This can then be the subject of a specific search or set of searches and can be reported as one section in the review. However, not all research issues are susceptible to the development of such a theme and some researchers choose to allow the structuring themes to emerge as material is searched. Overall, the paramount issue is to ensure that the structure of the review follows a logical and defensible pattern (this is especially true for doctoral students or those conducting funded research who may have to defend the way that they have presented their material in a viva, interview or presentation to a funding agency).

Box 3.2   Ask yourself

- What is the overarching concept or issue that underpins your study?
- What are the key research questions/aims/or sub-issues that develop out of this?
- What are the four or five key themes that you need to explore in more detail?

(Continued)

(Continued)

- Which key words are the most likely to produce relevant material when you undertake a literature search for each theme?
- How might you combine those words in order to explore the issues in more depth and to exclude extraneous results?

Conducting a systematic review

The notion of conducting a systematic review of the literature as part of a research study, or even as the principle methodological approach in its own right, has grown significantly in recent years. There are a number of reasons for this:

- the importation of the systematic review approach from biological and medical sciences into the social sciences;
- the growing recognition of the importance of a systematic search of previously published studies as a way of creating a conceptual framework of further research;
- the increasing ability to interrogate enormous amounts of extant literature because of easy access to electronic database searches; and finally
- the introduction of new frameworks of qualifications such as professional masters and doctoral degree programmes within which a systematic literature review may be undertaken as a discrete element of a degree.

Critical appraisal and synthesis of research findings in a systematic manner emerged in the 1970s under the term 'meta-analysis' in the areas of psychotherapy and medicine. The Evidence for Policy and Practice Information (EPPI) Centre was subsequently established in 1993 to address the need for a systematic approach to the organisation and review of evidence-based work on social interventions and has subsequently become highly influential in the growth of systematic review as an accepted method. The EPPI Centre approach argues that the key features of a systematic review or systematic research synthesis are that:

- Explicit and transparent methods are used.
- It is a piece of research following a standard set of stages.
- It is accountable, replicable and updateable.

(EPPI Centre, 2007a)

The structure of a systematic review has been outlined by Gough et al. (2012), who suggest that a clear and coherent pathway should be designed which includes the stages of:

- *Review initiation* (forming the review team and engaging stakeholders).
- *Review question and methodology* (formulating the question, the conceptual framework and approach).
- *Search strategy* (searching and screening for inclusion using eligibility criteria).
- *Description of the study characteristics* (coding to match or build a conceptual framework).
- *Quality and relevance assessment* (applying quality and appraisal criteria).
- *Synthesis* (using the conceptual framework, study codes and quality judgements).
- *Using reviews* (interpreting and communicating findings to stakeholders).

(Gough et al., 2012: 8)

The same authors note that two main types of such reviews may be discerned including *aggregative* reviews, which commonly use quantitative data and where the synthesis is predominantly adding data to answer the review question, and *configurative* reviews, which commonly use qualitative data and where the synthesis is commonly organising data from the studies included to answer the review question (Gough et al., 2012: 9).

A systematic review is different from a traditional literature review precisely because it attempts to be systematic in its approach. Some of the key ways in which this is achieved include:

- Systematic reviews are *transparent* about how their conclusions are generated. Each piece of research is evaluated and its quality and relevance are made clear.
- A *protocol* sets out how the review is to be conducted before the work starts that is designed to reduce bias.
- *Exhaustive searches* are undertaken to find as much as possible of the relevant research which addresses the review's research question. This is important if the review's conclusions are not to be over-influenced by studies which are simply the easiest to find (usually published research showing the benefit of interventions).
- A systematic review uses of a set of explicit statements, called *inclusion criteria*, to assess each study found to see if it actually does address a review's research question.
- *Potential users of the review are involved* to make sure that the research is relevant through the use of advisory groups.
- The *findings of sound research are synthesised* to produce clear and easily accessible messages about the reliable evidence available on a given topic by appraising individual studies and pooling results.

This latter point is one of the most important characteristics of a systematic review in that it includes a synthesis of its results usually presented in the form of a structured narrative, summary tables or a statistical combination (meta-analysis). This synthesis is then used to formulate conclusions and recommendations (EPPI, 2007b). Some systematic maps can be in-depth with a large degree of analysis of the research field. Syntheses are nearly always in-depth, as detailed scrutiny of the available research is necessary to be clear about the trustworthiness of that research and the relevance and direction of the findings. This time-consuming, but essential, activity means that systematic reviews including a synthesis often answer a more narrowly focused question. Reviews asking complex questions may be theory testing reviews using more iterative methods of review such as in critical interpretative and realist synthesis (EPPI, 2007c).

Once searches have been carried out, electronic records of the results can be downloaded from databases and imported into reference management software such as EndNote (www.endnote.com/) or Reference Manager (www.refman.com/). More detailed information on studies may be held in a database constructed by the researcher or research team or a commercial package such as Microsoft Access may be employed. Equally, analysis of the results of searches may be carried out manually or may use systems such as NVivo (www.qsrinternational.com/products_nvivo.aspxand) or NUD*IST (www.qsrinternational.com/) (EPPI, 2007d). However, there is still much to be said for using some simple approaches to structuring the material that is found, especially if the work is on a comparatively small scale where the use of sophisticated electronic packages may in itself be time-consuming and unwieldy. Some basic methods that are often useful are:

- Keep separate files for the different research themes (these can be both physical files for paper-based materials and electronic files for downloaded materials).
- Use a simple method of coding documents to filter out the material that is of most use such as highlighting the titles of documents that appear to be most relevant or use a 'star' system to rank each document according to its relevance.
- Structure the material in some way so that some form of logical nomenclature can be applied to it such as placing items in date order within themes and sub-themes.
- Above all, make sure that full references are kept for all items since it is an all too frequent problem of research to find that a host of material that needs to be included in the final review is lacking all or part of a reference, thus necessitating many hours of further searches to retrieve a name, date, full title or other.

(Brundrett and Rhodes, 2013)

The synthesis needs to be presented systematically and the researcher needs to be explicit about how studies are singled out for description in a review and to be methodical when presenting detail of different studies. The synthesis is usually presented in the form of a structured narrative, summary tables or a statistical combination (meta-analysis) which is then used to formulate conclusions and recommendations. The EPPI model requires that the synthesis should be more than a listing of the results of individual studies and may take a variety of forms.

- *Statistical meta-analysis* – a set of statistical procedures designed to combine the numerical results of primary research studies addressing similar research questions.
- *Narrative empirical synthesis* – brings together the results of empirical research that are in a narrative form to provide an accessible combination of results from individual studies in structured narratives or summary tables.
- *Conceptual synthesis* – where different understandings or concepts about the world are brought together to create a new concept or concepts. For example, meta-ethnography combines the results of different ethnographic studies to create a greater understanding of the phenomena under study than from the individual ethnographic studies.

(EPPI, 2007e)

The systematic review model is undoubtedly becoming increasingly influential across the social sciences. Nonetheless, such an approach is not without its difficulties and remains contested, especially by positivist researchers who, quite rightly, have concerns that any research study that relies solely on such methods may merely compound and collate the inadequacies of previous research studies. This is especially true in social research literature searches, however systematic, which may throw up articles and reports that are polemic in nature or the result of qualitative studies, such as ethnographic approaches, that may make no claim to generalisability. Nonetheless, it is also true that in social research one of the purposes of the literature review is to 'pay homage' to those that have gone before and whose work has been influential (Thody, 2006: 91) and the systematic approach will offer insurance that an analytical, thorough search has take place even if the aims do not include the desire to complete a formal meta-analysis of previous outputs. Indeed many funding agencies expect or require a systematic study of the literature as a precursor to subsequent empirical study.

Making literature reviews more systematic

Whether or not the researcher decides to undertake a systematic review rather than a literature review the development of an orderly and methodical approach to searching for and, subsequently, examining the literature is a vital element in the likelihood of success in a research project. For this reason researchers should strive to make any exploration of the literature as systematic as possible. Figure 3.1 outlines a toolkit for making literature searches more systematic through a logical process of identifying key themes based on using research aims to inform research themes, leading to a rationale for database searches.

Systematic Literature Review Toolkit

What is the overarching theme of the study?

Define four or five themes derived from research questions/issues/themes:

1.
2.
3.
4.
5.

Brainstorm five keywords for each of the themes to be explored:

	i.	ii.	iii.	iv.	v.
1.	i.	ii.	iii.	iv.	v.
2.	i.	ii.	iii.	iv.	v.
3.	i.	ii.	iii.	iv.	v.
4	i.	ii.	iii.	iv.	v.
5.	i.	ii.	iii.	iv.	v.

Note the electronic databases to be explored:

1.   2.   3.

Outline the key areas to be explored in the review document for each item scrutinised, including:

• Full reference with author/s, title, place of publication, edition, page numbers
• Source (database)
• Methodology employed by authors
• Key themes
• Key findings
• Notes

List the key features that make your approach *systematic*:

Figure 3.1   Systematic literature review toolkit

Once the relevant literature has been identified the researcher should adopt a critical approach to reading materials which will help them to focus their thoughts. The following points should be borne in mind:

- Skim the headings and the abstract of the piece, and perhaps look at the first line of each paragraph and the conclusion.
- Keep a critical focus. Who are the authors of this piece? What do you know about them?
- What is the perspective of the writer? (Think about the contexts of gender and culture.)
- Are the arguments logical?
- Is there reliable evidence to support the author's contentions?

(University of Melbourne, 2007b)

The extent to which this critical approach is followed will help to determine the final quality of the written review. The problems of acquiring and storing material have been minimised in recent years since most journals are now held in digital as well as hardcopy and, provided searches are carried out via an accredited university or other institutional search system, whole articles and documents can be downloaded from publisher's websites. Nonetheless, this mass of material itself presents challenges and the researcher should try to be systematic in the way that documents are stored. A simple system of creating folders and sub-folders that reflect the themes in searches, possibly allied to the actual key words entered, will enable speedy subsequent retrieval and obviate the need for much agonising when trying to locate 'lost' documents.

The systematic review process has as one of its elements the notion that a clear and consistent method of review for each retrieved item should be set up. The single researcher may decide to employ a wide range of alternative techniques such as simple note-taking but there is no reason why even the smallest of studies could not employ a simple review document to record the seminal details of the items examined. Figure 3.2 provides a simple example of such a document.

Whether or not such a document is used the researcher should try to make connections between the project aims and the material being read and should compare and contrast the views of the authors of the material as the 'narrative' of the research unfolds. In this way the researcher will be able to collate the mass of material that is available in order to formulate a conceptual map of the topic.

Using the literature review to develop a conceptual framework for a research study

The conceptual framework of a research study is that group of ideas, concepts and theoretical perspectives that give overall structure and coherence to a study. In developing such a conceptual framework the researcher will draw on their original conception for the project, their discussions with

Review Document
Title:
Authors:
Full reference:
Methodology:
Key themes:
Key findings:
Notes:

Figure 3.2 Literature review/systematic review document

colleagues, mentors, funding agency or supervisor, and the emerging ideas and previous research findings that derive from the literature. As outlined earlier, the aim of a literature review is to show that the writer has studied existing work in the field with insight and it is not enough merely to show what others in the field have discovered. In order to use this material as the basis of the conceptual framework the researcher will need to:

- compare and contrast different authors' views on an issue;
- group authors who draw similar conclusions;
- criticise aspects of methodology;
- note areas in which authors are in disagreement;
- highlight exemplary studies;
- highlight gaps in research;
- show how your study relates to previous studies;
- show how your study relates to the literature in general;
- conclude by summarising what the literature says.

The idea of the literature review is to develop a good working knowledge of the research in a particular area. The final written review should reflect the results of this preliminary research. So, a good literature review raises questions and identifies areas to be explored (University of Melbourne, 2007a). The resulting assessment of previous studies enables the researcher to explore their area of interest in considerable depth. The ideas, findings and theoretical perspectives that are the result of this process enable the researcher to refine and develop the conceptual framework for their research. This will be an iterative process since, as noted earlier, the initial research ideas and aims will serve to define the key themes and parameters in the literature survey. However, the literature survey may serve to contradict previous conceptions and this may shut off lines of inquiry or open up entirely new areas of interest that need to be explored. Thus the research questions or issues may themselves need to be adjusted or even altered considerably. This is a complex process since judgement is required about which new avenues of exploration may be valuable and relevant. There is always a danger that a study of the literature may expose whole new vistas of research that, although potentially fascinating, may actually lead the researcher away from their initial purposes, or may be so broad as to make the study untenable in terms of the time and resources available. The new researcher will find such issues especially problematic and consultation with a supervisor or research mentor may be invaluable at this point since experience will enable more practised investigators to judge which avenues of inquiry are likely to be helpful and manageable and which are not. The process of developing the conceptual framework is outlined in Figure 3.3.

Some researchers take great care to frame their initial aims very carefully, while others leave initial aims, or issues, more general and less concise with the deliberate intention that the final research aims will emerge as part of the literature review process. Such processes often reflect the methodological positions of the researcher. Positivist researchers tend to want to define research questions very precisely from the outset with the intention of 'testing' the issues. On the other hand, highly qualitative researchers frequently leave initial aims comparatively vague and avoid the use of terms like 'questions' altogether with the intention of allowing topics to reveal themselves in the process of research and writing.

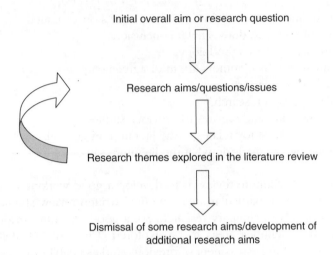

Initial overall aim or research question

Research aims/questions/issues

Research themes explored in the literature review

Dismissal of some research aims/development of
additional research aims

Figure 3.3   Development of conceptual framework

   Whichever approach the researcher chooses to take the most important factor is that the resultant set of ideas are articulated and defended clearly so that the research funder, auditor or examiner can see very clearly the interconnecting theoretical structure that underpins the final research report and other outputs.

Conclusions

It is important to differentiate between a search, which is the process of accessing one or more manual or electronic databases or search engines, a literature review, which is an analytical summary of literature, and a systematic review, which employs techniques that enable researchers to conduct a meta-analysis of previous research and is recognised increasingly as a methodology in its own right. Almost all studies will require one or more database searches, even if only to confirm that comparatively little literature has been generated on a topic in the past; most serious studies undertaken as part of postgraduate study or during funded research will require a number of structured searches against a clearly identified set of criteria. The subsequent analysis of the material elicited from such searches, whether in the form of a traditional or more systematic review, will inform the research process and help to develop the conceptual framework for the study.

   An initial exposition of this conceptual framework should underpin the introductory statement of a research report or thesis, even if the term is not employed at that stage. This underpinning theoretical construction should then be subject to further clarification during the analysis of previous research embodied in the literature review and should be exemplified in the discussion, analysis and conclusions of the study. The processes whereby this exemplification takes place may be both overt and subtle. For instance, the researcher may provide clear and signposted statements of the theoretical or methodological 'position' that they intend to take and how this relates to a particular intellectual tradition. Such statements will usually come early in the study and scaffold the later analytical framework. Later on it is unlikely that there will be room for such direct exposition but the conceptual framework will guide the direction of the study and will be revealed by reference back to key literature explored earlier, by comparison with previous research findings, and through the general line of argument presented by the researcher.

Further reading

Bell, J. (1993) *Doing Your Research Project*. Buckingham: Open University Press.

Blaxter, L., Hughes, C. and Tight, M. (1996) *How to Research*. Buckingham: Open University Press.

Edwards, A. and Talbot, R. (1999) *The Hard-Pressed Researcher: A Research Handbook for the Caring Professions*. London: Addison Wesley Longman.

Gough, D. (2004) 'Systematic research synthesis to inform the development of policy and practice in education', in G. Thomas and R. Pring (eds), *Evidence-Based Practice*. Buckingham: Open University Press, pp. 44–62.

Oliver, S. and Peersman, G. (eds) (2001) *Using Research for Effective Health Promotion*. Buckingham: Open University Press.

Potter, S. (2002) *Doing Postgraduate Research*. London: Sage.

Thomas, J. and Harden, A. (2003) 'Practical systems for systematic reviews of research to inform policy and practice in education', in L. Anderson and N. Bennett (eds), *Evidence-Informed Policy and Practice in Educational Leadership and Management: Applications And Controversies*. London: Paul Chapman, pp. 39–54.

References

Birley, G. and Moreland, N. (1998) *A Practical Guide to Academic Research*. London: Kogan Page.

Brundrett, M. and Rhodes, C. (2013) *Researching Educational Leadership: Methods and Approaches*. London: Sage.

EPPI Centre (2007a) *Reviews of Research Evidence Are Not Necessarily Rigorous or Explicit in Their Methods of Review*. At: http://eppi.ioe.ac.uk/cms/Default.aspx?tabid=67 (accessed 3 December 2012).

EPPI Centre (2007b) *Why Is It Important to Be Systematic?* At: http://eppi.ioe.ac.uk/cms/Default.aspx?tabid=69 (accessed 3 December 2012).

EPPI Centre (2007c) *Different Types of Review*. At: http://eppi.ioe.ac.uk/cms/Default.aspx?tabid=1915 (accessed 3 December 2012).

EPPI Centre (2007d) *Administrative Systems*. At: http://eppi.ioe.ac.uk/cms/Default.aspx?tabid=1918 (accessed 3 December 2012).

EPPI Centre (2007e) *Synthesis*. At: http://eppi.ioe.ac.uk/cms/Default.aspx?tabid=178 (accessed 3 December 2012).

Gough, D., Oliver, S. and Thomas, J. (2012) *An Introduction to Systematic Reviews*. London: Sage.

Taylor, D. and Proctor, M. (2007) *The Literature Review: A Few Tips on Conducting It*. University of Toronto. At: www.utoronto.ca/writing/litrev.html (accessed 3 December 2012).

Thody, A. (2006) *Writing and Presenting Research*. London: Sage.

University of Melbourne (2007a) *Conducting a Literature Review: Getting Started*. At: www.lib.unimelb.edu.au/postgrad/litreview/gettingstarted.html (accessed 3 December 2012).

University of Melbourne (2007b) *Conducting a Literature Review: Tips on Critical Reading*. At: www.lib.unimelb.edu.au/postgrad/litreview/criticalreading.html (accessed 3 December 2012).

SECTION 2
GATHERING YOUR EVIDENCE

Section 1 of this book broadly focused on 'what to ask'. By analysing the context you are able to focus down onto the 'key issues' that will form the basis of your study. Through a thorough exploration of the literature you will have become aware of alternative theories and the outcomes of past research performed in this field. From these entwined beginnings you will have established the key questions that must be preserved at the heart of your research if it is to maintain consistency and rigour.

This section takes you to the next phase – the research design and implementation of evidence-gathering techniques. From a consideration of the various approaches to collecting the information required to address your research problem, the following chapters will guide you through the decision-making process to adopt the most appropriate research approach and tools, including the means of constructing and deploying them.

Before you are able to make the 'best choice' you will need to ensure that you are fully aware of all of the options that are potentially available to you – given the focus of your study and the contextual constraints that you are working within. You are strongly advised to consider *all* of the options laid out in this section to enable you to make a fully informed decision.

CHAPTER 4

MODELS OF RESEARCH

Before exploring some of the more practical applications, this chapter will offer a brief overview of different approaches to research that can be gained through an appreciation of theory. By the conclusion of this chapter you will:

- be aware of different approaches to research;
- be able to match the approach to the context and research aims;
- appreciate the need to justify the model, approach and method adopted.

Models of research – a philosophical starting point

If it is possible to draw a line between 'researchers' and 'practitioners' (who 'dabble' in research activity), then this is where it is probably drawn. This text is geared towards the requirementss of teaching professionals who need to use research skills to enhance their knowledge and understanding of their professional contexts in order (mainly) to make good, confident decisions which will lead to improvements. It is not designed for professional educational researchers. All professions, to a greater or lesser extent, become 'precious' of their terminology to a point where communication of key ideas with 'lay people' becomes problematic. In Chapter 1, some of this terminology was hinted at. While it is the intention to explore the terminology in greater depth here, other texts, such as Punch (2009) and Cohen et al. (2011), make this a primary focus.

There are a growing number of models of inquiry (*paradigms*), but here we will focus on the two most frequently associated with educational research: the so-called positivistic/scientific and the interpretive paradigms. With this in mind we have constructed a simplified diagram (see Figure 4.1 below) to provide an overview of the key concepts and terminology associated with each paradigm.

For centuries, positivism has been the prevailing paradigm, while interpretivism has established itself relatively late as an alternative, challenging traditional assumptions underpinning research. Both paradigms represent opposing worldviews with regard to the way in which reality is understood (ontology) and the production of knowledge (epistemology) is perceived. Reality is believed to be objective and external to the observer. Accordingly 'the purpose of research is to develop ... confidence that a particular knowledge claim ... is true or false by collecting evidence in the form of objective data of relevant phenomena' (Mertens and McLaughlin, 2004: 52).

A positivistic researcher seeks generalisations and 'hard' quantitative, measurable data by means of employing a scientific approach. In contrast, an interpretive researcher aims to explore perspectives and shared meanings and to develop insights and a deeper understanding of phenomena occurring in the social world by means of collecting predominantly qualitative data. Reality is perceived as a human construct.

In relation to the two paradigms, a further distinction can be drawn between a naturalistic and an experimental approach. While the former is conducted in a natural setting, the latter takes place under controlled conditions (clinical laboratory, control groups).

However, we need to include a caveat here, as the distinction between these two paradigms can be rather simplistic. Although certain research approaches and methods tend to reside in either the positivistic or the interpretive paradigms, there is overlap in the way in which methods are used within specific paradigms. Indeed, a mixed methodology is often adopted, combining qualitative with quantitative data. While an interpretive investigator will doubt whether a scientific/positivistic approach can adequately explore and explain human behaviour, a scientific/positivistic researcher will collect data which are of generalisable value. The probability of an

Interpretive		Positivist
Reality is a construct. It is multi-dimensional and ever changing and is dependent on different frames of reference.	1. How is reality defined? **(Ontology)**	Reality is to be discovered. It is objective, rational and independent from the observer.
The research process is underpinned by democratic principles, giving equal status to participants and welcoming diversity of perspectives. The researcher forms part of the research setting and affects and is affected by it (e.g. insider/outsider position). Issues related to status, power, ownership and control (gender, race, class, culture, political perspective) are important.	2. How does the researcher perceive him/herself in relation to the research setting? **(Positionality)**	The researcher is objective and independent from the research setting/experiment (outsider position). Negation of self, as personal values impair the scientist's objectivity/impartiality. The researcher operates within clearly defined parameters, following predetermined procedures. Observation is viewed as uncontaminated.
Qualitative data, but not exclusively. Insights, deeper knowledge and understanding of human behaviour and relationship. Exploring different perspectives relating to one phenomenon. Uniqueness.	3. What is (are) the purpose/aim(s) of the research? **(Rationale)**	Qualitative data. Generalisations. Proving/disproving of hypothesis. Searching for the 'truth'. Hypotheses are derived from theories and are submitted to empirical tests for verification and rejection.
The construction of knowledge is a democratic process, involving both researcher and research participants. Knowledge is constructed from multiple perspectives. The element of subjectivity and bias is acknowledged and declared – the 'belief' system underpinning the viewpoint of the research (e.g. feminist research).	4. How is knowledge created? **(Epistemology)**	The researcher is perceived as the 'guardian' and 'creator of knowledge' and as such occupies a position of authority in relation to the research 'subjects'. Only those phenomena that are observable and measurable can validly be warranted as knowledge (empiricism).
Theory building is perceived as an ever developing entity, not a perfect product. It is central to the research process and emerges from the dialogue between theoretical and professional perspectives and the data gathered (e.g. Grounded Theory). The conceptual framework around which the research is constructed emerges gradually (inductive method).	5. What role does theory play?	Theory and hypothesis testing provide the rationale for the research and inform its design. The conceptual framework underpinning the research design is predetermined (deductive method).

(Continued)

Figure 4.1 (Continued)

Interpretive		Positivist
Credibility and trustworthiness (building confidence in the accuracy of the data). Internal validity (thick description, rich, dense data through triangulation). Transferability, relatability, translatability of findings across similar settings.	6. What are the quality criteria of 'good' research?	External validity (the data are accurate and are also valid in relation to other contexts). Reliability (concerned with the consistency of measure). Generalisability (the research results also apply to other settings). Statistical significance.
Voluntary participation based on informed consent. Anonymity of participants and confidentiality of information divulged. Protection of research participants against potentially harmful consequences. Protection of privacy. Giving voice and ownership to the research participants.	7. What ethical issues need to be considered?	Voluntary participation based on informed consent. Anonymity of participants and confidentiality of information divulged. Protection of research participants against harmful, consequences (risk assessment).

Figure 4.1   Competing research paradigms

event will be calculated as a precise numerical value, i.e. its statistical significance. Consequently, each approach has its strengths and weaknesses and its appropriateness depends on the nature of the inquiry and the type of information that is required.

To enable you to distinguish clearly between an interpretive and positivistic framework it is important that you understand the underpinning philosophical principles and the methodological preferences generally associated with each of these two paradigms. With the intention of making the differences and potential overlap between the two paradigms apparent, we have devised a number of questions and provided answers in relation to each paradigm (Figure 4.1).

Finally, to help you distinguish between the purpose for adopting a quantitative or a qualitative methodology or approach to gathering data, it is useful to refer to the metaphors applied by Kvale (1996).

Accordingly, the qualitative researcher can be perceived as a

traveller on a journey that leads to a tale to be told upon returning home. The (researcher) traveller wanders through the landscape and enters into conversations with people encountered. The traveller explores the many domains of the country, as unknown territory and with maps, roaming freely around the territory ... (Kvale, 1996: 4)

In contrast, quantitative research can be likened to the process of mining. In this metaphor knowledge is understood as buried metal and the researcher is a miner who unearths the valuable metal ... the knowledge is waiting in the subject's interior to be uncovered, uncontaminated by the miner. (Kvale, 1996: 3)

Taber (2007: 34) helpfully refers to positivism and interpretism as ERP1 (educational research paradigm) and ERP2. In the same way that it is useful to be aware that you, as a teacher, are, for example, employing a 'positive behaviour management' approach to control a class, this awareness should also allow you to make direct links to complementary techniques; similarly, an awareness of research paradigms, in respect of what you hope to achieve, will provide an indication of the evidence-gathering techniques that are most likely to be appropriate and effective.

Box 4.1 Worked example

You wish to explore the development of speaking and listening skills within a nursery setting.

The use of predetermined criteria (developed from a published theory, model or research findings) would imply a positivist standpoint and suggest a choice from a particular range of approaches (focusing mainly on the need to collect and collate data of a comparative nature. Previous research will inform the ontology.

Entering the nursery setting with a more 'open' perspective would mean that all information being presented is, potentially, of equal importance and it is the role of the researcher to select and record appropriately. This is where epistemological issues about how and what kind of knowledge is produced have to be considered for the perspective of the researcher will inevitably influence the selection data collected and 'edit' the information to be retained and organised. For example, will the researcher focus on resource and organisational aspects which appear to impact upon the children's development or place more emphasis on the quality of social interactions between the children or children and adults? Will the information to be gathered consist of measurable 'hard' (quantitative) data generated through standardised testing or will it be made up of 'soft' (qualitative) data, reflecting the participants' feelings, experiences and opinions?

Approaches to research

In research literature there is wide range of terminology employed to describe paradigms, approaches, methodologies, strategies, techniques, methods, instruments and tools – all of which can be rather confusing to the practitioner researcher. Similarly in teaching, the use of acronyms and jargon is not always understood by pupils and parents and those outside the profession. While Denscombe (2010) distinguishes between a number of alternative research strategies, Cohen et al. (2011) list different 'styles', while Walliman (2011) prefers to use 'types' and Bell (2010) 'approaches' – lists with similar, but by no means identical content. This text, as the subheading above indicates, will use the term 'approach'.

Interestingly both Cohen et al. (2011) and Denscombe (2010) list 'Internet-based research' at this organisational level (alongside ethnography, case studies and action research), but it might also be argued that this is simply the technology by which the researcher gains access to the research population (or published information) – there are not similar sections for 'telephone' or 'library' for example. Walliman's inclusion of feminist and cultural approaches perhaps could be construed as being particular per-spectives from which to perform ethnographic research.

Cohen et al. (2011) then continue by examining various evidence gather-ing *strategies* – which Bell (2010), Walliman (2011) and Denscombe (2010) refer to as *methods*, a further confusion of terminology which can be found

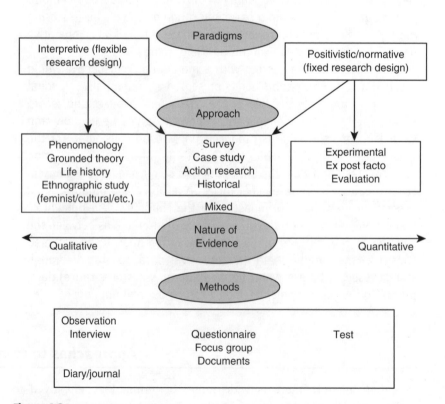

Figure 4.2   Research terminology

when comparing almost any two texts written on educational research. Here we will use 'methods'. The structure given in Figure 4.2 may help to clarify some of the terms used. Particular approaches complement the paradigms through the nature of the evidence that is related to the methods. A case study, for example, may be adopted via either paradigm; however, the nature of the evidence and the actual methodology will reflect the philosophy underpinning the chosen paradigm (qualitative or quantitative) for the research activity.

The examples given in Figure 4.2, discussed below, will also help you to distinguish between an overall methodology and specific methods residing within it. Thus the adoption of a research perspective should be considered of a higher order than the selection of a research approach/strategy and be considered to inform that selection.

- *Grounded theory*, developed by Glaser and Strauss (1967), is a pragmatic approach to the development of theories which are useful to those working 'on the ground' (Locke, 2001: 59). However, the term 'grounded' refers to the development of theory from the data, thus grounding the emergent theory in the data. At the same time it must be acknowledged that theory does not immediately spring from the data but is subject, according to Hayes (2000: 184), to 'a cyclical process in which theoretical insights emerge'. In other words, the process of data collection and analysis will involve a dialogical relationship between the data and existing (literature, professional knowledge and experience) and emerging concepts. In this sense it is firmly located within the interpretive paradigm. In its purest form, a grounded theory approach requires the researcher to enter the research setting without holding any preconceptions or socio-cultural/political biases. However, practitioner research is usually provoked by a hunch, an issue or a problem that has arisen within the context of professional practice and may also be informed by government frameworks, policy and literature.
- *Action research* also relies upon a cyclical process which is iterative in nature – the 'multi-cycle' model outlined in Figure 1.3 in Chapter 1. The aim is usually to bring about some desired change over a period of time which involves a series of interventions by the researcher(s), each one being informed by an analysis of the impact of the previous one and, as such, is possibly the most familiar to teachers, as it closely resembles the *plan–teach–assess/evaluate–plan* cycle. The approach will be explored in much greater detail in Chapter 10. The aim of action research is thus not primarily to generate knowledge but to improve professional practice within a democratic context of collaboration and inclusion.
- The *experimental* approach is worth examining not least because of the concerns that it throws up when attempting to gain ethical approval for

a piece of research! As with scientific experiments, a variable is changed and the effect is gauged, judged or measured by comparison with a control group – clearly there is direct connection to the 'single-cycle' (impact analysis) model in Figure 1.2 in Chapter 1. The concern revolves around the concept of 'harm' that can be caused to the research participants, either by being subjected to the variable or by not having access to it – a particular learning resource or strategy for example. An allied approach which is less intrusive and problematic, from the perspective of the researcher at least, is *ex post facto*. This involves a retrospective analysis of the impact of a change or specific factor – for example, the improvements in reading in Year 2 classes that have been using a particular reading strategy over the past year against those that haven't (assuming allowances for any other factors). This is also an approach preferred by professional researchers with access to large databases of evidence which are open to analysis and interpretation.

- According to Bogdan and Biklen (1982, cited in Wellington, 2000: 38), 'a *case study* is a detailed examination of one or more settings, or a single subject, or a single depository of documents or one particular event' (my emphasis). In some respects it is as much a defining of the scope and scale of the research population as it is an approach to the research. Essentially it is a concentration on the specific rather than the general – a choice of depth over breadth, and so is consistent with all of the models outlined in Chapter 1. As such, it does not dictate a particular paradigm, nor does it preclude the use of any methodology, indeed it actively encourages a multi-method approach in order to gather the necessary depth and range of data. However, interviews or questionnaires, perhaps in the form of commissioned diaries, will often form a foundation.

- While a *survey* is often used as the collective term for the gathering of evidence via interviews and questionnaires (more on which in Chapter 9), it is a distinct approach which seeks out generalised relationships between variables and influential factors and (possibly) trends over time – to compare and contrast in order to predict. It has the potential to identify and explore 'cause and effect' without the need (or where it is not possible) to construct an experimental approach.

- A *historical* approach seeks to explore the past to find explanations for contemporary issues or to find solutions to current problems. Inevitably, as it is dealing with the past, it frequently finds itself connected to documentary evidence (i.e. pre-existing data), but this is just one of many forms of recording of events in the multimedia age and the use of video or audio recordings should also be considered in addition to collecting primary data from those who experienced the situation first hand.

- Generally (as there are several divergent views expressed in the literature here) *ethnographic* approaches are an attempt to reveal, describe and (in some cases) explain a culture that the intended audience of the research is unlikely to be familiar with in these terms. As an approach it is highly susceptible to the interpretations placed upon the evidence by the researcher. These interpretations will usually be revealed by the way that the evidence is selected or presented.

- *Feminist* research often adopts an ethnographic approach filtered through a particular editorial and philosophical perspective, with the aim of giving voice to the research participants.
- The *cultural* approach, as defined by Walliman (2011), concentrates on the way that a context can be interpreted and analysed through an examination of the linguistic content or through the interaction of language and the social setting (discourse analysis).
- *Evaluation* can be taken to be the purpose of research activity, but Walliman (2011) argues that it should be considered a distinct approach with two separate strands. With *systems analysis* a holistic approach is taken to the examination of complex situation (classroom or organisational dynamics for example), which is progressively deconstructed into more manageable (explainable) chunks. *Responsive evaluation* focuses on an impact analysis of initiatives (e.g. a new scheme of work) on particular stakeholder groups (e.g. students, teachers). Perceived in this way, it falls within the realms of the positivist paradigm, although the evaluation of the implementation of new programmes and initiatives may well justify a qualitative case study approach. In either case, evaluation can be adopted for 'snapshot' or 'single-cycle' research activities.

Box 4.2   Have we made a decision yet?

Before progressing it is worth taking stock:

- An appreciation of the models of inquiry (research paradigms) requires us to consider the perspective our research will take – recording and measuring (positivist) or explaining and interpreting (interpretive).
- Next we need to consider the value and appropriateness of the different approaches/strategies to the aims and focus of the research.
- Finally, the relative merits of different data collection methods should be considered before constructing the actual research tools that will be used to gather the data.

Let's see how this process might work in practice.

Deconstruct the question

As teachers we are repeatedly asked to start from the learning objectives and then work towards the construction of the learning activities and the delivery strategies (although there is increasing pressure to adopt particular teaching strategies and certain learning resources). In some key respects research activity has similar pressures. There may be an 'inner desire' to use a questionnaire or interview someone – but you have to hold yourself back from jumping in with a specific methodology and consider what is most appropriate for what you hope to achieve (your research aims).

We can start by examining some generic starting points for research activity and considering how they might be approached and what methods might be adopted. Look for similarities between the generic questions in Box 4.3 and your own proposed piece of research.

Box 4.3

How did we get to where we currently are? (a 'snapshot')

Why are our exam results so poor? What makes our school popular? What makes our staff (or student) retention so bad?

- Either paradigm could be appropriate – positivism if the aim is to detect a trend or pattern in relation to a particular phenomenon, or interpretivism if the outcomes are to provide an insight into or a deeper understanding of it, including explanations.
- This type of focus strongly indicates a historical approach to examine factors and decisions to gain a deeper understanding of our current situation, but it might also be approached through a longitudinal study (if still contemporary) or as a case study.
- Methods are likely to include analysis of documents, questionnaires, interviews, focus group discussion.

Where are we? (a 'snapshot')

How do we identify and address the needs of gifted and talented learners? How do we manage the performance of 'inadequate' teaching staff?

- Although an interpretive approach is possible, a mixed methodology including qualitative and quantitative data may generate a more complete picture.

- A static evaluation/examination of the current position in preparation for making a change would probably indicate a case study or survey approach. However, if the perceptions of the key players are the focus (the gifted learner/the line manager/the 'poor' teacher) then an ethnographic approach would be appropriate.
- Documents (policies and procedures) would offer reference points which could be compared with professional practice through interviews, observations or possibly participant diaries.

What are our options? (a 'snapshot')

Which scheme is 'best'? Which mode of delivery will be most effective? What management structure should we choose?

- There is a positivist suggestion here of comparing opposing options in some criterion-referenced format. Even so, there will probably be a strong focus on the opinions of the stakeholders.
- As there is an emphasis on matching the appropriateness of differing potential lines of progression to current and proposed positions of a specific context, it is important to fully explore the nature of that context, suggesting a case study. However, the 'matching' element would probably suggest a survey approach to compare opinions.
- Evidence will be gathered from documents to specify the options, and surveys and observation could be employed to gain greater understanding of the context.

What is happening? (a 'snapshot' or multi-cycle)

What is induction like for new member of staff? How do we manage the change towards vertical pastoral groups? What is actually involved in planning a residential trip?

- The passive tracking of a development through a focus on processes rather than outcomes does have a strong interpretive feel about it.
- While an ethnographical approach may well provide a wider perspective of all the factors which impact on what is happening, a narrative approach may provide a much more personal perspective.
- Once again documents (policies, etc.) should provide a secure foundation on which to base discussion and analysis. Surveys should offer a wider perspective, while critical diaries can provide personal insights, with observation as a means of connecting the strands together.

(Continued)

(Continued)

What happens when we do this? (single- or multi-cycle)

Does 'BrainGym' (or 'Activ8') have an impact on learner concentration spans? What has been the effect on staff morale of 'learning teams'? What has been the impact of parental involvement in morning 'reading time'?

- Depending upon the specific interests of the researcher either paradigm is appropriate. In this case it is driven by the nature of the evidence being sought rather than the nature of the investigation itself.
- An interventionist approach to change where the researcher manipulates the situations to progress towards a desired outcome as an iterative process would suggest an action research approach. However, if it was approached from a more dispassionate and objective perspective, where the intervention, once started, was allowed to run its course, the approach would be more experimental in nature.
- Documents may provide an important 'baseline' by which to judge the impact of subsequent initiatives – standardised test results for example. However, it may be necessary to gather evidence through 'before and after' tests (surveys) or record change through participant observation. For more detailed and intimate responses and perceptions critical diaries should be considered alongside interview techniques.

What happened? (a 'snapshot', or single cycle)

Did setting for maths improve the standardised test results? Has the personal tutorial system improved student retention? Did the peer mentoring system help to embed assessment for learning?

- Educational organisations frequently progress onto the 'next big initiative' before the effects of the previous one have been fully analysed and appreciated. Given this particular emphasis, the research module is likely to be positivist in attempting to accurately record the outcomes of an initiative.
- Evaluation of the effectiveness of a particular intervention or change strategy could be considered a *de post facto* approach. Adopting an evaluative approach suggests a more interventionist style or greater ownership of the issues than the first example given above.
- Often documents will be useful in tracking what happened (minutes of meetings to lesson plans or examples of children's writing), but interviewing or distributing questionnaires to the key stakeholders would provide detailed and specific information about processes and the context within which they occur.

Working from pros and cons

The success of a research activity frequently hangs on the choice of an approach which appropriately meets the needs of the research aims. The examples offered above provide an indication of the way in which you need to be thinking to ensure that you think through the implications of what you are trying to achieve and that you are fully aware of the options available to you. If, for example, you are determined to compare the way that your school manages social inclusion with another school working with a similar intake, you need to consider very carefully issues of access to information – while your position in your school may mean that you have access to a full range of potential sources of information, you need to ask yourself whether you will you be afforded similar access in the other school. Would, for example, a case study of your own school linked to a review of policy documents publicly available from other schools be a more realistic and achievable approach?

Choosing a set of research methods is always a compromise between the ideal and the achievable, while maintaining a keen focus on the purposes of the research and its practicability. It is important to place any research on a secure foundation by ensuring that there will be the opportunity to access important sources of information – during the early stages of planning it is therefore essential that access is agreed to key sources, e.g. documents held by the organisation, children in the focus class, parents/carers of the children, etc. Once the potential sources have been identified and access secured, it is then a matter of exploring the options for collecting appropriate evidence, of various types, from those sources (see Chapter 6).

The most frequently mentioned methods for gathering research evidence discussed and explained in the standard texts (Cohen et al., 2011; Bell, 2010; Denscombe, 2010, for example) include:

- observations
- interviews
- focus groups
- questionnaires
- documents
- diaries
- tests.

Each one is examined in more detail in later chapters, along with a further examination of action research as a specific form of research in an educational setting. However, Box 4.4 provides a brief listing of the key merits and drawbacks of each.

Box 4.4

Observations (Chapter 8)

Pros:

- Teachers are usually skilled observers as a result of their professional practice.
- Facilitates a focus on what actually happens.
- A single observer can produce comparative evidence.
- Video offers the potential of recording for later or repeated observation.

Cons:

- A single observer may have inherent bias and will necessarily filter information prior to recording.
- Those being observed may change behaviour as a result of the observation.
- The observer may misinterpret what they are observing (objectivity and selectivity).
- Impossible to record everything and time-consuming!

Interviews (Chapter 9)

Pros:

- Useful for obtaining sensitive or in-depth information from a knowledgeable respondent.
- Interactive – allows the interviewer to probe and pursue relevant themes.
- Most effective when there is a positive relationship and trust between interviewer and interviewee.

Cons:

- The interviewer requires the skill to keep the interview focused.
- Very time-consuming to perform, record and collate.
- May be difficult to arrange.

Questionnaires (Chapter 9)

Pros:

- Can generate a lot of information very quickly and easily.
- Can be structured to provide comparable information in an easily collatable form.

- Allows remote access to respondents.
- Provides respondent with privacy, anonymity and space for reflection.

Cons:

- Must be very carefully checked and trialled prior to use to ensure that instructions are unambiguous, responses are in the form expected and that it is manageable for the respondent.
- Response rate can be very low.
- Unlikely to obtain detailed or profound information this way.

Documents (Chapter 7)

Pros:

- Useful as a baseline to other sources.
- Low cost and unobtrusive.
- Useful insight into past events.

Cons:

- Documents are unlikely to fit the precise needs of the research.
- Documents are not 'value neutral' and may have been written with a particular agenda or perspective in mind.
- Credibility and authenticity need to be assured.

Diaries (Chapter 7)

Pros:

- Can provide detailed, insightful information over a period of time.
- Can provide the basis for detailed interview.
- Comparative information from diarists (if a semi-structured approach is employed).

Cons:

- Significant effort, engagement and involvement required of the diarists.
- Non-standard responses/language/format can make comparisons very challenging through potential ambiguities in interpretation.
- Diarists may be atypical or have their own agenda.

(Continued)

(Continued)

***Tests* (Chapter 7)**

Pros:

- Useful means of establishing a learning baseline or demonstrating improvement.
- Standardised criteria for ease of comparison.

Cons:

- May need to be adapted to make it appropriate for different learners.
- May not test the precise skills or knowledge under examination in the research.

Selection or de-selection?

While it may be easier to explain why a certain research methodology has been chosen to gather specific information from a particular research population, it is perhaps more challenging to explain why others were rejected. For example, the choice of a semi-structured interview with the ICT coordinator/leader to discuss the implementation of a cross-curricular ICT initiative may be entirely reasonable and appropriate, but the decision would be much more secure if it could be shown that alternate methodologies were considered but rejected for good reason. A critical diary, for the coordinator to complete during specific stages of the implementation process, while offering contemporaneous insights, may have been deemed too onerous or time-consuming. But this at least demonstrates that the researcher is aware of other means of gathering evidence and can make rational decisions about how to proceed.

By approaching the final stages of the research design in this way it not only demonstrates your awareness of the options that you have available to you, and your knowledge of their strengths and weaknesses, but it also enables you to discuss this in close connection to the context of the research activity. This allows you to avoid resorting to a 'textbook' style of explanation to demonstrate to your tutor or mentor just how much you know about research methodology in general, and to concentrate on justifying your research decisions in relation to your specific practice setting.

To be able to understand the different research approaches sufficiently to be able to make informed and appropriate choices tends to suggest that you have taken the time and effort to read about them! It is important to acknowledge how your reading has influenced your decision-making process by making reference to these sources as you explain how you intend to gather your evidence.

Summary

While it is not always necessary to progress through all of these stages, you should be aware of them so that you can appreciate their impact on the final construction and outcomes of your research activity. In your considerations you will demonstrate the influence of existing theories, different theoretical perspectives and conceptual constructions and past research in the field, along with an awareness and sensitivity to the context in which you are working and the research population that you are working with.

- *Paradigm* – what is your model or framework of inquiry?
- *Approach* – what type of research strategy best fits what you hope to achieve?
- *Method* – what are the most appropriate techniques for you to gather evidence?

From this, you then need to be able to construct *research tools* (observation/interview schedules, questionnaires) through which the evidence will actually be gathered.

References

Bell, J. (2010) *Doing Your Research Project*. Buckingham: Open University Press.

Bogdan, R. and Biklen, S. (1982) 'Qualitative research for education', in Wellington, J. (2000), *Educational Research: Contemporary Issues and Practical Research*. London: Continuum.

Cohen, L., Manion, L. and Morrison, K. (2011) *Research Methods in Education*, 7th edn. Abingdon: Routledge.

Denscombe, M. (2010) *The Good Research Guide*, 4th edn. Maidenhead: Open University Press.

Glaser, B. and Strauss, A. (1967) *The Discovery of Grounded Theory*. Chicago: Aldine.

Hayes, N. (2000) *Doing Psychological Research: Gathering and Analysing Data*. Buckingham: Open University Press.

Kvale, S. (1996) *Interviews*. London: Sage.

Locke, K. (2001) *Grounded Theory in Management Research*. London: Sage.

Mertens, D. M. and McLaughlin, J. A. (2004) *Research and Evaluation Methods in Special Education*. Thousands Oaks, CA: Corwin.

Punch, K. (2009) *An Introduction to Research Methods in Education*. London: Sage.

Taber, K. (2007) *Classroom-Based Research and Evidence-Based Practice*. London: Sage.

Walliman, N. (2011) *Your Research Project*, 3rd edn. London: Sage.

CHAPTER 5

CONSIDERATION OF ETHICAL ISSUES

This chapter will focus on the following learning outcomes:

- development of a critical understanding of the principles underpinning research involving human beings, especially vulnerable groups;
- identification of potential ethical issues that you need to take into consideration prior to, during and following completion of data collection;
- production of appropriate documentation regarding gatekeeper's permission and informed consent.

(Continued)

(Continued)

By the time you have read this chapter you should be able to employ ethically appropriate strategies in:

- your selection and recruitment of research participants;
- seeking gatekeepers' permission;
- obtaining participants' informed consent;
- conducting data collection (e.g. interviewing, observation);
- your dissemination of research findings.

Ethics and the professional practice context

In a drive to raise standards in education and academic achievement, schools and teachers working within them have come under increasing pressure to strive for continual improvement of their practice with the aim of enhancing teaching and learning. Practitioner research, and within that action research, have been widely advocated as a means of facilitating teachers' professional learning and development. Teachers and other education professionals are expected to inform and enhance their professional practice with evidence-based research which they themselves have undertaken. This places upon them not only a responsibility to ensure that the research process is trustworthy and relevant, but also that it is ethically sound. In other words, their key concern must be to minimise any potential risk that might endanger the physical, emotional, financial or general well-being of the potential participants or stakeholders.

Ethics have always been recognised as a central element in medical and scientific research, but during the past ten years or so, there has been a growing awareness of ethical issues in relation to practitioner research in educational settings, particularly action research. In view of the increase in this practice-based research at postgraduate and doctoral level, higher education institutions increasingly require students to apply for ethical approval prior to commencing their investigation and to comply with a set of prescribed procedures and principles as set out in the university's ethics code. A particularly useful source of information on ethical issues which should be addressed is the *Revised Ethical Guidelines for Educational Research* (2011) published by the British Educational Research Association (BERA). It is unambiguous, easily accessible and provides a useful reference point for practitioners intending to conduct research in their professional practice setting. For example, it recommends that the researcher's behaviour should be underpinned by a respect for the person, knowledge, democratic values, the quality of research and academic freedom. In practice this means that participants' dignity must be preserved at all time, including when data collection has been completed and findings are reported (Mauthner et al., 2002; Oliver, 2003). They must be treated fairly and sensitively, regardless of age, gender, religion, ethnicity, class or disability. Researchers thus accept responsibility not only towards those participating in their research as participants (e.g. students, colleagues) or key informants (e.g. policy-makers, administrators), but also towards gatekeepers (e.g. heads of department, head teachers, local authority) and those who may have sponsored the research.

Taking responsibility for sound ethical practice is particularly important in a competitive climate and a culture of accountability, where teachers, subject leaders and head teachers are under constant pressure to improve their league table position or, following an Ofsted inspection, need to address areas identified for further development in their school improvement plan. While these internal and external imperatives can function as genuine incentives to undertake a critical inquiry into educational practice with the aim of finding solutions to problems, they can also exert pressure on the practitioner conducting the research to achieve the desired outcome. For example, distorting evidence by selectively focusing on some aspects and not others, abusing one's insider position or failing to declare a conflict of interest would constitute unethical behaviour on the part of the researcher.

We will now focus on four distinct aspects that are central to an ethically sound research practice and that are particularly pertinent to practitioners conducting research in their own practice setting. They concern:

- gaining access to the research setting;
- obtaining participants' informed consent;
- the researcher's positionality (insider/outsider role);
- ownership and balance of power.

Gaining access

There are two, more likely three, levels of access to be negotiated before any evidence is gathered in order to ensure the ethical standards of the proposed research are adequate. The first is the need to confirm that the gatekeeper of your proposed research population (if one can be identified) is in agreement with your research aims and the tools that you intend to use – the head of department or head teacher of the school for example. If you are working towards an academic qualification, you will also need to satisfy the ethical requirements of the organisation you are studying with. A prerequisite teachers normally possess, and one that all those working with or being in contact with children need to fulfil, is a valid Criminal Records Bureau (CRB) check.

In the complex mechanism of bureaucratic, technical and logistical difficulties, gatekeepers and key informants play a crucial role in the process of gaining access, with issues of building trusts and developing relationships lying at the heart of the process. As much as they can hamper the process of data collection, they can equally well function as 'catalysts' in the process of reaching compromises, taking short-cuts and bringing about serendipitous occurrences (Walford, 1991), which can enhance the quality and quantity of data you collect. As a teacher you may consider your 'insider' position as a distinct advantage. This is often based on the assumption that access is automatically granted and students and/or colleagues are only too willing to participate in your study. Particularly researchers in senior managerial roles must be mindful of their positions of power and control and must ensure that potential participants are made aware of their rights not to take part or to withdraw from the research at any stage and that participation is based on informed consent.

However, before you start approaching any potential research participants you need to obtain the gatekeeper's permission to proceed. Particular care needs to be taken where the research outcomes may have an impact on part of or the whole school. It is therefore not only courteous, but is also considered good research practice to consult the head teacher and any other colleagues whose department may be affected by your study. This will also allay any potential concerns and anxieties among those who may be involved or be indirectly affected by your research and it is thefefore important that you adhere to the ethical principle of informed consent. Providing gatekeepers with detailed and accurate information about your intended research is an absolute must and should include the following key points:

- background to the project in terms of the local, regional or national context;
- purpose of the research, including key objectives;
- criteria used in the selection of participants;
- phases of the research;
- procedures involved in data collection/intervention;
- audience to whom the research outcomes may be of interest or benefit;
- dissemination of research findings (e.g. conference presentations, journal articles);
- contact details for further information.

Where a cluster of schools is involved, as might be the case in an evaluative study concerned with the social inclusion of children with SEN in mainstream education, it would also be appropriate to seek the local authority's approval. As Measor and Woods (1984) highlighted in their study in a comprehensive school, any shortcuts taken at this stage may result in blockage at a later stage of the research process, which can result in the breakdown of relationships and trust between the researchers and gatekeepers and ultimately in the end of the investigation. Gaining access to the research setting is thus closely linked to establishing trusting relationships with gate-keepers and key informants. Box 5.1 is an example of a letter requesting the gatekeeper's permission to conduct an evaluation of an intervention in the primary PE curriculum that seeks to improve the inclusion of children with disabilities.

Box 5.1　Letter to gatekeeper

Dear Head Teacher/Head of PE

Re: Study of the Football in the Community Pan-Disability Coaching Programme

I am writing to you in connection with the *Football in the Community* Pan-disability Coaching Programme, which will take place in your school in the autumn term 2011. The programme allows children with disabilities to take part in an enjoyable, high-quality physical activity programme as part of their PE lessons and aims to provide young people with disabilities with a positive experience of sport, in order to increase their fundamental physical skills and to raise self-esteem. I would like to ask your permission to conduct the evaluation of this programme.

To evaluate the quality and impact of the programme on children with and without disabilities I would like to carry out a study which will investigate the perceptions and experiences of the participating children and those directly or indirectly involved in its delivery. I would also like to examine the unique techniques and methods used by the coaches from XXXX Football Club to engage a wide range of children and adolescents with disabilities in physical activity with the aim of developing a resources pack for teachers, teaching assistants and coaches involved in the delivery of such activities.

The study will involve the collection of data from pupils participating in the pan-disability programme, their parents/carers, teachers and teaching assistants involved in the delivery of PE and external coaches. The following strategies will be used:

- observation of sessions delivered by the coaches;
- questionnaires and face-to-face recorded interviews with pupils, parents/carers, teachers and teaching assistants.

(Continued)

(Continued)

Data collection will take place in the PE lessons during which the pan-disability coaching programme will be delivered. In order to obtain parental and carers' informed consent we would be grateful if the distribution and collection of relevant documentation could be facilitated via the school. Enclosed you will find the participant information sheets and consent forms / assent forms as well as for your information the interview schedules and questionnaires to be used with parents/carers and pupils.

This study will allow pupils participating in the pan-disability programme to express their views about any benefits derived and challenges encountered. It will give those participating in the programme a voice to explain which aspects of the programme were beneficial and which would benefit from further development and improvement. By giving your permission for this study to be conducted in your school, you are making a valuable contribution to the future design of pan-disability programmes and relevant learning resources for staff delivering such programmes, which will be of benefit for children and young people of all abilities.

Thank you for your time and giving this matter your consideration.

Yours sincerely

[Signature of project leader]

If you have any further questions please contact:

Contact details:
Tel:
Email:

Informed consent

In order to ensure that all potential participants can make an informed decision on whether they wish to take part in your research or not, you will need to provide them with clear and detailed information about the project you intend to undertake and explain how they will be involved. This will include:

- an explanation of the purpose of your research to your potential participants and why they have been invited to take part so that they are fully informed about the reasons for the data collection processes;

- assurance that the information they provide will be held in confidence, securely stored and destroyed;
- assurance that their anonymity will be maintained where their responses might be reported in any published form (the purpose of any identifier placed on any questionnaire or test will need to be explained);
- confirmation that participation is entirely voluntary and that they can withdraw at any stage of the research process, if they wish.

This information should be communicated to all potential participants in a participant information sheet (P-I sheet), or, if they have difficulty accessing a written text, a verbal introduction explaining the data collection can be given instead. Cohen et al. (2007: 339) provide a fairly definitive list of what should be included in such letters. Projects that include different groups of participants, such as children/young people, parents/guardians/carers and teachers, will require a participant information sheet for each participant group to ensure that the style of presentation and language used is appropriate in terms of level of comprehension. Particular care needs to be taken where members of vulnerable groups (e.g. children/young people under the age of 16 or with special needs) are involved. Research involving children is generally considered a risky undertaking (Hood et al., 1996).

In order to ensure that the information given is fully understood by all participants, it may be necessary to produce a customised participant information sheet for each sub-group of the entire sample, which takes account of their specific characteristics and needs in terms of the way in which the information is presented. This may involve the use of appropriate language, clear layout and a larger than usual font size. It may also include a specific colour scheme, for example blue script on a yellow background to cater for participants with dyslexia or colour blindness. Boxes 5.2 and 5.3 show two examples of participant information sheets. The first is for children and the second for their parents/guardians/carers, whose consent is required before the children can decide whether or not they wish to participate in the research.

Box 5.2   Participant information sheet for children

Title of project: Evaluation of a Pan-Disability Coaching Programme

Name of researcher: John Smith, Social Inclusion Officer, Riverside Primary School

You are being invited to take part in a research study. Before you decide it is important that you understand why the research is being done and what it involves. Please take time to read the following

(Continued)

(Continued)

information. Ask me if there is anything that is not clear or if you would like more information. Take time to decide if you want to take part or not.

1. What is the purpose of the study?

Coaches from XXXX Football Club are coming into your school this term to get all children involved in sport in a fun way. I would be interested in what you think about the programme and would therefore like to talk to you about how it was for you, what you enjoyed and what you think could be made better.

Do I have to take part?

Whether you take part in this study is up to you. If you do want to take part, you will be given this information sheet and asked to sign a consent form. You can still decide to stop taking part at any time and without telling us why.

What will happen to me if I take part?

I would like to know what you think about the programme to help me to find out what works well in involving all children in sport. This will help me in making learning materials for teachers, teaching assistants and coaches. There are two activities which you might wish to do:

1. Complete a *questionnaire*.
2. Volunteer to take part in a recorded *interview* with a member of the research team. The interview will last approximately 15–20 minutes.

The questionnaire and interview will take place at your school. You don't have to do both. On the consent form, you can put a tick by what you want to do.

2. What are the benefits of being involved?

There are no risks to taking part in this study. I hope that you will enjoy participating in the Pan-Disability Coaching Programme. By taking part in this study you will be able to tell me how you felt about the programme, letting me know what you liked about it and what could be improved. Thus you can help make pan-disability programmes better.

3. Will my taking part in the study be kept confidential?

The questionnaires you complete and what you say in interviews will be kept securely so that no one outside the research team will be able to find out what you said or wrote. No one will ever be able to know that what you said or wrote is your words, as your name will not be kept with what you say or write (that is it will be stored anonymously).

If you have any further questions please contact one of the Principal Investigators below:

Postal address:
Email address:
Telephone number:

Box 5.3   Participant information sheet for parents/guardians/carers of children

Title of project: Evaluation of a Pan-disability Coaching Programme

Name of researcher: John Smith, Social Inclusion Officer, Riverside Primary School

You and your child are being invited to take part in a research study. Before you decide it is important that you understand why the research is being done and what it involves. Please take time to read the following information. Ask me if there is anything that is not clear or if you would like more information. Take time to decide if you want to take part or not.

1. What is the purpose of the study?

The school of your child has agreed to participate in the Pan-Disability Coaching Programme which allows children with disabilities to take part in an enjoyable, high-quality physical activity programme as part of their PE lessons. The programme aims to provide young people with disabilities with a positive experience of sport, to increase their fundamental physical skills and to raise self-esteem.

The study I intend to carry out will examine the unique techniques and methods used by coaches from XXXX Football Club to engage a wide range of children with disabilities in physical activity in primary schools.

(Continued)

(Continued)

2. Do I have to take part? Does your child have to take part?

Participation in this study is entirely voluntary and it is up to you to decide whether or not you or your child wants to be involved. If you do, you will be given this information sheet and asked to sign a consent form. You or your child is still free to withdraw at any time and without giving a reason. A decision to withdraw will not affect your rights/any future treatment/service you receive.

3. What will happen to me/my child if I/s/he take(s) part?

The pan-disability initiative is a physical activity programme that involves children with and without disabilities. I would like to know how beneficial it is for the participants and would therefore like to investigate the experiences of those participating in it. I am also keen to know the views of parents/carers whose children are involved in the programme in order to develop the programme further and produce learning materials for teachers, teaching assistants and coaches.

This is what your child/you will be invited to do if you agree to be involved:

All pupils participating in the programme will be asked to complete a *questionnaire* with the assistance of one of the university research team, if appropriate. Your child will also be invited to take part in a *focus group* and/or a one-to-one recorded *interview* with a member of the research team. The one-to-one recorded interview (30 minutes) and focus group (60 minutes) will take place during a Pan-Disability Programme session on school premises and last approximately 15–20 minutes. The focus group and interview will be conducted by a member of the university research team, all of whom have had a Criminal Records Bureau check.

In order to help me identify those techniques and practices which children with disabilities find particularly beneficial and enjoyable, I would like to *video record* some of the sessions. The purpose of doing this would be to identify examples of good practice, which could be used in the production of training materials for new teachers, teaching assistants and coaches and thus provide better opportunities for children with disabilities to engage in physical activity and sport at school.

I would therefore be delighted if you gave your permission for your child to be involved in this study. Your child need not participate in all three research activities. On the enclosed consent (for parents/carers) and assent (for your child) forms you can indicate your and your child's options.

4. What are the benefits of being involved?

There are no risks involved in participating in this study. I hope that your child will enjoy participating in the Pan-Disability Coaching Programme. By taking part in this study the children will have the opportunity to express their views about the programme in terms of benefits derived and challenges encountered. It will give them a voice to explain which aspects of the programme were beneficial and which would benefit from further development and improvement. By participating in this study you and your child could make a valuable contribution to the design of pan-disability programmes that benefit children with and without a disability.

5. Will my taking part in the study be kept confidential?

All information about your child will be treated with the strictest confidence and stored securely. Only the researcher will have access to the information generated. Unique identifying codes will be used to protect the participants' identity. Pictures or video clips of activities involving your child will only be used with your permission.

If you have any further questions please contact one of the Principal Investigators below:

Postal address:
Email address:
Telephone:

The question of whether you always need to obtain parents'/guardians'/carers' consent has generated critical debate among educational researchers and is not easy to answer. BERA (2011) provides a helpful guideline with reference to the United Nations Convention on the Rights of the Child. Accordingly, 'the best interests of the child must be the primary consideration' (Art. 3) and 'Children who are capable of forming their own views should be granted the right to express their views freely in all matters affecting them, commensurate with their age and maturity' (Art. 12). Given that the law relates to the notion of 'competence' (see Masson, 2000; Anderson and Morrow, 2011), it seems reasonable to suggest that parent/guardian consent can be waived where a child can be judged to understand what participation in a particular project will involve. This introduces a further consideration in relation to participants' competence, which may be determined by their age, intellectual ability, level of emotional maturity and their social and cultural background. In such circumstances the question arises whether the parent/guardian has the right to override the child's wishes. According to Fine and Sandstrom (1988) it is the nature of the research that is critical. They, along with Lindsay (2000) and Hill (2005), believe that the head teacher's consent is sufficient unless the children are involved in an extreme form of research. Masson (2004) defends the view that a social researcher who does not seek parents'/guardians' consent for an under16-year-old participant should not be at risk of legal procedures brought by parents/guardians unless it is about causing harm to the child.

Providing potential participants with unambiguous and detailed information about the research needs to be accompanied by a strategy to obtain their written (or, where not possible, verbal) consent, clearly articulating the specific research activities and dissemination modes for which consent is sought. Boxes 5.4 and 5.5 provide two examples, a consent form for parents/guardians/carers and an assent form for children.

Box 5.4   Consent form for parents/guardians/carers

Project title: Evaluation of a Pan-Disability Coaching Programme

Name of researcher: John Smith

1. I confirm that I have read and understand the information provided for the above study. I have had the opportunity to consider the information, ask questions and have had these answered satisfactorily.   Yes/No

2. I understand that my participation is voluntary and that I am free to withdraw at any time, without giving a reason, and that this will not affect my legal rights.   Yes/No

3. I understand that any personal information collected during the study will be anonymised and remain confidential.   Yes/No

4. I agree to take part in recorded face-to-face interviews.   Yes/No

5. I understand that the interview/focus group will be audio recorded and I am happy to proceed.   Yes/No

6. I understand that parts of our conversation may be used verbatim in future publications or presentations but that such quotes will be anonymised.   Yes/No

Name of Participant	Date	Signature
Name of Researcher	Date	Signature
Name of Person taking consent	Date	Signature

(*if different from researcher*)

Note: *When completed 1 copy for participant and 1 copy for researcher.*

Box 5.5   Assent form for children

Project title: Evaluation of a Pan-Disability Coaching Programme

Name of researcher: John Smith

Child (or if unable, parent/guardian on their behalf)

Have you read (or had read to you) information about this project?	Yes/No
Has somebody else explained this project to you?	Yes/No
Do you understand what this project is about?	Yes/No
Have you asked all the questions you want?	Yes/No
Have you had your questions answered in a way you understand?	Yes/No
Do you understand it's OK to stop taking part at any time?	Yes/No
Are you happy to take part?	Yes/No

If **any** answers are 'no' or you **don't** want to take part, don't sign your name!

If you **do** want to take part, you can write your name below

Your name: _____

Date: _____

Your parent or guardian must write their name here if they are happy for you to do the project.

Print name: _____

Sign: _____

Date: _____

The researcher who explained this project to you needs to sign too:

Print name: _____

Sign: _____

Date: _____

The researcher's positionality – the insider/outsider role

Teachers and researchers share one common responsibility, namely 'duty of care' in relation to all those involved in the teaching and learning process and any related research. Behaving in an ethical manner will also increase the chances of maintaining positive relationships between researcher and research participants for the duration of the study. As Groundwater-Smith and Mockler assure us, 'quality action (and practitioner) research is in its very nature an ethical business' (2007: 209).

Given that practitioner research is conducted by teachers already located within the research setting, gaining access is often considered not to pose any great challenges. In fact, classroom practitioners may have difficulty distinguishing between data collection they undertake as a classroom practitioner with the aim of reviewing, analysing and improving teaching and learning processes and similar activities commonly associated with practice-based research. For example, information gathered via pupil observation, a questionnaire survey involving parents/guardians/carers or face-to-face interviews with colleagues may be used internally to inform and improve professional practice, but, equally, could be made available in the public domain to a much wider audience. In this case, we would view the process as being more akin to research rather than merely constituting an aspect of professional practice. As such, it would require careful exploration of the potential ethical issues inherent in the research setting and the selection of strategies that address them appropriately. 'Insider' research can thus be problematic and raise issues of balance of power, ownership and voice, anonymity and confidentiality, and informed consent, to which we will return later in greater detail. Mauthner et al. (2002) explore such issues from a feminist ethics of care perspective, which is equally relevant to practitioner research in educational settings. Nevertheless, the distinction between an ethical, moral and legally defensible approach is not always clear-cut, as all three are concerned with the protection of individuals, physically, psychologically, emotionally or in any other conceivable form. For example, suppose the introduction of a new strategy designed to assist pupils in developing their reading skills is to be evaluated. To ensure the quality of the research, one group of pupils will be exposed to the new strategy while a control group will not have the opportunity of enjoying the potential benefits of this innovative intervention. While such a procedure is perfectly legal, it raises ethical issues of fairness and inclusion. Similarly, deliberately misleading a group of participants, for example to test their resilience to powerful means of persuasion in the safe knowledge that no one will come to any harm, is predominantly a moral issue. In contrast, the observation and video recording of children's behaviour in the playground would first and foremost constitute a legal issue, although as part of their professional role teachers regularly observe and record pupils' behaviour. What is at issue here is the future use of the material, i.e. whether it will be available in the public domain.

Ownership

To ensure a sense of inclusion and ownership among all stakeholders it is vital that all their perspectives are considered in the design of the action and its implementation. This presents challenges to the person leading the project in terms of providing effective leadership and in managing potential ethical issues. We would now like you to consider the scenario presented in Box 5.6 which raises potential issues and poses pertinent questions of how they should be addressed.

Box 5.6

Within the agenda of raising achievement as well as *Every Child Matters*, a school's senior management team has identified issues with regard to pupil transition from Key Stage 2 to Key Stage 3. To assist pupils in managing the transition it was decided to implement a new curriculum for Year 7 pupils, which will mirror some of the conditions prevailing in a primary education setting.

Year 7 teachers will be attached to a mixed-ability class in a designated classroom, teaching across a range of subjects. It is hoped that, within a stable learning environment and through regular contact with their teacher and peers, pupils in 'their own base' will be helped to form positive relationships, develop a sense of cohort identity and belonging and, as a consequence, will be better equipped to manage the challenges of transfer from primary to secondary school and from Key Stage 2 to Key Stage 3. The aim of this intervention is to enhance the quality of pupils' learning experiences, to generate a sense of well-being and ultimately to raise achievement.

However, the response from school staff is divided. While some teachers are excited at the prospect of stepping outside the boundaries of their subject specialism, others are very unhappy at the prospect of having to confine their teaching almost exclusively to Year 7 and of losing the intellectual stimulation of working with older GCSE and AS/A level students. Furthermore, they expressed concern about having to teach subjects in which they lack knowledge and expertise.

An assistant head teacher, who is aspiring to take on a headship in the foreseeable future and who is currently selecting a topic for his MA

(Continued)

(Continued)

dissertation in Education and Management, would like to take this opportunity for conducting an action research project as part of his dissertation.

Points you will need to consider:

- the composition of the research team to ensure ownership across stakeholders
- the kind of data should that should be collected
- inclusion of a range of perspectives via triangulation
- potential ethical issues arising from insider action research
- seeking consent.

Balance of power

Conducting action research in your own institution can lull you into a false sense of security, as you are familiar with the setting and know the actors within it. Insiders often have knowledge not only about an institution but also about the people who work within it and those who are designated to participate in the action research (Costley and Gibbs, 2006). The combination of these factors may engender ambivalent feelings towards you among your colleagues. In your role as researcher, you may suddenly be perceived in a different light, namely as someone who has a hidden agenda and can therefore not be trusted unconditionally. In addition, you may occupy a position of power within your institution's management system, inadvertently affecting colleagues' behaviour towards you in a number of ways. There may be a faction within your school who perceive the research exercise as a fortuitous opportunity to promote their own interests and air their personal or departmental grievances in the hope that they can influence the outcome of the research and thus have an impact on strategic decisions relevant to them. Others may want to demonstrate their loyalty to you by giving you the responses which they believe you expect, while some may feel intimidated and will be less likely to share their views with you in an honest manner. As in teaching, the appropriate use of language is therefore critical. For instance, referring to participants as 'subjects' would not only be wholly inappropriate from a professional point of view but be incompatible with the democratic principles inherent in the philosophy underpinning practitioner research. Particularly within an action research context, the notions of inclusion and ownership are central and the representation of marginalised and vulnerable groups is one of the core aims.

If the research involves children, the issue of balance of power can be even more pronounced. By asking them to complete a questionnaire or take part in an interview, there is the danger that they do not perceive the researcher in you, but the teacher, and that instead of 'honest' they may feel that they have to give 'right' answers, which would impair the validity of their responses. Similar issues may arise in undertaking focus group discussion involving a mix of pupils, some of whom have established themselves as leaders who voice their opinions openly and vociferously while others, under the influence of peer pressure, lack the confidence to do so. As a consequence the data gathered will reflect a certain bias in favour of a certain group of pupils. How can you, as their teacher, ensure that the focus group allows all pupils to express their views without restriction and thus minimise the potential of bias in favour of a dominant group?

While these issues are of an ethical nature in relation to the balance of power and control, they can also have serious epistemological and methodological implications in terms of the way in which they affect the quantity and quality of data generated and introduce bias into the construction of knowledge. Furthermore, ethical issues, such as protection of participants'

Boys 19					
British born 17			Born outside UK 2		
White 11	Asian Muslim 4	African Caribbean 2	White Polish 1	Asian Muslim 1	African Caribbean 0
Girls 15					
British born 14			Born outside UK 1		
White 7	Asian Muslim 6	African Caribbean 1	White Polish 0	Asian Muslim 1	African Caribbean 0

Points to consider:

- Appropriate group size
- Composition of the group
- Suitability of venue
- Length of conversation
- Recording of data

Figure 5.1 Focus group discussion involving Year 9 pupils (Scenario 5.2): a male form tutor would like to investigate the incident of bullying among 34 Year 9 pupils. This is the composition of his form.

identity and confidentiality of information divulged, are of the utmost importance with regard to the dissemination of findings in the public domain. The strict adherence to ethical guidelines, which stipulate voluntary participation, informed consent and the right to withdraw from the research without suffering any negative consequences as the key aspects to consider, are therefore paramount.

Summary

Having considered a wide range of issues in relation to sampling, gaining access and informed consent, we should take heed of the caveat presented by Stanley and Sieber (1992), who remind us that not everything that is legal is ethical and that 'ethics has to do with the application of moral principles to prevent harming or wrong others, to promote the good, to be respectful and to be fair' (Sieber, 1993: 14). As in teaching, there is a strong pragmatic dimension inherent in practitioner research, requiring the researcher to display attributes commonly associated with Schön's (1983) concept of 'reflective practice,' and a professional and moral responsibility to those in their care.

> In essence, the aims of an ethical approach to research involving human beings are to develop and maintain non-exploitative social and personal relationships and to enhance the social and emotional lives of those who participate. (Stringer, 1999)

For education practitioners who intend to conduct research in their own or other colleagues' institutions the following list of guidelines may be helpful and should be considered prior to starting the research:

1. All research participants need to have a full understanding of the research purpose, the activities in which they will be involved (time, venue, additional disruption to daily routine), any potential risks involved and what will happen to the data with regard to publication.
2. Participation must be entirely voluntary. Incentives to participate (raffle, prize draw, vouchers) should be kept within reasonable limits.
3. Participants must be made aware of the right to withdraw at any stage of the research without any negative consequences or incurring loss of services received.
4. Informed consent must be obtained from all those participating in the investigation and where this involves vulnerable groups and children, it includes their guardians, such as parents, carers and/or teachers.
5. Any intrusion of the participants' privacy must be avoided.
6. Additional stress, such as investigating sensitive issues requiring participants to spend time in addition to their normal work schedule, must be kept to a minimum.

7. All information divulged by the research participants must be stored securely.
8. Unless agreed otherwise, any records, such as audio/video recordings and transcripts, must be destroyed following completion of the research.
9. Anonymity of participants and confidentiality of information must be assured.
10. There must never be any coercion on participants to behave in a certain way.

Further reading

Campbell, A. and Groundwater-Smith, S. (eds) (2007) *An Ethical Approach to Practitioner Research*. Abingdon: Routledge.

Farrell, A. (ed.) (2005) *Ethical Research with Children*. Maidenhead: Open University Press/McGraw-Hill.

Mauthner, M., Birch, M., Jessop, J. and Miller, T. (eds) (2002) *Ethics in Qualitative Research*. London: Sage.

References

Anderson, P. and Morrow, G. (2011) *The Ethics of Research with Children and Young People: A Practical Handbook*. London: Sage.

BERA (2011) *Ethical Guidelines for Educational Research*. BERA. At: www.bera.ac.uk/publications/ethical-guidelines.

Cohen, L., Manion, L. and Morrison, K. (2007) *Research Methods in Education*, 6th edn. Abingdon: Routledge.

Costley, C. and Gibbs, P. (2006) 'Researching others: care as an ethics for practitioner researchers', *Studies in Higher Education*, 31 (1): 89–98.

Fine, G. A. and Sandstrom, K. L. (1988) *Knowing Children: Participant Observation With Minors*. Newbury Park, CA: Sage.

Groundwater-Smith, S. and Mockler, N. (2007) 'Ethics in practitioner research: an issue of quality', *Research Papers in Education*, 22 (2): 199–211.

Hill, M. (2005) 'Ethical considerations in researching children's experiences', in S. Greene and D. Hogan (eds.), *Researching Children's Experience: Approaches and Methods*. London: Sage, pp. 253–72.

Hood, S., Nayall, B. and Oliver, S. (1996) *Critical Issues in Social Research: Power and Prejudice*. Buckingham: Open University Press.

Kemmis, S. and Taggart, R. (2000) 'Participatory action research', in N. K. Denzin and Y. S. Lincoln (eds), *Handbook of Qualitative Research*, 2nd edn. London: Sage, pp. 567–605.

Lindsay, G. (2000) 'Researching children's perspectives: ethical issues', in A. Lewis and G. Lindsay (eds), *Researching Children's Perspectives*. Buckingham: Open University Press, pp. 3–20.

Masson, J. (2000) 'Researching children's perspectives: legal issues', in A. Lewis and G. Lindsay (eds), *Researching Children's Perspectives*. Buckingham: Open University Press, pp. 34–45.

Masson, J. (2004) 'The legal context', in S. Fraser, V. Lewis, S. Ding, M. Kellett and C. Robinson (eds), *Doing Research with Children and Young Prople*. London: Sage, pp. 43–58.

Mauthner, M., Birch, M., Jessop, J. and Miller, T. (eds) (2002) *Ethics in Qualitative Research*. London: Sage.

Measor, L. and Woods, P. (1984) 'Breakthroughs and blockages in ethnographic research: contrasting experiences during the changing schools project', in G. Walford (ed.), (1991) *Doing Educational Research*. London: Routledge, pp. 59–81.

Oliver, P. (2003) *The Student's Guide to Research Ethics*. Maidenhead: Open University Press/McGraw-Hill.

Schön, D. (1983) *The Reflective Practitioner*. New York: Basic Books.

Sieber, J. E. (1993) *Planning Ethically Responsible Research*. Newbury Park, CA: Sage.

Stanley, B. and Sieber, J. E. (eds) (1992) *Social Research on Children and Adolescents: Ethical Issues*. London: Sage.

Stringer, E. T. (1999) *Action Research*, 2nd edn. Thousand Oaks, CA: Sage.

Walford, G. (1991) 'Reflexive accounts of doing educational research', in G. Walford (ed.) *Doing Educational Research*. London: Routledge, pp. 10–18.

CHAPTER 6

SOURCES OF EVIDENCE

Once you have used your analysis of the context and existing literature and research findings to define the two to four key research questions that you intend to address, you must consider where the 'answers' might be sourced. This chapter will ask you to consider the range of sources that might be available to you in order for you to systematically evaluate the usefulness and viability of each to make a fully justified decision. While research methodology and tools will not be a prime focus, an awareness of them and the potential strengths and weaknesses of each will be a factor in the decision-making process.

(Continued)

(Continued)

By the time you have read this chapter you should, for your chosen research focus:

- be able to identify potential respondent groups who will be able to address your research questions;
- appreciate the need to justify the choice of sources;
- understand that compromises may need to be made due to issues of access or logistics;
- demonstrate a critical awareness of how your decisions to accept or reject particular sources will impact the outcomes of the study.

Identify a convenient starting point

Let's recap how you get to a 'starting point'. In our consideration of possible research topics we are usually guided by a personal or professional interest in issues and problems of which we have become aware and wish to investigate further. For example, as a teacher you may have become increasingly aware of inconsistencies in pupil behaviour which you attribute to factors inherent in the classroom environment. In order to explore your hunch more systematically you would like to conduct a study. This study will need to be constrained within parameters in order to make it manageable, both in terms of scale and duration (how long it will take you to complete).

- *Scale of the study*. Focus down to a point where you will have meaningful access to data – use your professional position within the educational system to guide you. For example, if your work in educational administration at a local or regional level, it is likely that you will have access to generalised multi-school data, but would have difficulty gaining access to individual classrooms. School leaders are likely to have the greatest access to school-wide data, but can also gain entry to classrooms. Age or subject leaders are likely to have the greatest access to information within their particular subjects or age groups. Class teachers have their classes – but this does not prevent you from working with colleagues on joint enterprises!
- *Aspect of the theme*. 'Inconsistencies in pupil behaviour' does cover an awful lot of ground! Use an initial 'trawl' of anecdotal evidence to achieve a more precise focus. Is it perceived as an issue of gender, ability, time of day (e.g. before school, lunch times, between lessons …), year group, subject area … It is likely that you will be able to gain an indication of the potential underlying aspect(s) to focus on through a combination of informal discussions with practitioners and reading published research findings in the area.

So, from a general starting point concerning 'pupil behaviour', depending on the positionality of the researcher (you!), the resultant study may range as follows:

- An examination of potential correlating factors of pupil exclusions in X town secondary schools. (*local administrator*)
- Evaluating the effect of staff training on measures of pupil behaviour in X school. (*school leader*)
- Analysing the impact of 'Think4All' initiative on Year 10 girls' behaviour in science classes. (*subject leader*) (NB: 'Think4All' is not a real initiative!)
- Comparing the effect of different strategies to improve engagement of Year 4 low-attaining boys in maths sessions. (*class teacher*)

While behaviour management is the generic theme for each of these studies, each will require a different approach to gain access to a different range of evidence from a different research population.

Breaking the starting point into manageable 'bits'

It is helpful – essential really – to unpick the starting point (or 'title', if you happen to be performing this research for an academic or professional qualification) so that the specific elements within the study can be brought into sharp focus. For example, the research focus of 'effective management of pupil classroom behaviour' may be deconstructed into four sub-themes: perceptions of what might be construed as 'undesirable pupil behaviour'; strategies to promote positive pupil behaviour; factors influencing pupil behaviour; and means of supporting teachers to promote desirable pupil behaviour. Adding this level of structure to the study would provide both added focus to any review of existing published research and conceptual models. Ultimately these sub-themes will need to be converted into questions in a form that will allow them to be addressed through empirical study.

In the same way that a teacher, in a classroom context, must consider how evidence will be gathered in the classroom to confirm that learning objectives have been met, these initial research questions should be used to guide the construction of the research methodology. To take this analogy further, if the learning objective were for pupils 'to explain what happens to particles of water as it evaporates', there would be a number of ways this might be assessed:

- pupil produced documents – e.g. annotated individual or group drawings to show the process;
- group observation – of pupils discussing and explaining to each other the process;

- individual/group interview – questioning the class to obtain a verbal response (you might want to think about sampling and reliability here!);
- questionnaires – a multiple-choice or short-answer 'test' to check understanding.

There are several different ways of achieving the same end – the teacher has to use their experience, availability of time and resources and knowledge of the particular group of pupils to adopt the most appropriate approach for the circumstances. Likewise the researcher must make similar choices.

Figure 6.1 provides a worked example of how the initial research questions (1–4) can be mapped against the means of data collection (A–D). Please be assured that '4' is not a magic number! Four initial research questions can usually be regarded as a maximum – more will often mean that the research goal will not be achieved as there will be too many elements to keep track of. Our experience suggests that between two and four is, in most cases, appropriate. The same applies to the means of data collection. While it is always advisable to employ more than one tool to more than one source, the

Research focus: Effective management of pupil classroom behaviour

Research questions/objectives:

1.   What are the perceptions of desirable/undesirable pupil classroom behaviour?
2.   What strategies do teachers employ to promote desirable pupil behaviour?
3.   What factors are believed to influence pupils' classroom behaviour in a positive/ negative way?
4.   How could teachers be supported in the effective management of pupil behaviour?

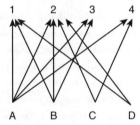

Data:

A.   Teachers' questionnaire – perceptions, attitudes, beliefs and behaviours
B.   Pupils' group interviews – perceptions, attitudes, influences and behaviours
C.   Researcher observations – behaviours, strategies, ethos/culture
D.   School policy documents – ethos/culture, strategies

Figure 6.1   Mapping research questions to sources of evidence

abundance of evidence, particularly to the lone researcher, can also be very problematic and four is often pressing the limits of manageability.

The most productive way to approach this is to identify all the potential sources of evidence for each of the key questions – you may well find that there is a considerable number. Then begin a process of reduction. Try to narrow it down by focusing on those sources which will

- address more than one of the key questions;
- be able to be accessed by you;
- provide the most meaningful data;
- minimise your effort!

The simple mapping process, as shown in Figure 6.1, should provide reassurance that all of the initial research questions are gong to be adequately addressed through the evidence to be collected. The analysis of school policy documents (D), for example, anticipates that they will reveal what the school expects of pupil behaviour (Q1) and might also provide an indication of the behaviour management strategies (Q2) that teachers will be expected to employ.

In supporting research activity with teachers, both for the purposes of academic qualifications and for reasons of professional or school development, we have found this matching process a very useful checking point to ensure that sufficient evidence will be collected in order to meet the aims of the study. It is also of great use later in the research process when analysis is being performed to ensure that appropriate comparison of evidence from different sources and means of collection is being achieved. In presenting and analysing evidence to respond to Q4 ('… how could teacher be supported …'), the teachers' perceptions of what they needed (from the questionnaire) would be able to be compared and contrasted with the researcher's own observations, linked back, of course, to what the review of literature suggested would be the case.

Through this direct connectivity between the research focus and the sources of information, you are providing clear justification for your choices and offering confidence in your evidence base. When deciding upon and justifying your choice of research approach and methodology (be it in the methodology section of an assignment or to assure the 'robustness' of your approach to data collection to a line manager), employing an approach similar to that presented in Figure 6.1 will confirm the direct link between what you intend to achieve (the research questions) and the means of achieving it (the data collection).

To sample or not to sample

To some extent, sampling is an inevitability of the research process which will already have been acknowledged within the title or focus of your study: you will be concentrating upon a single school among many, or a year group, subject or class within that school. But is there a need to sample within that focus?

As the primary concern of practitioner research is generally considered to be the improvement of professional practice within a specific context, it normally precludes large-scale surveys for the generation of generalisable outcomes. Clearly there are situations where large-scale data sets will be entirely appropriate – the analysis of assessment data for a whole school (or year group) will quite frequently be required, but this is data that is usually already collected and so can be regarded as documentary evidence rather than a survey performed specifically for a particular study. Population in this respect does not exclusively denote people, but is to be understood as 'the total number of possible units or elements that are included in the study' or 'the totality of people, organisations, objects or occurrences from which a sample is drawn' (Gray, 2004: 82, 403). This can, for example, include the selection of venues, times and type of data sources.

With this in mind, it can be seen that the focus for the study in Figure 6.1 is still far too wide for it to be achievable. The 'title' needs to provide a much more specific indication of the actual research population – a particular school, and within that possibly a particular year group. However, for practical purposes it has to be recognised that a school with 60 pupils is less likely to require a sampling phase than one with 3,000. As suggested above, the potential population might be reduced through the narrowing of the focus (to a specific year) or through the selection of the data collection approach – information from a large population can be collected much more readily through a questionnaire than through individual interviews.

Justification for sampling

There is an inevitability that evidence that you collect for your study will only represent a 'sample' of what is available. Either the sample will be predetermined with a conscious (and hopefully justifiable!) decision to select some sources of evidence and reject others, or it will be a part of the evidence-gathering process. Selection of evidence at the point of collection is addressed in other chapters, in particular Chapters 8 and 9 (observing and interviewing) where the researcher will select from the evidence presented what is actually recorded and presented. Data collection will always result in a compromise of some degree – tools that are more appropriate for large numbers of respondents, such as questionnaires, are unlikely to offer the 'depth' of response that more individual approaches, such as interviews, can achieve, but will require significantly more research time.

Time (or rather the lack of it) will frequently be the most important determinant in deciding upon a particular research tool and research sample. The time invested in the construction of a well-focused, multiple-choice style questionnaire (which will reduce analysis time) may allow you to access a much larger number of respondents than an open-ended questionnaire or group or individual interviews. Given that the time that you have to offer to a research project will be relatively fixed, the nature of the research tool will have a significant impact on the need to sample.

A starting point would be to consider whether sampling could be avoided, with evidence being gathered from the entire research population. When focusing on a research population which consists of a class of children or the teaching staff in a subject department, year group or even a school it can be virtually impossible to select a sample that is representative in order to obtain a reliable evidence base. As Cohen et al. (2011) point out, in order to achieve outcomes in which you can have strong confidence (i.e. 99 per cent of the time you would get the same response) then out of a population of 30 (a class) you would need to select a sample of … 30! Indeed, to achieve the same level of confidence with a population of 100 you would need to randomly select a sample of 95 – why go to the trouble of deselecting five potential respondents? It is only when you get to populations of 30,000+ that the sample size begins settle around the 1,800–2,000 mark (this is why YouGov (2012) surveys of the UK population are based on a sample of 2,000 respondents). Clearly a sample of less than the 'whole class' cannot, in statistical terms, be considered a particularly reliable indicator of the class as a whole. Any sampling 'system' which selects 'two from the top, two from the middle and two from the bottom' of the ability range within a class certainly cannot be justified in terms of being representative of the class.

So, with regard to the question: 'Do I need to sample?' consider the appropriateness of evidence-gathering techniques – questionnaires, group interviews – that will avoid the need to sample. If sampling is unavoidable – individual interviews, observation – then you will need to justify the selection of your sample.

Selecting your sample appropriately is therefore key, particularly where there is no research funding and minimal or no clerical support available. First, you need to familiarise yourself with a range of sampling methods to enable you to make an informed decision on their appropriateness for your investigation. The research literature distinguishes between two major categories: probability or representative sampling, used in surveys with the intention to produce generalisable outcomes in the form of statistical inferences, and non-probability samples, usually employed in small-scale studies such as practitioner research.

Deconstructing the population

Before applying any specific sampling techniques it is worthwhile considering the nature of the population that you are studying. Are there any particular sub-groups that you wish to focus in on, or need to ensure that their views or perceptions are included in the final analysis?

For example, a head teacher may wish you canvass the views of staff concerning the induction processes within the school. While a universal questionnaire would elicit responses from the whole population, it may lack the necessary detail that interviews would achieve. To ensure that the detailed views of the various sub-groups (inductees, mentors, teaching and non-teaching staff) are included, *stratified sampling* may be appropriate. Once the membership of each of the different population sub-groups (teachers/non-teachers, inductees/mentors) has been identified then further selection of actual respondents may be required. However, sub-groups are unlikely to be the same size, so *proportionate stratified sampling* may be employed to reflect the proportion of the various sub-groups involved and thus prevent skewing of the data in favour of a group that actively engaged with the process as opposed to one where only a minority of group members responded.

Another approach is to identify a specific sub-group within the research population on which to focus the study. Rather than drawing on the whole school population, the focus may be narrowed to a particular cluster selected on the basis of key stage, year group, subject area, gender, position and so on. This *cluster sampling* allows the population to be segmented (Walliman, 2005) using criteria relevant to the thrust of the research. A study focusing on literacy across the curriculum in a secondary school might narrow the focus to the Humanities Department, drawing on an evidence base constructed around the views of humanities teachers and teaching assistants and classroom observations within this department.

Given the nature of practitioner research, the most frequent means of reducing the scale and size of the research population for a study is the use of *opportunity or convenience sampling*. The researcher reduces the scale of their study simply through focusing on those respondents that they have access to. A maths teacher focusing on the use of a 'rewards systems' to improve behaviour and motivate learning might use the 'convenience' of focusing on teachers and classes in their own department. A primary school teacher exploring the impact of peer assessment might well choose to focus on their own class. As Wilson (2009) indicates, this approach cannot be considered as 'representative' or offer a basis for generalisation beyond the particular group, but it is, well, convenient.

Even, where possible, when the research population has been manipulated and reduced to a more manageable scale, it may be necessary to reduce the number of respondents still further by applying further levels of selection and sampling.

Probability sampling

In probability sampling the sample must be representative of the population from which it was drawn. As such it must share the same characteristics. If a population is sufficiently homogenous *random sampling* can be applied, in which each member of the population has a chance of being selected.

As indicated above though, the sample size required for statistically representative data from a population suggests that this form of sampling is only really useful when dealing with large populations. The table supplied by Cohen et al. (2011) would suggest that random sampling only becomes viable for selecting a reliable sample with high levels of statistical confidence when populations approach 1,000. Even for lower levels of reliability, where you might expect the outcomes to be replicated 90 per cent of the time, this form of sampling is only useful when the population passes 300.

Non-probability sampling

As most practitioner research is conducted in the researcher's own practice setting, it will involve relatively small, non-probability samples and be predominantly of a qualitative nature. (It is likely that any quantitative data will be constructed from responses from the whole population rather than a sample.) Nevertheless, samples and sampling methods have to be selected with care, always bearing in mind the purpose of the investigation and potential logistical, methodological, epistemological and ethical issues. The most commonly employed non-probability sampling methods are the following:

- *Purposive sampling.* The researcher uses his/her own judgement in the selection of participants in relation to certain characteristics or traits. For example, a study investigating the perceived crisis in modern foreign languages could include all those pupils who have decided against continuing their studies beyond Key Stage 4. In effect, this could also be considered as a means of narrowing the focus of the study to a more manageable population.
- *Quota sampling.* Often used as an extension to stratified sampling, it contains sub-groups of the total population in the proportion in which they occur in the particular research setting. Returning to the example above, a quota sample could take into account distribution of gender, ability, ethnic background and socio-economic status of Year 11 pupils within a school. If, for example, gifted and talented (G&T) learners represented 8 per cent of the school population, then the proportion of G&T in the sample should also be approximately 8 per cent.

- *Volunteer sampling.* By taking advantage of personal or professional contacts and relationships researchers choose individuals who are relatively easy to reach. According to Robson (2002: 265) it 'is probably one of the most widely used and least satisfactory methods of sampling' and, heeding the caveat supplied by Gray, 'need to be treated with extreme caution' (2004: 88), as the representativeness of the sample cannot be determined. For example, sixth formers are invited to provide monthly feedback on the any aspects of their learning environment (quality of teaching, learning environment, assessment, guidance and support systems, social events, etc.). However, there is no way of ascertaining how representative the comments are of the total student body. What about those who do not reply? However, it is not unusual to adopt this process following a questionnaire to the wider population. The final question of the questionnaire asks the respondent to identify themselves, should they be willing to participate in a subsequent round of group or individual interviews or possibly an observation. In this way, the more detailed responses will come from those who have self-selected or volunteered.
- *Snowball sampling.* As the term implies, this sampling method starts with a small number of individuals who have been selected by the researcher on the basis of specific characteristics relevant to the study and who can identify other individuals potentially eligible for inclusion in the research. Often this method is employed when it is difficult to identify suitable participants or where highly sensitive topics can raise the issue of intrusion of privacy, emotional upset and loss of dignity. However, it is possible that a group with similar characteristics, but without connections to the initial group, may be completely missed. Examples relating to this category might include investigations into drug abuse, eating disorders, sexual behaviour or bullying.

These sampling strategies are not designed to result in a reliable evidence base that can be generalised from to a much wider population. You should not make any claims beyond the scope of the evidence that you are working with. What you are doing with these techniques is reducing the working population of your research to a more manageable scale.

In helping you select the appropriate sample type it is useful to consider the following aspects:

- ease of access to the research setting and research participants (negotiation with gatekeepers);
- the number of perspectives to be represented in relation to the research focus (e.g. teachers, parents/carers, pupils, support staff, managers);
- your positionality in relation to the research setting and participants, particularly critical in insider research (balance of power between researcher and researched);

- the participants' competence to give informed consent to participate (ethics guidelines);
- legal requirements regarding the involvement of children in research;
- logistical challenges, such as travel, availability of venues (interviewing);
- funding of data collection (postal distribution of questionnaires).

Summary

Once you have decided upon the focus of your research (the key research questions) and the context in which you will be carrying out your study, systematically approach the issue of deciding who (which respondents or documentary evidence base) will be able to provide you with the means of addressing your questions.

Use a diagram similar to Figure 6.1 to map out the links between your sources and your questions.

Consider how the evidence might be gathered and decide whether or not this will require you to further restrict the scope of your study (narrow the research population) or sample from your research population. You need to be aware how your means of gathering evidence will impact upon your decisions here – a well formed questionnaire will reduce your need to sample but may also reduce the depth of evidence you would otherwise have gained via an interview.

Justify your decisions through reference to the purposes of your research and the constraints under which your research is being performed to explain how your compromise was arrived at. If the study is part of an academic qualification, then ensure that the choices that you have made are also supported by reference to educational research methodology texts.

References

Cohen, L., Manion, L. and Morrison, K. (2011) *Research Methods in Education*, 7th edn. Abingdon: Routledge.

Gray, D. E. (2004) *Doing Research in the Real World*. London: Sage.

Robson, C. (2002) *Real World Research*, 2nd edn. Oxford: Blackwell.

Walliman, N. (2005) *Your Research Project*. London: Sage.

Wilson, E. (2009) *School-Based Research: A Guide for Education Students*. London: Sage.

YouGov (2012) *Panel Selection*. Available at: http://research.yougov.co.uk/services/q-a/ (accessed on 2 January 2013).

CHAPTER 7

DOCUMENTARY EVIDENCE

Documentation, in one form or another, is an essential source of information for a large proportion of research studies. However, you do need to be aware of the disagreements that exist between authors working in the field of education research methodology as to what actually constitutes 'documents' (in the context of research) and how they can be incorporated as a research methodology. Cohen et al. (2011), for example, only include documentation as an element of a historical research approach, due mainly, it is presumed, to the pre-existing nature of documents. This chapter attempts to establish the parameters of 'documentary evidence' and the type of information that it can provide, identify the potential strengths and weaknesses and provide an indication of how to construct recording formats to collect and collate evidence in this form.

By the conclusion of this chapter it is anticipated that you will:

- be able to recognise the strengths and weaknesses of documents and appreciate the appropriateness of the approach to support other formats;
- be able to construct recording formats suitable to the contextual and conceptual foci of the research.

What is a 'document'?

This is a fairly simple and straightforward question on the face of it, but it is inextricably linked to the context and focus of the research. In essence all sources which can be used as part of the evidence base for your research, but were not produced specifically for your research, can be classed as documents. This will include all forms of publication and recording including:

- printed materials (text and images);
- electronic media (text, images, audio and video);
- artefacts (models, equipment, physical resources, and so on).

Interestingly Denscombe (2003) lists books and journals within his definition of 'documentary evidence'; indeed Denscombe (2003: 212) refers to it as the 'first port of call' for researchers. Well that's as maybe, but not as a source of evidence. We feel that it is important to draw a clear line of distinction here between sources which inform the direction and content of the research and sources which *are* the research. The review of existing published literature on a specific theme – a 'literature review' of theory, conceptual frameworks and published empirical research – will be used by you to help you to construct your research activity, it will not *be* your research activity. While a review of literature is a form of research, since we here are supporting you as a practitioner/researcher, we consider it as part of the background to your research. In our view these literature-based sources deserve to be treated quite differently, hence our focus on this as 'reviewing existing theories and findings' (Chapter 3). Structurally this then gives us:

- contextual documents:
  - national/government publications – used to establish the national context;
  - documents produced by the organisation – used to set the local context of the study;

- conceptual documents:

  - books, journal articles (paper and electronic publication) and web-based articles (of appropriate providence) – used to establish the conceptual framework through theory, models and past research findings.

If any, it is those documents listed as 'contextual' that are more likely to be redesignated as 'evidence'. If the focus of your study is at the national policy level, then the documents produced by the various government offices will form a significant part of your evidence base. Similarly, if you are focusing on the (re)development of school policy, then these policies will be central to your research effort, rather than simply contextualising it.

Types of document

After putting these 'distractions' to one side we can concentrate on an examination of those sources which provide evidence for your research but which were produced for other reasons. In many respects, the enormous increase in the levels of accountability within state-funded education over the past 25 years has resulted in the production of quite staggering quantities of documentation. At all stages of the education process, from pre-school to higher education, planning, assessment and evaluation – and much more – have to be recorded for various levels of inspection. At a national level, vast data sets now exist as a result of government data collection requirements, which allow specialist researchers the opportunity to perform significant and influential studies purely based on this secondary evidence. All of this provides the researcher with a rich, if not confusingly excessive, potential source of data.

- *Pupil level*. Evidence of learning, for example, can be obtained through a review of the written work or artefacts produced by the learners, the teacher assessment and feedback given to those submissions, the assessment records maintained by teachers, self-assessment/evaluation activities completed by the learners, reports and references written by teachers/tutors, plus a host of collated, statistical data from formal testing.
- *Teacher level*. This includes lesson and scheme planning and evaluation documents, teaching materials (including 'favourite websites' and IWB (interactive whiteboard) materials), class/group/pupil assessment records, staff training (CPD) materials and records, performance management documentation, among others.
- *School/management level*. This includes meeting minutes, memos, emails, policy documents, briefings, curriculum and syllabus documents, room and equipment booking sheets, risk assessment forms and job descriptions. Additionally there is also all of the documentation produced for public consumption such as brochures, web pages, newsletters and mission statements.

However, it is not just the educational organisations themselves that supply documents; there are many supporting organisations, particularly given the broader educational agenda as a result of Every Child Matters, that also produce paper and electronic-based documentation which might be of relevance to an education-based researcher. Included within this would be video-based materials available via the Internet, particularly those produced for Teachers TV (TES, 2013) of school and classroom-based activities up to 2011 when it closed.

To sum up then, documentary evidence:

- already exists in a definitive form (e.g. a diary that has already been written, independent of the research, is a document; one which has been commissioned for the purpose of this research is an extended form of questionnaire);
- cannot be individually designed to suit a particular research purpose;
- must be drawn on as a source of data in the form in which it stands;
- is an unobtrusive or non-reactive research tool;
- is not affected by the fact that it is being used for research purposes.

Using documents in research activity

As documents are a recording, in one format or another, of events, thoughts or perceptions, they represent a particular point in time. A lesson plan, for example, represents the *expectations* for learning and activities, not what actually *did* happen or was learnt. Similarly, an evaluation following a lesson is likely to be layered and effected by the perceptions of the person writing the evaluation. As such most documents offer a baseline against which other sources can be compared and contrasted. For example, a lesson plan and evaluation can be compared to an independent observation of the lesson in question or a pupil evaluation.

 Case Study 7.1   Evaluating the effect of giving written feedback to KS2 learners in a large primary school

New deputy head teacher (MA student) 'Nina'

Being new to the school when she was asked to perform this evaluation, Nina referred to the school's policy document on assessment to establish what was actually 'supposed' to be happening. This was then

(Continued)

(Continued)

compared to what teachers thought that they were meant to be doing, what was actually being written in pupils' books (further documentary evidence) and, through interviews with the children, what impact it appeared to be having on their learning.

Policy documents, particularly in the case of classroom-based research, do offer a very fruitful starting place as they provide a strong indication of what *should* be happening. Admittedly this does depend on the perspective from which the policy was written and how dated it is. Some policies are written to represent the current reality (or, more likely, the best of current practice), whereas others might be more aspirational in their tone, giving an indication of what is being striven for rather than actually achieved. In either case, the documentary source provides a 'known point' against which evidence from other sources can be compared.

A lesson plan may provide an excellent foundation for an interview following an observation of that lesson. In particular it would provide the teacher with the opportunity to discuss and justify any divergences from the original plan.

Many teachers in the compulsory phases of education will adopt a similar process when faced with a class of relatively unknown children and a set of standardised test results achieved at the completion of the previous school year. The documentary evidence is accepted as a starting point, but is then modified as this is compared and contrasted with evidence from other (more current) sources, such as direct observation, interviewing (asking the learners pertinent questions) and subsequent documentary evidence (artefacts and other tangible 'work' completed by the learners).

Most documents offer a 'snapshot' in time, reflecting or capturing a particular reality. This offers not only the researcher the opportunity to reanalyse the documents with changed perceptions following the passage of time, but also to identify and respond to change. Learning is all about change, so written work (or videoed interviews as a further example) collected from learners before and after a 'learning opportunity' presents the researcher with a useful set of comparative data. For example:

- concept maps showing children's ideas on a particular scientific concept before and after the use of a specific learning technique;
- video of a class of children before and after the teacher has applied and embedded a set of behaviour management techniques;
- comparing the lesson plans produced by a PGCE trainee at the beginning and end of their course to compare the level of sophistication and pedagogic knowledge being demonstrated.

Going beyond those documents that are for the classroom-based researcher, many others support research into educational management issues.

Case Study 7.2   Establishing a vision for a new academy sports college: analysing the competition

Assistant head teacher responsible for sports college status (MA student) 'Mike'

Having been charged with bringing a paper to the governing body concerning how the college should present itself 'renewed' to the community following its change of status, Mike chose to collect, collate and analyse documentary evidence from two distinct populations – local colleges/schools (potential competitors) and existing academies with a sports 'specialism' in other areas of the country. The sources of the documents were the websites of these schools/colleges which were used to publicly declare their educational and organisational values and aims. From this Mike was able to offer suggestions that were consistent with many of the mission statements from the sports colleges, but made his academy distinct from other local schools.

Case Study 7.3   What are primary schools looking for when appointing new science subject leaders?

Primary BEd dissertation student 'Tim'

In an attempt to discover the extent to which the course he had attended for four years had been preparing him and his peers for the 'science subject leader' role, he used the 'jobs section' of the *Times Educational Supplement* to obtain the details for all promoted-post primary science subject leaders (i.e. advertisements which indicate a salary enhancement for the post) over a six-month period. He analysed the requirements in terms of science subject knowledge, leadership/management skills/experience and general teaching skills/experience.

Educational establishments collect and retain a significant amount of information that is not directly concerned with learning and teaching – although
much of it will have a substantial influence:

- Attendance records – are some days/times more 'popular' than others?
  (For example, is Monday more poorly attended than any other day? ...
  for both staff and students!).
- Minutes of meetings – do different departments discuss similar issues?
  What proportion of meetings is actually spent on debate and decision-
  making as opposed to information giving?

Documents are useful to the researcher, not only in terms of the content,
but also in terms of the presentation (the style, language, format, etc.).
Documents are clearly meant to convey information – evidence that is presented 'wittingly'. But it may also be possible to extract information that the
author did not knowingly include – 'unwitting' evidence. For example, the
minutes of a meeting may not simply reflect what happened and who said
what; the status of individuals may also be conveyed in the language
(teachers being referred to by surname and teaching assistants by their
given name). Different authors may adopt different styles for different types
of document (for different audiences or purposes) and it is the researcher
who needs to be aware of this and learn to 'read between the lines' to
assess the significance.

In all of these examples given above, the researcher has to rely on others
to produce the evidence that they will be using in their research. But just
how reliable is it?

Assessing documents

As was the case in Chapter 3 that researchers need to assure themselves of
the providence of the literature that they are using to base their conceptual
arguments upon, you must also be sure of the validity and accuracy of the
evidence your intend to collect from documents. In assessing the value of
documentary evidence there are two levels at which you need to operate:

- *external criticism* – conformation of the 'authenticity or genuineness'
  (Cohen et al., 2007: 195) of the source;
- *internal criticism* – conformation of the value and accuracy of the content of the document (how credible is it?).

The first imperative is to confirm that the document is from a sound source
(i.e. not faked, forged or knowingly distorted) and is authentic. One
researcher, examining the way that local KS2/3 schools risk assessed study

trips into the local community to teach aspects of geography, found herself in receipt of risk assessments from eight schools – five of which were identical (complete with a spelling mistake) other than date, school name and the signatory! While it is quite frequent to find that policies, curricula and certain other documentation have been 'based' on those used in other institutions and suitably adapted and amended prior to adoption, there have been cases where the adoption has taken placed with only perfunctory levels of engagement, which really questions their validity if not rightful ownership.

Credibility can be a problem with certain documents in education, particularly those written for more than one purpose. Lesson plans and evaluations may be written more for the mentor or tutor than the teacher and so may not accurately represent what the teacher intends, or is able, to deliver. Similarly, departmental minutes may be written knowing that senior management are expecting certain issues to be discussed and so minutes will reflect expectations rather than reality.

Sampling is a particular issue with documentation. As Denscombe (2003: 220) asks, 'is the document typical of its type?'. Choice may be restricted by access – you may only be offered those lesson plans, for example, that respondents feel 'confident' with – the best examples, rather than those which are more representative of the general level of quality.

Given that documentation is often written with the expectation that it will only be viewed by an internal audience, accurate interpretation of them can require significant levels of 'insider knowledge'. It may not just be a matter of the language and possible codes used, but also what could be implied and what is omitted. Interpretation by the author or someone with the requisite 'insider knowledge' may be required to bridge potential gaps between the intended meaning and the received meaning.

Above all else, the key determinant in assessing the values of a document must be 'does it help me with my research?', specifically 'does it help me to answer my questions?'. If not, it should be rejected as a source of evidence.

Accessing documents

Ethically, you need to inform your potential research population of the purpose of your research when you request information from them. As suggested above, this may significantly impact on the willingness of your potential respondents to participate – or it may at least mean that you are presented with a 'selection' of the documentation or an edited version of it. It is possible that you have access to the documentation, but not for this particular purpose. For example, as head of a year group or subject area within your organisation you may have access, in your professional capacity, to all planning, curriculum schemes, assessment feedback and so on produced by your team. However, if you are also using the documentation, which you are examining and analysing for professional purposes, as an evidence base for an assignment towards an academic award, you will need to discuss your access issues with your tutor to clarify your ethical position and your potential use of the evidence. Clearly your relationship, particularly the level of trust, with the research population will have a significant impact on this process.

To gain access to documentary sources that would not normally be within your reach (a different organisation or even department), you would be advised to work through a member of the senior management team who will have access. As suggested in the first section to this book, to ensure that your research effort is welcomed, it is worth working with a senior manager from the very earliest stages so that they can act as your 'gatekeeper'.

A full examination of the ethical issues surrounding access and the reporting and presenting of evidence can be found in Chapter 3.

Developing documentary research tools

The development of research tools specific for documents is dependent upon the research paradigm that is being adopted. The interpretive model suggests that researchers adopt an approach by which they immerse themselves in the data to begin the search for what is important. This approach is frequently used in the early stages of a research activity to get the 'feel' for the nature and scope of the issues that need to be addressed through the research activity, in much the same way that you might have a preliminary 'chat' with colleagues to discover if they have the same perceptions of a 'problem' as you. The positivist researcher would clarify what they are seeking from the evidence base and focus upon that. Interpretism may appear to be the 'easy option' but the data can quickly become overwhelming. Positivism may mean that many 'interesting' points found in the evidence must be disregarded as irrelevant, but it can make the whole process more manageable and focused. Pragmatically, it would be prudent, when adopting a positivist approach, to maintain an explicit focus, but make a note of any 'interesting' points of information that arise out of the data collection.

Robson (2002) suggests that the whole process is broken down as follows:

- Start with a research question.
- Decide on a sampling strategy.
- Define the recording unit.

- Construct categories for analysis.
- Test the coding on samples of text and assess reliability.
- Carry out the analysis.

Robson uses the research question as an anchor with the conceptual literature being implicit in the identification and construction of the 'recording
units' and 'categories for analysis'.

In the same way that interview and observation schedules ensure that the
researcher maintains a focus which is consistent with the aims of the
research, so documents must be treated the same way. As the documents
will not have been constructed for the purpose of the research that you are
carrying out, you can maintain your focus much more successfully by constructing a research tool which will keep you on track. As with interview
schedules and questionnaires (see Chapter 9), it can be helpful to construct
your research tool in three sections:

- biographical – information about the document (authorship, title/identi-
  fier, age, source, etc.);
- factual – information that you wish to gain from the source (from your
  conceptual reading based upon the focus from the research question),
  both witting and unwitting;
- opinion – your (as the researcher) informed opinion of the validity and
  reliability of the source and any additional witting and unwitting evidence to be gleaned from it.

This general recording structure can be used regardless of the format, from
paper and web-based text documents, through visual and video images to
physical artefacts.

**Box 7.1   Data collection schedule for Case Study 7.3
(science subject leader)**

Biographical details: [Name of school]

Date of advert:	applications by	interview date
Size of school:	authority	salary point
Information sent:	job description ☐ job/person spec. ☐	school brochure ☐
	application form ☐	other ....

(Continued)

(Continued)

Factual:	essential (numbers)	desirable (numbers)
Science	☐	☐
Management	☐	☐
Teaching	☐	☐
Other	☐	☐

Specific statements: ....

Opinion:

Job specification style and structure: ....

Language used: ....

Personalisation: ....

Other: ....

The schedule, constructed to collect and collate information sent out by primary schools seeking to appoint a science subject leader, is designed to offer the researcher a consistent format for comparing the documentation. A separate schedule is completed for each set of documentation, in much the same way that individual respondents complete questionnaires. Inevitably there is an element of interpretation of the documentation as the schedule is completed, which brings in the potential of researcher bias, but with a single researcher it would be hoped that any bias would be acknowledged – and at least be consistent!

The factual element of the schedule seeks to identify key terms or phrases within the documentation and record them quantitatively. This 'content analysis' will need to link directly back to the key ideas identified in your examination of the conceptual and empirical literature.

Box 7.2   Research tip

Photocopy the original document and then, using a selection of different coloured highlighter pens for the different categories, mark the key points and tally them.

If the document is in an electronic form (scanning with OCR (optical character recognition) software will do nicely!) then there are various software packages available that will find the key terms for you – if you tell it what to look for. Word from Microsoft Office will even do this in a limited way using the *Edit-Find-Highlight* option. For video-based material software such as Dartfish offers similar means of coding evidence (see Chapter 11).

Content analysis can be used for many purposes, for example:

- sentence length in text books (as an indication of readability);
- 'ethnicity' of names in reading books;
- positive/negative language in reports and student feedback;
- suitability of websites;
- use of behaviour management techniques used in exemplar lessons (on video) for training purposes.

An interesting example using an analysis of images involved a student exploring how universities encourage 'widening participation' through the images used in their undergraduate prospectuses (i.e. 'older' or non-white students). One university scored a high 'black male' count; unfortunately it was often the same black male student who appeared to be on several different courses across all faculties!

 Case Study 7.4   To what extent are maths teachers planning lessons to meet the needs of all their students?

Head of Maths in a large secondary school (MA student) 'Jude'

As part of a year-long initiative to help teachers in the department become more responsive to the learning needs of the students Jude wanted to supplement the observations of lessons with an examination of a sample of lesson planning.

Biographical details: [Name of teacher]

Date of lesson:	topic	time	day
Year:	group	support?	

(Continued)

(Continued)

Factual:

Objectives:	knowledge	☐	skills	☐	differentiated	☐
Phases:	intro	☐	activity	☐	plenary	☐
Teaching:	VAK	☐	group	☐	whole class	☐
Timings		☐				
Key questions:		☐				
Resources		☐				

Other content:

Opinion:

Lesson plan style and structure:

Language used:

Evaluation:

Case Study 7.5   Student learning through PowerPoint presentations – are tutors making effective use of the medium?

Learning 'advocate' in an FE college (MA student) 'Krish'

Tutors at the college were increasingly making use of this presentation format which they were placing on the college's 'virtual learning environment' (VLE) to allow the students further access and to print off handouts prior to sessions. But were the tutors aware of the best ways to use the format? A sample of presentations were downloaded from the VLE and analysed.

Biographical details: [Name of tutor]

Course: Year: Subject:

Factual:

Presentation:	background colour(s)		☐	style	☐
	title font	☐	size	☐	colour ☐
	text font	☐	size	☐	colour ☐

Transition: slide   ☐   elements ☐

Content: word density ☐   graphics ☐   objectives   ☐

              session length   ☐   number of slides ☐

Opinion:

Presentation colour scheme:

Language used:

Embedded notes:

In each case, it is helpful to consider each document as a 'respondent' who is providing information for your research and to help you keep to your focus the schedule will be invaluable.

Analysing documentary evidence

This is different from assessing the validity and reliability of the documents themselves (a particular focus for many research methodology texts) and relates purely to the evidence that you have collected from the documents.

Content analysis has already been referred to above and, as suggested, can take both quantitative and qualitative form. In this respect, it is little different from evidence collected by any other means and presented as text (e.g. an interview transcript) or video (e.g. a lesson observation). Textual documentary analysis does offer a particular form of detailed analysis not open to other formats – even a transcript of an interview cannot adequately account for the facial expression, body language or even vocal inflection (in the particular case of non-face-to-face interviews) that will have been an integral element of the communication within the interview. Linguistic analyses of written text can become incredibly detailed and self-involved; in most situations, the research that you will be performing will be focusing on the extent to which the language (word and structure) adequately conveys meaning to the intended audience (also see Chapter 11).

As suggested above, it should be acknowledged that there is an element of analysis through selection within the data collection process (note-taking in an interview or observation may be considered similar in this respect).

Finally, we may expand upon the pros and cons of using documentary evidence given in Chapter 4 as follows:

Summary of strengths:

1. It is an unobtrusive method (when you don't have to ask to gain access).
2. You can collect data without the act changing the behaviour of respondents (be aware of ethical considerations).
3. The data are in permanent form and can be subject to re-analysis, allowing reliability checks (as long as you have stored and organised it).
4. It may provide a low-cost form of longitudinal analysis (where the same data is collected over time).
5. Enables inquiry into past events where there is no access to contemporary participants (validity and reliability may be hard to check).
6. May help to triangulate other evidence (offers a good baseline).

Summary of weaknesses:

1. The documents available may be limited or partial. (Try to find out why they are incomplete and the nature of the evidence that is missing or have been withheld.)
2. The documents have been written for purposes unconnected with the research and may be biased or distorted. (Examine the rationale of the author.)
3. Documents are not neutral reports and may be shaped by the context and the assumptions of participants. (Examine the rationale of the author.)
4. The documents may not be credible, authentic or representative. (The documents are the record of the author's perceptions – it offers a viewpoint, not reality.)

References

Cohen, L., Manion, L. and Morrison, K. (2007) *Research Methods in Education*, 6th edn. Abingdon: Routledge.

Cohen, L., Manion, L. and Morrison, K. (2011) *Research Methods in Education*, 7th edn. Abingdon: Routledge.

Denscombe, M. (2003) *The Good Research Guide*, 2nd edn. Maidenhead: Open University Press.

Duffy, B. (2005) 'The analysis of documentary evidence', in J. Bell (ed.), *Doing Your Research Project*. Buckingham: Open University Press.

Glaser, B. and Strauss, A. (1967) *The Discovery of Grounded Theory*. Chicago: Aldine.

Hayes, N. (2000) *Doing Psychological Research: Gathering and Analysing Data*. Buckingham: Open University Press.

Locke, K. (2001) *Grounded Theory in Management Research*. London: Sage.

Robson, C. (2002) *Real World Research*, 2nd edn. Oxford: Blackwell.

Taber, K. (2007) *Classroom-Based Research and Evidence-Based Practice*. London: Sage.

TES (2013) *Teachers TV*. Available at: www.tes.co.uk/MyPublicProfile. aspx?uc=447531&event=21 (accessed 3 January 2013).

Walliman, N. (2005) *Your Research Project*. London: Sage.

CHAPTER 8

OBSERVING INDIVIDUALS, GROUPS AND ENVIRONMENTS

By the conclusion of this chapter it is anticipated that you will have considered and be able to:

- understand the nature of observational research and be able to differentiate this approach from the normal act of watching or observing everyday activity;
- recognise the strengths and weaknesses of observation as a research approach;
- develop systems to record observations in a systematic way and construct observation schedules suitable to the context and the conceptual focus of the research;
- understand the key issues in analysing data and drawing conclusions and recommendations based on observation.

The nature of observational research

Put simply, observation 'involves the researcher watching, recording and analysing events of interest' (Blaxter et al., 2010: 199). However, a special kind of watching is required in order for such activity to be considered research and the key to making the step from simply looking at the situation to real observational research is to make this watching systematic in nature and focused on particular aims and objectives. A further important issue to be taken into consideration is the way in which this observation will be recorded and, finally, how the consequent data will be analysed if proper research-based conclusions are to be drawn that can lead to helpful recommendations for the improvement of practice.

The places where this 'watching' takes place can be almost anywhere provided sensible ethical rules are taken into consideration and so may include classrooms, early years settings, playgrounds, treatment rooms, consultation rooms, homes, staffrooms, corridors, offices, etc. It is a flexible approach that provides information about the 'real world' in which we operate (Robson, 2011: 316). It is a flexible approach which allows the researcher to change focus if necessary and can be used to produce both quantitative and qualitative data of high quality (Lambert, 2012: 106). Observation can thus be one of the most powerful tools in research and this is especially true for practitioner researchers in the social sciences.

Observation – the natural research tool of the educational profession

The training and experience of those engaged in the caring professions requires close attention to the details of their professional context. For instance, teachers must constantly monitor the progress of children in relation not only to their academic development but also the progress of social skills and general behaviour. Teachers quite naturally observe children on a minute-by-minute basis or over the longer term in order to make sure that their methods of teaching are effective and that children are on task and engaged in their learning. For other professions such as nursing and social work, the observation of the patient or client is central to professional processes which are part of the job. The creation of national regimes of accountability, such as that practised by Ofsted, are based on a methodology that has at its heart the process of systematic observation to judge the quality of individual teachers and schools. Increasingly within-school activities have also employed forms of observation as part of mentoring and coaching activities or for performance review.

Observation comes naturally to many, if not all, of those undertaking research in educational, health and social settings, but it is really surprising how infrequently observation forms part of the research methodology.

There are three main reasons for this. Firstly, the reluctance to integrate observation into an approach is a hangover from notions that research should be 'scientific' in character and many researchers seem to feel that simply looking at what is going on around them will not be viewed as 'good research'. This is, of course, somewhat ironic, since observation has been central to the scientific method, especially in the biological sciences, for hundreds of years. Secondly, 'familiarity breeds contempt' and many aspirant researchers are reluctant to use a research tool which they employ every day in their professional lives, sometimes quite understandably because they wish to try out other less familiar and more esoteric research techniques. Thirdly, and finally, there is often a concern that observational approaches will be time-consuming and that research tools will be complex and difficult to develop. Again, this last point is quite understandable since the kind of unstructured everyday observation that practitioners undertake as part of their work may not seem appropriate for a formal research project which may have both money and personal prestige invested in it.

Observation can, nonetheless, be used as part of any number of research approaches and is one of the most flexible of means of conducting a research study:

- Comparatively unstructured observation can be employed as part of a highly qualitative approach to research. It can be employed to support diary writing or field note taking as part of one or more of the interpretive paradigms.
- Systematic observation can lead on to the use of statistical analysis as a means of calculating frequencies that may lead to generalisable conclusions about events that may assist in the analysis of learning success or failure, behaviour modification, the comparative efficacy of 'treatment' or social adaptation and change.
- Observation can be employed as one element of a blended or mixed methods approach and can be used as a first research approach that provides the basis for subsequent positivist research tools. Alternatively it may be employed as a second research tool that will add richness to the data-gathering process, or can be operated simultaneously with other research approaches and thus allowed to both inform and be informed by other data-gathering techniques.

Table 8.1 lists the relative merits of observational methods.

Types of observation

Observation is especially helpful in providing deep, rich data that provide verisimilitude to the research process since 'it provides a degree of life experience that is lacking in most academic environments' (Hammersley, 1993: 197). Thody (2006: 133) suggests that observation is especially useful

Table 8.1   Applicability of observational methods

Advantages	Disadvantages	Paradigm	Uses
Can reveal behaviours, characteristics and group interactions that the subjects/respondents may not themselves be aware of.	Time-consuming, and lengthy and subjective in interpretation.	Largely qualitative but observation schedules can include carefully thought-out mapping techniques that are susceptible to quantitative analysis.	Especially appropriate for examining teacher–pupil/pupil–pupil interactions in the classroom, playground or other social situation.

Adapted from Burton and Brundrett (2005).

in the 'openings' to research reports since it is unrivalled in attracting reader attention and in establishing the atmosphere of the context within which the research took place. Whether used as an opening that leads on to other types of data collection and analysis or as the totality of the method employed, it is undoubtedly true that observation is unrivalled in enabling the researcher to immerse themselves in the research environment and correlatively in drawing the reader into the world of the researcher and researched. For these reasons observation is fundamental to the processes of ethnographic methods and is also often associated with the grounded theory approaches made famous by Glaser and Strauss (1967). The increasing use of first-person narrative in research reports and theses has enabled observation to come to the fore in both undergraduate and postgraduate research. Not too many years ago such methods of reporting and writing-up would have been frowned upon by many in the academic community but such responses are now, thankfully, rare. Anyone researching the complex social setting of the classroom, the home or other caring contexts will need to consider whether observation should form part of their approach.

Observation can enable the researcher to gather data on a range of settings including the physical setting (so the physical environment of the organisation); the human setting (the way people are organised, the numbers and types of people that are employed); the interactional setting (the forms of interactions and exchanges that are taking place and the ways they are planned); and the programme setting (such as resources, teaching or other professional styles or approaches) (Morrison, 1993: 80). Even more importantly, observation can take several forms (Cohen et al., 2000: 305) as listed in Table 8.2.

In slight contrast Robson (1993: 316–19) distinguishes between the following:

- the *complete participant*, where the observer actually conceals that they are a researcher in order to become a full member of a group;
- the *participant as observer*, where the researcher makes clear that they are observing the situation from the start but still tries to establish close relationships with the group;

- the *marginal participant*, where the researcher adopts a largely passive role and merely watches what is going on but is nonetheless a participant in the group; and
- the *observer-as-participant* where the researcher takes no part in the activity whatsoever, although their role is known throughout.

Table 8.2 Forms of observation

Form of observation	Key features
Highly structured	The researcher works out exactly what features they are looking for prior to commencing observation. Observation categories will have been worked out and structured observational tools will have been developed to record data. Observation will be highly systematic and methods of analysis are likely to be statistical.
Semi-structured	The researcher will have worked out the main issues that they wish to explore and so will have a clear conception of what it is they wish to observe. The observational tool used to record data will also be worked out in advance but is likely to allow note-taking rather than highly structured responses. Observation will be semi-systematic and methods of analysis are likely to be qualitative, although some basic numeric analysis may be undertaken.
Unstructured	The researcher will only have a generalised conception of what is to be observed, probably relating to an overall research theme or issue. Research tools for recording data are likely to be unstructured and likely to take the form of notes. Methods of analysis will be qualitative.

Such a continuum will reflect the nature of the research being carried out and will almost certainly imply whether the researcher wishes to operate within the interpretive or positivist paradigms with consonant effects on methods of analysis. For instance, the complete participant is most likely to be engaged in some form of highly ethnographic process whereby the researcher wishes to be immersed fully within a particular culture. At the other extreme, the observer-as-participant is far more likely to be interested in a scientific or semi-scientific approach that will enable appropriate statistical procedures to be applied to the data that is gathered.

In choosing which type of observation to undertake the researcher will draw on a variety of variables in order to make their decision. These will include their research aims and which method is most likely to fulfil them, their background training and whether it predisposes them to qualitative or quantitative approaches, the access that they are likely to be able gain to the group and even their ethical standpoint with regard to informing those under observation of their intentions.

> ### Box 8.1   Ask yourself . . .
>
> What methods of observation do you employ during your professional practice? How do you analyse such observations? Are any of the processes you use 'formal' and systematic?
>
> What problems might you encounter if you tried to employ observation in your current (or a related) work setting? What sensitivities would you encounter? Who might object?

Research tools and methods of recording data

The flexibility of the observational method means that an extremely wide variety of data recording approaches may be employed. The nature of such tools will depend on the original aims of the research project and the intended research paradigm or paradigms that the researcher intends to operate within. Crucially, the research tool must be structured in such a way as to enable the methods of analysis that the researcher intends to employ. For this reason methods of recording will vary widely within the method according to the skills, training and personal predilections of the researcher. Indeed observation is an area of research which enables the widest set of approaches of almost any of the many available to the researcher. Even a general research text such as Cohen et al. (2000: 311–13) lists two detailed pages of methods of recording, while, similarly, Sarantakos (1998: 214–17) offers almost three pages on the topic. These include approaches such as:

- quick jottings of key words or the use of symbols;
- detailed note-taking or field notes which may be on predetermined themes or in response to events as they unfold;
- pen portraits of participants;
- descriptions of events, behaviour or activities;
- 'chronologs' describing events or episodes along with the time of occurrence or recording of observations at predetermined times;
- context maps, sketches or other non-verbal representations;
- rating scales, checklists or taxonomies;
- sociometric diagrams that indicate relationships between people or show key shifts in control such as the changing speakers in a staff meeting.

At its simplest the recording of observation may take the form of simple jottings in a diary which note phenomena as they occur. Some researchers employ new diaries for this purpose, others merely use footnotes in general diaries – although one would expect that such an ad hoc approach would form just one element in a more carefully constructed approach. The paramount concern is that important events or occurrences are captured along with the related chronology so that the evolution of patterns can be determined. Contemporaneous diary writing will provide an opportunity to record observations in an extremely rich form that will be especially useful in the more reflexive forms of research. The advent of accountability activities such as appraisal and performance management has increased the prevalence of observation activities as a normal part of institutional life. For this reason researchers frequently adopt an observation schedule that enables structured observation according to key themes in a manner which is reminiscent of external accountability approaches. Figure 8.1 offers an example of such an observational tool that focuses on curriculum development in schools and might be employed by a researcher interested in the efficacy of certain curricular approaches, innovations or action research activities. A simple form such as this should contain key information such as the names of the observer and observed along with the date and time, and provide a matrix for note-taking against predetermined themes that relate to the research aims.

Curriculum development observation research project	
Name of observer: Individual observed: Group observed:	Date: Time: Focus of lesson:
Quality of teaching and learning and of the curriculum:	
Pupils' attitudes, values and personal development:	
Classroom management:	
General observations:	

Figure 8.1   Curriculum development observation schedule

A modified version of such a schedule is suitable for critical incident/ critical event observation (see Figure 8.2). Such events or occurrences are deemed to be particularly important since they may typify or illuminate a particular feature of organisational culture or social interaction. Such approaches are most often employed by those interested in behaviour management, student integration problems or issues relating to the student–student, client–client or staff–client interface.

Some academic commentators such as Bryman (2004) emphasise a more systematic approach to observation with a concomitant requirement for an observation schedule with clear focus and simple system of recording that takes account of subsequent systems of coding of data and shows due consideration for reliability and validity (Bryman, 2004: 169–70). Such approaches will enable highly structured methods that may employ diacritical marks to record events in a manner which will be familiar to those trained in psychology. For instance, Figure 8.3 provides an apparently simple representation of how much time off task individuals in a group of

Critical event analysis	
Critical event number:	Date:
Name of teacher:	Time:
Group/class:	Focus of event:
What precipitated the event:	
What took place:	
Outcomes:	
Notes on interviews with participants:	

Figure 8.2 Critical event analysis schedule

		\multicolumn{15}{c}{Time in one-minute intervals}

		1	2	3	4	5	6	7	8	9	10	11	12	13	14	15
Name of child	1. Joanne		X	X	X				X	X	X	X				
	2. Diane															
	3. Neil	X					X	X								
	4. Chris			X											X	X
	5. Freddie		X	X	X	X	X	X								
	6. Jane															
	7. Pat												X	X	X	X
	8.Richard															
	9. Hattie					X						X				
	10. Paul								X	X	X					

X indicates time off task

Figure 8.3   Chart of time off task over a 15-minute period

ten children spent during a 10-minute period of observation. The chart will provide very a straightforward numeric representation of the number of occasions that children failed to pay attention to their work. At first sight the chart may seem to be useful in providing a fairly precise indication of which children within the group are attentive to their work and which are not. However, such a schematic representation might lead to a series of other important question. For instance, children numbers 1 and 5 seem to be off-task for the greatest amount of time during the 10 minutes of observation but does the chart give a hint as to why they were off task? For instance, is child number 3 instigating an interaction that may cause a breakdown in concentration? Why is child number 7 apparently attentive until the final minutes of the period of observation? Has she, for instance completed all the work given to her and become bored? Why does child number 9 appear to be on-task for most of the period but have brief periods when she is off-task and then, apparently, get back to work? Such questions are tantalising and cannot be answered by such a chart in isolation. They need to be followed up by further observation which may focus on the types or forms of interaction of only one or two individuals at a time in a way what will allow for much more detailed qualitative analysis. This is not to say that such an observation chart is not of value in itself. In its own right it will provide clear and precise indications of the length of time that a particular individual or a whole group of children are undertaking a particular task and this can be analysed through the use of simple statistical techniques in a way that may inform the researcher about the efficacy and interest levels of particular curriculum approaches or pieces of work. The technique could be employed as part of a pre- and post-test to see whether some change in materials or pedagogic technique encouraged engagement by pupils. Or it could be used as one in a variety of methods to investigate complex sets of relationships among children.

Minor modifications to such a chart enable it to be used for very different purposes. So, instead of measuring 'negative' activities such as time off task the observations could be to see the extent to which young children are socialising and cooperating in their work (see Figure 8.4).

		Socialisation/interaction level			
		High	Medium	Low	Notes
Time in five-minute intervals	10.00				
	10.05				
	10.10				
	10.15				
	10.20				
	10.25				
	10.30				

Figure 8.4 Socialisation/interaction level

Box 8.2   Ask yourself . . .

What would be the key features of an observation schedule for a small-scale project relevant to your own professional context? Is the schedule susceptible to quantitative or qualitative data analysis or both?

Analysing data from observation

The forms of observation that are susceptible to qualitative analysis may be addressed either by the use of 'traditional' methods of data interrogation or through the use of the increasing number of electronic data analysis packages. The decision whether to employ electronic means is both individual and pragmatic. Some experienced researchers continue to use manual means even if they have the skills to employ electronic approaches since they wish to remain in close personal contact with the data while others regularly use electronic means even when exploring comparatively small amounts of material. However, a general rule is that small-scale pieces of research that have elicited comparatively little qualitative data may not be worth the time and effort of coming to grips with the complexities of electronic approaches unless learning such techniques is itself a goal of the researcher. Whether using electronic or manual means the essence of qualitative analysis remains the same: to look for key commonalities within the data that indicate linkages, illuminate research questions or point to emerging themes within the data. This process is facilitated by close reading of the material that has been derived from observation and where this is in the form of notes, diary or other verbal means of recording, the researcher will seek to allocate key phrases, utterances or incidents to predetermined or emergent themes or nodes. The process might follow a straightforward path of transcription of original notes and primary data followed by close reading of the material during which the main concepts are highlighted, either manually or electronically, and the resulting material is categorised and ordered. A simple stem and branch analysis would include the creation of key themes from original research objectives which might then form the basis of a series of matrices with emergent sub-themes.

Wragg (1999) cautions those untrained in statistical approaches should consult a statistician rather than misuse a procedure. However, he suggests that the following techniques are the most common and most appropriate ways of analysing observational data through statistical methods:

- *Relationships between measures* – used to calculate the relationship between two measure such as the amount of misbehaviour and number of pupils applying themselves to a task.
- *Comparing groups* – dependent on the type of measure involved. If a frequency count has been taken a chi square may be appropriate but other techniques such as a t test, Mann-Whitney U or Kruskal-Wallis analysis may be appropriate.
- *Measuring change* – especially useful in calculating 'value-added' and thus for comparing the progress of unmatched groups.
- *Predicting* – multiple regression analysis.
- *Reducing complexity* – factor analysis or cluster analysis.
- *Aggregating findings* – used to put together findings from several different pieces of observational research. Most commonly associated with 'meta-analysis'.

(Wragg, 1999: 123–7)

A chapter on observation is not itself the place for a detailed outline of either qualitative or statistical techniques of analysis but there are a range of excellent texts that provide detailed instructions on where and how to apply such approaches that are accessible to the non-specialist.

Those interested in qualitative approaches might examine the work of Miles and Huberman (1994) or Silverman (2004) while those seeking guidance on quantitative approaches could consult, for instance, Solomon and Winch (1994), Clegg (1994), Cohen and Holiday (1996) or Bryman and Cramer (1997).

Ethics and observational methods

It is easy to overlook ethical issues when employing observational techniques since observational methods do not employ intervention and may be perceived to be part of 'normal professional duties'. Nonetheless, as noted earlier, observation may be employed as a result of critical incidents or may be the precursor to intervention as part of an action research cycle. Even when disassociated from intervention the act of observation is itself a matter of extreme sensitivity since it will involve at least an element of judgement-making that may be deemed to be sensitive within the social context of the workplace. For instance, when observing a classroom judgements may be made about the quality of teaching and learning, thus potentially impugning the professional competence of the colleague observed or the abilities of the student. Moreover, any observation of child subjects will always contain potential problems since child protection issues will be paramount. For this reason permission for research should be sought and any relevant ethics applications made, as explained in Chapter 4, as a 'precaution'. Additionally it is crucial to recognise and acknowledge that observation as part of research processes should never be confused with observation for accountability or other managerial processes. This should form part of the 'contract' between the observer and the observed so there should be no doubt that data gathered in the process of research observation will be used solely for the purposes of the research project and will not be employed as part of competence or capability procedures.

Intervention?

The subject of whether or not to intervene during the process of observation is a vexed one and is not infrequently the subject of lively discussion and conjecture among academic colleagues involved in such data-gathering processes. Of course there are no real issues if the researcher has chosen to undertake the role of 'participant observer' since intervention, discussion and engagement form part of the research process. The situation is far more complex for the non-participant observer who determines to operate without taking part in the activity that is the focus of observation. The nub of the issue usually revolves around when and whether it appropriate to interject if the observer sees something occur or about to occur that is inappropriate or dangerous. There are several disadvantages to such intervention including the fact that the researcher will inevitably cease to function as a researcher since they will themselves become part of the activity under scrutiny. Further, any such intervention may be very distressing to those being observed since it may be seen to imply some lack of ability by those in charge of the activity. All researchers will face such a situation at some time during the process of observational research and they will make a professional decision whether or not to act to intercede based on circumstance. In general the decision will focus on whether there is likelihood of injury, whether physical or emotional, to the subjects.

Summary

Observation is one of the most powerful and most overlooked of research approaches. Frequently, those undertaking research projects in the social sciences have finely honed skills of observation through years of training and professional practice within which the scrutiny of colleagues and, most importantly, clients, pupils or students forms an integral part of their role. The use of observation does not predetermine or even imply the dominant research tradition within which the researcher intends to work since data gathered through such methods can be employed as part of either a positivist or interpretive approach to data interrogation. Such decisions about paradigmatic approaches will, however, be inherent in the nature of the actual research tools developed since only certain forms of observational recording will be susceptible to qualitative or quantitative approaches. However, some forms of data gathering will be susceptible to both quantitative and qualitative methods or, even more commonly, will enable an interaction between methods. Alternatively, one research tool that employs observation may be employed as the concomitant of another element within a blended approach.

Researchers using observational techniques must be extremely sensitive to ethical considerations since the process of observation may easily be confused with some form of onerous surveillance by the subject or subjects of observation. It is essential that all those involved in the research process are completely clear how the data derived from such methods will be employed and that there will be no question that such material will be used for other purposes such as appraisal or performance management.

Despite such complexities and challenges observation can be one of the most rewarding of research approaches. Although observation may, and has, formed the main research tool for major, funded research studies it can also be a particularly relevant method for small-scale research by the practitioner researcher.

Further reading

DeWalt, K. M. and DeWalt, B. R. (2001) *Participant Observation: A Guide for Fieldworkers*. London: Altamira.

Fine, G. A. and Sandstrom, K. L. (1998) *Knowing Children: Participant Observation with Minors*, Qualitative Research Methods Series. London: Sage.

Hopkins, D. (2007) *A Teacher's Guide to Classroom Research*. Milton Keynes: Open University Press.

Montgomery, D. (2002) *Helping Teachers Develop Through Classroom Observation*. London: David Fulton.

Rodriguez, N. M. and Ryave, A. L. (2002) *Systematic Self-Observation: A Method for Researching the Hidden and Elusive Features of Everyday Social Life*, Qualitative Research Methods Series. London: Sage.

Sharman, C., Vennis, D. and Cross, W. (1995) *Observing Children: A Practical Guide*, Cassell Studies in Pastoral Care and Personal and Social Education. London: Continuum.

References

Blaxter, L., Hughes, C. and Tight, M. (2010) *How to Research*, 4th edn. Maidenhead: Open University Press.

Bryman, A. (2004) *Social Research Methods*, 2nd edn. Oxford: Oxford University Press.

Bryman, A. and Cramer, D. (1997) *Quantitative Data Analysis*. London: Routledge.

Burton, N. and Brundrett, M. (2005) *Leading the Curriculum in the Primary School*. London: Sage.

Clegg, F. (1994) *Simple Statistics: A Course Book for the Social Sciences*. Cambridge: Cambridge University Press.

Cohen, L. and Holliday, M. (1996) *Practical Statistics for Students*. London: Paul Chapman.

Cohen, L., Manion, L. and Morrison, K. (2000) *Research Methods in Education*, 5th edn. London: RoutledgeFalmer.

Glaser, B. G. and Strauss, A. L. (1967) *The Discovery of Grounded Theory: Strategies for Qualitative Research*. Chicago: Aldine.

Hammersley, M. (ed.) (1993) *Social Research: Philosophy, Politics and Practice*. London: Open University Press.

Lambert, M. (2012) *A Beginner's Guide to Doing Your Education Research Project*. London: Sage.

Miles, M. B. and Huberman, A. M. (1994) *Qualitative Data Analysis*, 2nd edn. Thousand Oaks, CA; Sage.

Morrison, K. (1993) *Planning and Accomplishing School-Centred Evaluation*. Norfolk: Peter Francis Publishers.

Robson, C. (1993) *Real World Research*, 2nd edn. Oxford: Blackwell.

Robson, C. (2011) *Real World Research: A Resource for Users of Social Research Methods in Applied Setting*, 3rd edn. Chichester: Wiley.

Sarantakos, S. (1998) *Social Research,* 2nd edn. China: Macmillan Limited.

Silverman, D. (2004) *Qualitative Research: Theory, Method and Practice.* London: Sage.

Solomon, R. and Winch, C. (1994) *Calculating and Computing for the Social Science and Arts Students*. Buckingham: Open University Press.

Thody, A. (2006) *Writing and Presenting Research*. London: Sage.

Wragg, E. D. (1999) *An Introduction to Classroom Observation*. London: Routledge.

CHAPTER 9

DIRECT QUESTIONING – SURVEYS, INTERVIEWS AND QUESTIONNAIRES

By the end of this chapter you should be able to:

- understand the advantages and disadvantages of surveys, interviews and questionnaires;
- differentiate between different types of interview and know which type of interview is most suitable for use in which project;
- have a clear overview of the main theoretical concepts associated with interviews;
- understand how to construct an interview schedule;
- know how to conduct and interview and how to record what you hear;
- plan and construct a questionnaire;
- understand the difference between and relative merits of open and closed questions;
- understand the importance of good data collection processes and appropriate response rates.

Asking questions

This chapter focuses on asking questions with respondents whether as part of a survey or through the use of interviews and questionnaires. The link between these approaches is the issue of questioning itself since in all cases the researcher needs to be clear about what is being asked and what is expected of the respondent. As will be shown the different approaches require different kinds of questions if they are to be successful and the researcher must construct and select their language very carefully. The chapter will also outline key the main basic methods of constructing both an interview schedule and a research questionnaire.

Using surveys

The use of a survey or surveys is usually part of the 'descriptive' approach to research in that the researcher is trying to 'describe' and interpret a situation or phenomenon. Surveys are useful in gathering a considerable amount of data on a given topic at a given point in time and can either involve simple, short interviews or questionnaires whereby a given number of respondents, defined in the stated sample, are asked to respond to questions on the issue under scrutiny. The best known types of survey include political polls, opinion polls, marketing surveys and general preference surveys but they can also have a wide range of uses in wider research, often by gathering the opinions of a fairly large group of people prior to undertaking more intensive methods of research such as detailed questionnaire research or longer semi-structured interviews. Morrison notes that surveys have a number of key features including the fact that they gather data economically, they address a wide target population, generate numerical data, gather standardised information, make generalisations and can be processed statistically (Morrison, 1993: 38–40). The rest of this chapter will focus on how to ask questions in either a questionnaire or interview format, whether as part of a survey or a more detailed interview or questionnaire.

The advantages and disadvantages of interviews

Interviews are undoubtedly one of the most popular of research tools for those engaged in research in education generally and educational leadership specifically. The reasons for this are complex being partly pragmatic and relating to the skill sets possessed by many researchers and partly theoretical and relating to the requirement to gain a depth of understanding of the topic under scrutiny in the complex work of educational institutions. It is sadly the case that comparatively few educational professionals gain a strong grasp of the use of statistical techniques and so the use of quantitative methods is challenging if not impossible for many as a way of investigating educational leadership issues. By contrast, all teachers, lecturers, health professionals and social workers are, by virtue of their nature and training, articulate and skilled at interaction with others since the very act of teaching requires high levels of expertise in human communication. For these reasons, interviews are a natural method (probably *the* natural method) of undertaking research for most aspiring or expert researchers in the social sciences. However, the reasons for using such an approach are not merely a lack of ability in other approaches since interviews have a very great deal to commend them for many types of research project. As Kvale has noted (2007) interviews are helpful since knowledge is often generated between humans through conversations. This is especially relevant to schools, colleges and universities since such institutions are fundamentally social in nature and their activities relate to personal relationships built up in classrooms, staffrooms, meetings, offices and so on. By using interviews the researcher can swiftly gain large amounts of interesting and relevant material that is highly germane to their area of interest which may well offer the possibility of key insights that would not be possible to establish through the use of other techniques such as questionnaires or observation alone.

Although interviews pose challenges for the researcher in that they require high levels of skill if they are to be managed effectively, preparation is needed beforehand. However, interviews allow all participants to discuss their own interpretations of the world and to express how they view the situations they are examining from their own point of view (Cohen et al., 2007: 349). This means that it is inevitable that both the conduct of the interview and the process of analysis may be influenced or biased by the interviewer's own views. For this reason, it is always difficult for a researcher to argue for the generalisability and universality of the findings of a research project based solely on interviews. Robson argues that the interview is really an effective substitute for ethnographic research since the linguistic interchange embodied in the interview approach can open a virtually unique window on what lies behind our actions (Robson, 2006: 272). There are many books that focus solely on how to prepare for and conduct interviews, one of the most useful of which remains that by Drever (1995) which explains concisely but in some detail how to construct and carry out an interview.

The delivery format

A variety of formats are available for interviewing including face-to-face, telephone, video conferencing and online interviews. In general face-to-face interviews are considered the best approach wherever possible because the interviewer can interact with the interviewee and note their full response, including tone of voice, manner, body language and so forth.

Table 9.1 Interview formats

Type of interview	Methods	Advantages and disadvantages
F2F (face-to-face)	The 'traditional' format for interviews where the interviewer and interviewee pre-arrange a date, time, place and focus for the interview.	Generally most effective when the interviewer goes to the interviewee, particularly if it is 'neutral ground'. Convenient for the interviewee and avoids distractions.
Video conferencing	The interview takes place using a video link that is secure and so ensures confidentiality.	Means that more geographically distant potential respondents can be approached and may save on travel time and costs. It can be an expensive option and does require that both 'ends' of the interview have the necessary technology and skills available to them.
Telephone interview	The interview takes place using a normal telephone line at a time agreed between the interviewer and interviewee.	Generally easy to arrange and very convenient but does not allow for the observation of physical cues and mannerisms.
Online	Use of a web-based 'chat room' as the location for your interview.	Increasingly popular as researchers and respondents become more familiar with and reliant on digital technology and ICT. Confidentially and safely need to be ensured.

However, there are certain circumstances where constraints of time, finance or whatever can make it difficult or impossible to meet with some or all of the respondents in person and in such circumstances the only approach available may be to use some form of electronic communication. Despite the constraints that this approach may place on the process such interviews can still be a very valuable form of data gathering and such an approach is especially useful when a large number of brief interviews need to be undertaken comparatively swiftly. Tables 9.1 shows some of the strengths and weaknesses of different ways of undertaking interviews.

Each approach offers certain advantages but also poses challenges. Electronic forms of interview mean that a wide range of people can be interviewed swiftly and with comparative ease at low cost. Indeed, there are many circumstances where problems of time and finance mean that the only viable approach is to use telephone, video or internet approaches. However, all of these means lack the level of personal contact which can be essential for a really successful interview where an understanding of non-verbal cues and a calm and friendly atmosphere can help to ensure that the best data is gained. For this reason the immediacy and intimacy of a face-to-face interview remains the best way to undertake interviews where it is possible to do so. Nonetheless, many projects would not be possible and much valuable data would remain uncollected if electronic means were not used.

Types of interview

Interviews are really only appropriate for small samples since their conduct is time-consuming and can be costly in terms of travelling to and from interview sites. Their greatest strength lies in the fact that very large amounts of data can be gathered during each interview and the level of detail and quality of material can be considerable. In this sense, interviews are almost unique in the richness of data that can be gathered.

Table 9.2   Types of interview

Type of interview			
Unstructured	Allows the respondent to discuss a wide range of issues more or less under their own control with only light guidance from the interviewer. Can produce very rich and detailed data and allows issues to emerge as the conversation develops.	Can have a tendency to meander and lead to convoluted discussions that are not necessarily on topic. Can be difficult to manage and can lead to the gathering of a great deal of irrelevant data.	Useful in certain types of research such as grounded theory or ethnographic approaches where the researcher does not have any clear, preconceived ideas about what they expect to find.
Semi-structured	Enables the researcher to guide the interview and to ensure that the respondent addresses the key issues that have been defined in the interview schedule. Produces rich data on the topic under scrutiny.	Can lack spontaneity and cause problems for the researcher in trying to keep the respondent on topic. Issues that may be relevant but were not included in the interview schedule may be missed.	Useful in most situations where there is plenty of time to plan the interview and where the discussion can take place in a relaxed and private atmosphere.
Structured	Allows the researcher to gather a wide range of key data very swiftly according to preconceived questions.	Only allows for short questions and answers on questions identified before the interview. Comparatively little rich data is likely to be elicited and both the interviewer and respondent may feel that much has been left unexplored.	Can be very helpful when trying to gather data on very specific questions that require brief answers such as ages, preferences, roles, etc. Has the advantage of speed and clarity of purpose and can often be undertaken very quickly in ad hoc situations such as corridors, classrooms, rest areas. Some of the resulting data may be suitable for basic statistical analysis.

There three main types of interview:

- *Unstructured interviews* – where the interviewer simply engages with the respondent on the topic he or she is interested in with no predefined agenda and allows the interview to take whatever course it may.
- *Semi-structured interviews* – where the interviewer has a series of predefined questions under main headings but allows some degree of latitude in what is discussed.
- *Structured interviews* – where the researcher asks only a series of predefined and detailed questions and allows little or no latitude in exploring the wider issues.

As shown in Table 9.2, each of these approaches has its merits and demerits and each one is more or less suitable for different purposes.

Whichever approach to the interview is chosen, considerable preparation is not only recommended but is essential if the interview is to be successful in developing the right kind of relationship between the interviewer and interviewee that will ensure that as much relevant data is gathered as is possible.

Constructing the interview schedule

It has been noted that one major advantage of the interview is its adaptability (Bell, 2005: 157) by which we mean that interviews can be used to explore a very wide range of issues and gain a great a deal of data very swiftly. However, much depends on the interviewer's ability to pose appropriate questions and to respond to the answers that the interviewee gives in order to take the interview forward as a result of their responses. To do this successfully the interviewer will need to:

1. possess, and possibly demonstrate, considerable background knowledge;
2. use informed questioning (based on the ideas and research findings from previous reading);
3. react with sensitivity to new leads.

(Burton et al., 2008: 87)

An interview schedule is a document prepared by the interviewee prior to the interview which outlines the questions that will be asked in the interview itself. It is generally considered good practice to provide the interviewee with the interview schedule prior to the event so that they are aware of the questions that will be asked and they can give some thought to their responses. There is an art to preparing a good interview schedule and the formulation of this document can predetermine the likelihood of successful outcome of the project. It is often helpful if the first section of the document outlines key issues prior to the asking of the actual questions that need to be dealt with such as:

- the title of the research;
- the place and time of the interview;
- the name of the respondent (or number if this is preferred).

It is also good practice to have a standard preamble which will be read to the interviewee explaining the nature of the interview, the reasons why it is taking place and offering guarantees about anonymity (where agreed) and the security of the data.

The way that the subsequent questions which make up the main body of the document are posed can predetermine the kind of response that is received and up to seven different kinds of question and response have been identified (Tuckman, 1972). 'Closed' questions tend to limit the possible responses of the interviewee and are most appropriate when trying to find out simple, factual information such as asking how long a respondent has been in post, the number of students on roll, how many colleagues are in a certain department and so on. In contrast 'open' questions encourage the respondent to be expansive in their responses and are likely to involve prompts such as 'Tell me about ...' or 'What is your view ...' etc. Closed questions are likely to be most relevant in short, structured interviews while open questions are likely to form the majority of the interaction in a semi-structured or unstructured interview. However, the range of types of question involved in an interview can be very subtle and different types of questions can be identified that:

- introduce the theme of the study to the interviewer;
- ask for information;
- ask for an example;
- probe and follow up a response;
- interpret and reformulate a response (clarify and check understanding).

(Kvale, 2007: 133–5)

All of these kinds of question can be integrated into a successful interview and, as the list above suggests, the order in which they are asked can be very important.

The way that the questions are phrased is thus crucial to the outcome of the meeting but the number and ordering of questions is also very important. In a one hour semi-structured interview it is unlikely that any more than about five or six themes can be explored in any detail and so the schedule should fall naturally into five or six sections. The order of these sections can be very important and considerable thought should be given to the approach used. The first section of the interview should be used to gain any simple, relevant material that may only require brief, precise answers, such as length of time in post, main role of the respondent, previous roles, etc. Such material can be dealt with swiftly and allows the respondents to become engaged in the interview prior to any more detailed or reflective questions. The subsequent sections of the interview should be based on the major issues that are to be explored in some detail. Denscombe (2003: 179) suggests a process of questioning that links prompts, probes and checks to interviewer behaviours since the interviewer can encourage the interviewee to respond by remaining silent, repeating the question or the last few words of the response, or asking for examples.

Typically, each section may contain only one or two main questions with possible follow-up questions. Such questions fit into three categories:

- *Main questions* – which address the major issue under scrutiny and allow the respondent the broadest latitude for response. Such questions are intended to be open ended and to invite the respondent to reflect and respond at length.
- *Probes* – which are follow-up questions designed to explore issues in more detail.
- *Prompts* – which are simple and often quite direct questions whose aim is gain some data on key issues where the respondent has not addressed these matters in their response to the main question or the probe question. Such questions are far less open and literally 'prompt' the interviewee for a response.

The themes that underpin the questions in the sections of the schedule can be derived from a number of sources including:

- initial reading of previous research and ideas on the topic (the initial literature review);
- other sources of data gathering such as an initial questionnaire, observations, field notes, etc.;
- the previous professional experience of the interviewer;
- the content or relevant publications and documents such as national, regional or local policy documents, laws, etc. This is especially relevant when the purpose of the interview is to test out some current or proposed policy.

Crucially, the questions that you ask should relate closely to the main aims of the study. The reasons for this are self-evident since it is of little use to gather data on issues that are not directly related to what you are trying to test out or discover. However, structuring your questions very closely in

TITLE

Respondent:
Date:
Time:
Interview location:

Introduction

Section 1: Context
Main question 1.1:
Main question 1.2:
Main question 1.3:

Section 2
Main question 2.1:
Probe:
Prompts:

Main question 2.2:
Probe:
Prompts:

Section 3
Main question 3.1:
Probe:
Prompts:

Main question 3.2:
Probe:
Prompts:

Section 4
Main question 4.1:
Probe:
Prompts:

Main question 4.2:
Probe:
Prompts:

Closing statement: *Those are all of the questions that I have for you and we have reached the end of the session. Thank you for agreeing to be interviewed. I emphasise once again that everything that you have said will be kept in the strictest confidence. I will be in touch with you again in the near future with a transcript of our meeting and I would be grateful if you would read through the document and make any amendments to it you feel appropriate where you feel that you misstated issues or where the transcript is not clear about what was said. Do you have any final questions or issues that you would like to raise about the interview?*

Figure 9.1   Basic structure of an interview schedule

relation to your aims can have many other benefits since this approach can make subsequent data presentation and analysis simpler and help to give structural integrity to your final report. This is because such an approach can allow the researcher to compose the content of the main aims, then structure the literature review around the key themes derived from these aims, employ the same themes in constructing the interview schedule, and finally analyse and present findings according to the same issues. This can make analysis much simpler since the researcher can readily reflect back on his or her aims and the literature that has been read previously when analysing the data from the interviews and use this same approach when writing up the research report, dissertation or thesis thus adding a level of readability and accessibility that would otherwise not have been the case. An example of the basic structure of an interview schedule is shown in Figure 9.1. Note how the document is constructed to ensure that all the relevant information is gathered and that main questions, probes and prompts are provided.

Recording the interview

Care must be taken in your choice of recording techniques which should always be agreed in advance with the interviewee since some respondents will agree to certain types approaches and not others. Overall, audio recording remains the most common approach since it is simple to operate and unobtrusive but allows for the collection of a large volume of material speedily and in such a way that it can be played back and transcribed with comparative ease provided sound quality is good. Tape recording still remains popular with some researchers but digital audio recording is increasingly ubiquitous since digital recorders are comparatively inexpensive and offer excellent sound quality. The consequent audio files can be played back on the recording device itself or can be imported into personal computers and subsequently shared with other researchers in the research team. They can then be stored simply and safely, taking up no physical space whatever.

Contemporaneous note-taking will inevitably split the concentration of the interviewer between the process of writing and the conduct of the interview and will only produce a partial record unless the interviewer is a very skilled note-taker or trained in shorthand. Such notes will be based upon what appeared to be important to the interviewer at the time and may not record important issues, thus biasing the subsequent data and final report towards the personal predilections and beliefs of the researcher rather than being based on the actual material that the interviewee was trying to communicate. Nevertheless, for most interviewers the development of a good note-taking technique that does not distract too much from the conduct of the interview but allows for the recording of salient points is a skill which will develop over time and during a number of interviews.

The timing and manner of the interviewer

The 'manner' of the interviewer is important in all forms of interview, in terms of putting the interviewee at ease and encouraging them to discuss the issues in question with openness and confidence. Effective interviewing is a skill that needs to be developed and it is often only after a number of interviews on any given topic or project, when the interviewer has become really familiar with the issues and with the schedule, that the process becomes really efficient. In-depth interviews usually take around an hour to conduct but additional time may be required to set up recording devices and to prepare for subsequent interviews. However, if a large volume of interviews are to take place where comparatively small amounts of data are required from each respondent (often in structured interviews) then much shorter interactions may be appropriate that may only last a few minutes each.

The advantages and disadvantages of using questionnaires

Munn and Drever (1996: 2) offer a straightforward series of advantages of using a questionnaire. In summary, these advantages may be stated as:

- an efficient use of available time;
- allowing for respondent anonymity;
- the possibility of receiving a high return rate;
- the possibility to standardise questions to facilitate analysis.

In contrast, Munn and Drever (1996: 5) also suggest a series of disadvantages. In summary, these may be stated as:

- the information received tends to offer description rather than any deep explanation;
- the information received can be superficial given communication 'distance' between the researcher and the respondent;
- sufficient time must be spent in proper preparation and piloting or the questionnaire may have limited usefulness.

As previously stated, questionnaires can offer a rapid, effective, efficient and confidential means of collecting a large number of responses. The data collected can lend itself to quantitative analysis using descriptive or infer-ential statistics (see Chapter 11) and open-ended textual sections can give respondents greater freedom of expression and may be useful in capturing additional and valuable data outside the closed questions set by the researcher.

Planning and constructing a questionnaire

Munn and Drever (1996) describe a questionnaire as a written form of questioning, which emphasises the fact that this approach is more closely related to the interview approach than might at first be realised. A ques-tionnaire survey can used when the target population is generally large and quantitative data is needed that will lend itself to analysis using descriptive or inferential statistics. If the population is sufficiently large the researcher will be able to analyse for responses from any sub-groups present within the sample; for example, responses could be compared between males and females or between senior leaders and practioners. Although questionnaires may yield data which lack depth when com-pared to interview data, this does not preclude the use of some open-ended questions within a questionnaire to elicit more detailed textual responses. As with other methods, questionnaires can contribute to cross-site and cross-level studies; so, for instance, a research study could include staff in different local authorities, heads in a variety of schools located within the chosen authorities and associated university-based education staff who work with those heads in their schools (Brundrett and Rhodes, 2013).

If a questionnaire is to be successful then it is crucial that the overall aims of the study are known in advance of the construction and administration of the research tool (Youngman, 1994). In addition questionnaires need to be as accessible, not too long, not too onerous, well-presented and as inter-esting as possible to secure returns. Fowler (1998) points out that if the researcher is not present when questionnaires are completed – which may well be the case – this may lead to respondents not answering questions in a way that is useful to the researcher. Again, careful questionnaire construc-tion on the part of the researcher to ensure returns of value is emphasised. For a postal questionnaire, provision of a covering letter or an introduction to explain the nature and purpose of the research with clear contact and return details, a reassurance concerning the ethical standards upheld, a pre-paid return envelope and an acknowledgement with thanks for the time the respondent will take in completing and returning the questionnaire could all help facilitate provision of data for the researcher. The researcher can help manage questionnaire returns by attaching an appropriate identifica-tion number to each one.

It is often considered best to offer the respondent the most straightforward and least contentious questions at the start of the questionnaire, such as age, gender, employment, etc., in order to engage them with the issue and then the complexity can be increased later (rather in the same way as suggested for interviews earlier in this chapter) (Denscombe, 2003). All questions should be clear and care should be taken that none can be deemed overly intrusive or offensive to the respondent (Cohen et al., 2003) or else the respondent may withdraw from the process or may be influenced in the way they respond. Overall, Cohen et al. (2003) suggest a possible sequence of:

1. unthreatening factual questions;
2. closed questions gaining responses on attitudes and opinions;
3. open-ended questions seeking reasons for the responses given.

Advice concerning the construction of questionnaires appears frequently in the research literature. The final form depends, of course, on the nature and purpose of the research and on the sample of respondents who will receive the questionnaire. For example, the text used will need to accommodate the experience and realistic levels of knowledge of the intended respondents and any questions put to children, for example, will need to take this into account. Lambert (2008) examines the use of questionnaires in educational evaluation with very able pupils attending out-of-school classes. He suggests that materials need to be clear, concise and well-presented. He also advises that the researcher should always be open to questions from all those involved in the research whether these be pupils themselves or their parents. Appropriate behaviour and respect for the teacher's authority are needed when administering the questionnaires oneself and of course in any interaction with the pupils. He adds that questionnaires as a research instrument can appear invitingly deceptive, but cautions with regard to the potential complexity of the procedures involved from sending materials to analysis of data.

It is usual and wise to pilot a research instrument with a group of respondents drawn from the possible sample prior to using the full questionnaire since this will help to iron out any issues or inconsistencies in the questions and, in more technical terms, will help to ensure the validity and reliability of the research tool (Brundrett and Rhodes, 2013). Instructions to respondents need to be clear and questions must be unambiguous and suitable for the target group. For instance, it is perfectly reasonable to ask experienced professionals questions that include technical matters or that may contain acronyms relevant to their professional interest but such questions would be completely inappropriate for the general population or for individuals in other professions. The pilot will allow the questioner to check whether the questions are indeed relevant and easily understood and the researcher would be well-advised to change those that are not. Brundrett and Rhodes (2013) point out that certain types of questions should be avoided, including:

- double questions;
- leading questions;
- presuming questions;
- hypothetical questions;
- overly complex questions;
- double negative questions; and
- awkward questions.

If questionnaires are not well constructed then responses may be poor or the interviewee may even decide to disengage and move on or refuse to complete the questionnaire. It is important to remember that in many educational organisations there is a severe overload of data gathering, often for the purposes of accountability, which means that it is even more imperative that things are kept as straightforward and unfussy as possible in order to encourage a serious response since there will be little or no opportunity to check on the accuracy or seriousness of the responses obtained (Robson, 1999). Thomas (2009: 174) comments on the possibility for 'prestige bias' to occur where, for example, in order to 'look good' or 'informed' or 'ethical', respondents may try and offer the 'right answer' (Brundrett and Rhodes, 2013). However, if the questions are made to be direct, simple and unambiguous and any instructions are clear and easy to understand, then there is a good chance that responses will be sensible and, most importantly, useful to the researcher

This does not mean that all questions in a questionnaire survey have to be of the 'closed' type, with only one 'right' answer. The chosen questions may be 'closed' and attract answers such as yes or no but the questions may also be 'open-ended' and allow participants to respond in a variety of ways or allow them to be more expansive in their responses. Indeed, open-ended questions allow the respondent to provide details that may offer rich data that is more interesting than simple one word answers or yes and no responses. However, the disadvantage is in the added complexity in analysing such responses, especially if the sample is large. For this reason, as a general rule, the larger the sample being used the more likely it is that a closed questioning technique will be used so as to enable statistical analysis. With smaller samples open-ended questions are often included in the latter part of the questionnaire to gain greater detail about the subject under scrutiny.

Postal and telephone questionnaires

The researcher may be able to send out a great many questionnaires by post very swiftly but this can only be successful if the researcher can access a suitable database of addresses for the target group. Equally, the researcher needs to keep in mind that the increasing cost of postage can be a severe strain on a research budget, especially when one keeps in mind that pre-paid envelopes should be provided.

Telephone questionnaires involve asking respondents simple questions over the telephone and can be carried out by several researchers at the same time provided trials or pilots have been carried out and a strict protocol in administration is used. Otherwise there is a great danger of introducing variation and bias if the respondents are led in any way or are not clear about what is being asked. Telephone questionnaires can give rapid returns from respondents at distance at a reasonable cost. As with postal questionnaires, full permission from research sites and respondents is required and the respondent must be completely clear about what they are responding to and why. Anyone who has experienced a 'cold call', where someone from an unknown organisation starts to ask questions, will be aware how annoying and inappropriate such an approach can be and such tactics should never form part of any educational research that claims to abide by ethical standards. Nonetheless, if used properly, this approach can gather a very large amount of useful data very swiftly in a manner which is perfectly sound.

Online web questionnaires

Online questionnaires are increasingly popular and there are a number of web tools that will assist in the construction and administration of such a questionnaire. For example, Survey Monkey at www.surveymonkey.com is well known and will allow researchers to create and distribute a good quality basic questionnaire in a professional format very easily. However, more complex questionnaire surveys tend to need greater expertise and more advanced online services and some help with analysis may also be needed which is likely to incur financial costs.

There are drawbacks to this approach and it is important to remember that with web questionnaires samples are likely to be largely self-selected and not representative of the general population since those who respond are inevitably going to be the people who are interested in the topic and have the skills to respond (Wilson and Dewaele, 2010). This does not subsequently automatically invalidate the approach but statistical techniques may need to be employed to take account of the type and range of responses received. Such problems may reduce over time as access to the Internet and IT skills become increasingly widespread.

Response rate

Many first-time researchers ask what response rate is appropriate for their work and the inevitable answer is that it depends on what they are researching and with whom. Not surprisingly the evidence shows that research with highly educated professionals on a topic of relevance to their interests is more likely to gain a high response rate than research on an esoteric topic with the general public. However, response rate is important in terms of trustworthiness and analysis. Verma and Mallick (1999) state that an initial response rate of less than 20 per cent may not provide sufficiently detailed data and Gillham (2000) suggests that a return rate of less than 30 per cent could lead to uncertainty concerning validity. For this reason the 'general rule of thumb' that is often applied is that a minimum response of about 30 per cent is considered acceptable but there are circumstances where a much lower response rate may be tolerated – especially when the topic is considered to be one which is likely to be a difficult one on which to gather data. In other words, the researcher needs consider whether their research aims are sensible, their tools good and their sample selected well. If all of these things have been addressed then there is little more that they can do (Smith and Bost, 2007)

Summary

Surveys are one of the most common approaches to research in education since they allow the researcher to gather a lot of data swiftly. Whether the researcher chooses to use an interview or questionnaire approach, the construction of good, clear questions is the key to making the research successful. This can be a more difficult task than the new or early researcher realises and it is always wise to pilot a research tool thoroughly and to amend any elements that are confusing or not fit for purpose prior to full administration. Gaining sufficient return carrying the right kind of information to address the research issues is at the heart of success and the researcher must make sure that he or she selects the right sample, that the system of administration is suitable and that instructions are clear. If all these issues are taken into consideration then the likelihood of a successful outcome is high.

Further reading

Blaikie, N. (2003) *Analyzing Quantitative Data: From Description to Explanation*. London: Sage.

Cohen, L., Manion, L. and Morrison, K. (2011) *Research Methods in Education*, 7th edn. London: Routledge.

Creswell, J. W. (2008) *Research Design: Qualitative, Quantitative and Mixed Methods*, 3rd edn. London: Sage.

Denscombe, M. (2010) *The Good Research Guide*, 4th edn. Maidenhead: Open University Press.

Gilbert, N. (2003) *Researching Social Life*. London: Sage.

Gillham, B. (2008) *Developing a Questionnaire*, 2nd edn. London: Continuum.

Kamberelis, G. and Dimitriadis, G. (2013) *Focus Groups: From Structured Interviews to Collective Conversations*. London: Sage.

Munn, P. and Drever, E. (2004) *Using Questionnaires in Small-Scale Research: A Beginner's Guide*. Edinburgh: Scottish Council for Research in Education.

Roulston, K. J. (2010) *Reflective Interviewing: A Guide to Theory and Practice*. London: Sage.

Seidman, I. (2006) *Interviewing as Qualitative Research: A Guide for Researchers in Education and the Social Sciences*. New York: Teachers' College Press.

Silverman, D. (2004) *Qualitative Research: Theory, Method and Practice*. London: Sage.

Silverman, D. (2005) *Doing Qualitative Research*. London: Sage.

Survey Monkey – at: www.surveymonkey.com.

References

Bell, J. (2005) *Doing Your Research Project*, 4th edn. Buckinham, Open University Press.

Brundrett, M. and Rhodes, C. (2013) *Researching Educational Leadership: Methods and Approaches*. London: Sage.

Bryman, A. (2004) *Social Research Methods*. Oxford: Oxford University Press.

Burton, N., Brundrett, M. and Jones, M. (2008) *Doing Your Education Research Project*, 1st edn. London: Sage.

Cohen, L., Manion, L. and Morrison, K. (2000) *Research Methods in Education*. London: RoutledgeFalmer.

Cohen, L., Manion, L. and Morrison, K. (2003) *Research Methods in Education*, 5th edn. London: RoutledgeFalmer.

Cohen, L., Manion, L. and Morrison, K. (2007) *Research Methods in Education*, 6th edn. London: Routledge.

Denscombe, M. (2003) *The Good Research Guide*, 2nd edn. Maidenhead: Open University Press.

Drever, E. (1995) *Using Semi-Structured Interviews in Small Scale Research*. Glasgow: Scottish Council for Educational Research.

Fowler, F. J. (1998) 'Design and evaluation of survey questions', in L. Bickman and D. Rog (eds), *Handbook of Applied Social Research Methods*. London: Sage, p. 37.

Gillham, B. (2000) *Developing a Questionnaire*, 2nd edn. London: Continuum.

Johnson, R. B. and Onwuegbuzie, A. J. (2004) 'Mixed methods research: a research paradigm whose time has come', *Educational Researcher*, 33 (7): 14–26.

Johnson, R. B., Onwuegbuzie, A. J. and Turner, L. A. (2007) 'Towards a definition of mixed methods research', *Journal of Mixed Methods Research*, 1 (2): 112–33.

Kirsz, A. S. (2007) 'A Case Study of the Knowledge and Understanding of Leadership Amongst Leaders in the Scout Association in an English City'. Unpublished PhD thesis, University of Birmingham.

Krueger, R. A. and Casey, M. A. (2000) *Focus Groups*, 3rd edn. London: Sage.

Kvale, S. (1996) *Interviews*. London: Sage.

Kvale, S. (2007) *Doing Interviews*. London: Sage.

Lambert, M. (2008) 'Devil in the detail: using pupil questionnaire survey in an evaluation of out-of-school classes for gifted and talented children', *Education 3–13*, 36 (1): 69–78.

Mitchell, V. (1998) 'Improving mail survey responses from UK academics: some empirical findings', *Assessment and Evaluation in Higher Education*, 23 (1): 59–70.

Morrison, K. R. B. (1993) *Planning and Accomplishing School Centred Evaluation*. Norfolk: Peter Francis.

Munn, P. and Drever, E. (1996) *Using Questionnaires in Small-Scale Research*. Edinburgh: Scottish Council for Research in Education.

Rhodes, C. P., Brundrett, M. and Nevill, A. (2008) 'Leadership talent identification and development', *Educational Management Administration and Leadership*, 36 (3): 301–25.

Robson, C. (1999) *Small-scale Evaluation: Principles and Practice*. London: Sage.

Robson, C. (2006) *Real World Research*. Oxford: Blackwell.

Smith, S. C. and Bost, L. W. (2007) *Collecting Post-School Outcome Data: Strategies for Increasing Response Rates*, National Post-School Outcomes Center. Available online at: www.psocenter.org (accessed July 2009).

Symonds, J. E. and Gorard, S. (2010) 'Death of mixed methods? Or the rebirth of research as a craft', *Evaluation and Research in Education*, 23 (2): 121–36.

Thomas, G. (2009) *How to Do Your Research Project*. London: Sage.

Trochim, W. and Donnelly, J. (2006) *The Research Methods Knowledge Base*, 3rd edn. Mason, OH: Atomic Dog Publishing.

Tuckman, B. (1972) *Conducting Educational Research*. New York: Harcourt Brace Jovanovich.

Verma, G. K. and Mallick, K. (1999) *Researching Education: Perspectives and Techniques*. London: Falmer Press.

Wilson, R. and Dewaele, J. (2010) 'The use of web questionnaires in second language acquisition and bilingualism research', *Second Language Research*, 26 (1): 103–23.

Youngman, M. B. (1994) *Designing and Using Questionnaires*, Rediguide 12, Guides in Educational Research. Nottingham: Rediguides.

CHAPTER 10

ACTION RESEARCH

In the previous chapters there has been a degree of detachment between the researcher and the research context to encourage an objective research perspective. This and the use of mixed methods are also encouraged in an action research approach but are combined with active intervention. It is also commonly referred to as 'practitioner research' or 'critical inquiry' and can be conducted individually or collaboratively. Its key aim is 'collaborative knowledge building' (Groundwater-Smith et al., 2013: 1) for the enhancement of professional practice. As such, teachers undertaking action research not only strive to improve their professional practice, they also develop theories about their practice (McNiff and Whitehead, 2011). This involves asking questions about the learning strategies and teaching techniques they employ, what informs the selection of these practices and how effective they are in terms of achieving the desired learning outcomes. Inevitably, such a practice-based inquiry can involve not only other colleagues, but also students, either as active participants or as researchers in their own right. As with a series of connected lessons – subsequent lessons being shaped by the outcomes from previous sessions – action research can be described as an iterative process, with each cycle of iteration being informed and directed by an analysis of the evidence gathered and further consideration of the conceptual literature and relevant published research findings.

For example, challenging the belief that use of the foreign language must predominate in the MFL classroom, a teacher of modern foreign languages may wish to explore whether the use of English for the explanation and clarification of grammar points can result in increased learner engagement and improved learning outcomes across the entire ability range. A Year 7 Science teacher may be aware of the disparity of pupils' learning experiences in primary education and would like to investigate how this affects their progression and attainment at Key Stage 3. In collaboration with colleagues from primary feeder schools s/he would like to develop, implement and evaluate a transition intervention programme, which has the aim of bridging the perceived gap between the primary and secondary curriculum and facilitate smooth progression from Key Stage 2 to Key Stage 3 for all children.

The closeness of action research to 'reflective practice' is both a strength and a drawback for the educational professional, so it is important that by the end of this chapter you will have had the opportunity to:

- recognise the strengths and weaknesses of action research and its relationship to 'reflective practice';
- construct an appropriate action research strategy suitable to the research context and the conceptual focus.

The nature of 'action research'

An action research approach is commonly employed to shed light on a particular situation in relation to which you have identified issues that need addressing. The processes involved in such an inquiry are not dissimilar to those informing teachers' production of an end-of-year report.

Any judgements or evaluations of pupil performance must be evidence-based, but will also include supplementary information that has emerged outside the formal assessment procedure. It can include both formative and summative elements and should be guided by two concepts: assessment *for* learning and assessment *of* learning. Similarly, action research generates findings *for* practice (informing practice) as well as *of* practice (research report). In both cases the process of evidence-gathering will be positioned within temporal, conceptual and thematic boundaries, which provides a clear focus and enhances the validity of findings.

As in teaching, where the assessment of student learning will be conducted via a specific set of activities (written test, practical task, coursework, homework, classwork), action researchers need to select their methods for data collection carefully, taking into consideration the nature of the inquiry and participants involved. For example, by adopting a quantitative approach, non-participant observation would suggest itself as a possible strategy with the aim of obtaining an objective view of teacher and pupil behaviour in the classroom. If, however, the aim is to elucidate the behaviour patterns observed and examine the underlying motives, a qualitative approach by means of in-depth one-to-one interviews or learning journals would be appropriate.

Practitioner action research is commonly associated with the concept of 'reflective practice' (Schön, 1983, 1987), a process within which reflection can be 'triggered by the recognition that in some respects a situation is in need of special attention' (Eraut, 1984: 144). Most teachers engage in this process regularly in their day-to-day practice when they reflect on how a particular group of learners responds to a new teaching approach, learning strategy or resource and whether this new idea requires further modification, should be retained or abandoned. Sometimes, such reflection manifests itself in critical dialogue and may even provoke action within a department or across the whole school. Although teacher reflection is often followed by action, and action is followed by reflection, the generation of so-called evidence is often anecdotal and derived from ad hoc experiences. Like any other form of research, practitioner action research needs to satisfy a set of quality criteria by ensuring that the process reflects a rigorous and systematic approach. As such, it needs to go beyond practice with a focus on knowledge that informs action rather than the action itself and is concerned with practitioners' values, beliefs and motives and how these influence them in their actions (McNiff and Whitehead, 2009). The action cycle starts with an issue or a problem that has been identified in a certain situation (classroom or school as a whole) and that is in need of resolving through an intervention programme, a new strategy or the implementation of a new framework, policy or procedure. Practitioner action research is thus 'insider' research, which can provide teachers with a framework for inquiry into their professional practices. It can enable them to engage in critical reflection about issues related to their own and other practice settings in a systematic manner.

Practitioner-based action research can be conducted at different levels of critical engagement reflecting a technical, practical and emancipatory focus (Kemmis and McTaggart, 1992; McKernan, 1991; Zuber-Skerritt, 1996). It can be used to find solutions to technical problems, without questioning the legitimacy of these techniques or the framework within which they are to be applied. Effective implementation of the literacy hour springs to mind. Where the focus of the inquiry is practical it needs to take into account the social and cultural factors inherent in the practice setting and how they might affect learning. For example, the problem of truancy may not be effectively addressed by taking a harsher stance in terms of sanctions, but may require action and inquiry that incorporates a range of perspectives (pupils, parents/carers, teachers, children's services). By allowing those at the heart of the process a voice, it will also reflect an emancipatory agenda (Groundwater-Smith and Mockler, 2007), the core aims of which are empowerment of individuals and social groups that have been marginalised and whose voices need to be heard.

Definition of action research

During the past twenty years, action research has enjoyed immense popularity among practitioners in education and other professional fields, such as health, business and management. Its potential contributions to improving professional practice through critical inquiry and reflection have been brought to the fore in recent literature on teachers' continuing professional development and school improvement (Burton and Bartlett, 2005; Campbell et al., 2004; McNiff and Whitehead, 2009). Although action research takes a variety of forms, its key features manifest themselves in how researchers and research participants relate to and interact with each other and how knowledge is constructed. Unlike conventional scientific research the philosophy underpinning this research genre reflects a strong democratic dimension (Carr and Kemmis, 1986) in that it often includes 'service users' (pupils, parents/carers) in the research process (Beresford, 1999; Winter and Munn-Giddings, 2001) and seeks to give voice to those who are 'culturally silenced' (Winter, 1998).

In Education, the term 'action research' has become a key ingredient in the discourses concerned with the improvement and development of professional practice from within the profession, implying notions of ownership and participation in the generation of new insights into processes of teaching and learning. According to Kemmis and McTaggart (1982) 'action research is the way in which groups of people can organise the conditions under which they can learn from their own experience, and make this experience accessible to others' (1988: 7), or as Waterson describes it:

> to make improvements . . . by working with the organisational actors in a cycle of action, data gathering, analysis, reflection and planning further action, as the researchers and the organisation work together. Praxis and research go together, each taking account of the other, and influencing the way people think about an issue. (2000: 495)

In this sense action research is frequently employed to address issues arising from professional practice with the aim of constructing knowledge collaboratively in order to bring about change and improvement (Carr and Kemmis, 1986; Elliott, 1991; Lewin, 1952). It thus promotes ownership of the research process by those who will be most affected by its outcomes with the predominant aim 'to improve practice rather than to produce knowledge' (Elliott, 1991: 49). The key principle underpinning such research could be described as essentially democratic in that it implies the active participation of practitioners in the research process with the aim of trying to change practice and as such its success 'will depend, in large measure, on [...] success with working with other people' (Gray, 2004: 377). It can be conducted by individuals or a group of practitioners, who have identified an area in their professional practice that they consider in need of further development or improvement. Working with fellow practitioners and peers, however, requires a sensitive approach towards and respect for others' feelings and expertise in the field. In this respect it is important to highlight the strong philosophical underpinning in terms of the ethical/moral principles inherent in action research and how they are reflected in the four outcomes identified by McNiff et al. (1996: 8):

- personal development;
- improved professional practice;
- improvements in the institution in which you work;
- contribution to the good order of society.

Traditionally, though, insider action research is concerned with institutional improvement, development of practice and organisational learning and involves practitioners with a leadership or management role. McNiff et al. (1996: 17) highlight the point that when you undertake your own action research, you need to put the 'I' at the centre, which needs to go along with an explanation of how you are positioned in relation to the research setting and other research participants.

More recently, action research increasingly involves the active participation of pupils, without whose views, opinions and experiences many questions posed by teachers would remain unanswered. The inclusion of children's voices forms an integral element in 'participatory action research' (PAR), which has as its primary aim to transform situations and structures in an egalitarian manner (Gray, 2004: 375). But most importantly, before you develop your action research design, you need to identify the focus of your inquiry.

Identifying the general idea

As mentioned earlier, the general idea around which the research is to be constructed needs to relate to a situation which is deemed to be in need of improvement or change. This mirrors the teaching and learning situation in which teachers recognise a discrete area in their pupils' cognitive and socio-emotional development – or, indeed, in their own behaviour as teachers – which requires targeted action. The following examples illustrate how such 'general ideas' are derived from situations that are perceived to require action.

Box 10.1   Starting points

Example A

Students have expressed dissatisfaction with an overemphasis on the use of text-based resources in history, which they find boring and are not related to reality. How can they, and their teacher, collaboratively explore a more diverse way of teaching and learning?

Example B

Year heads have become aware of the fact that absenteeism among Year 7 pupils has increased dramatically. How can they reverse this trend by investigating the underlying causes in collaboration with pupils, parents/carers and secondary and primary colleagues and respond to pupil needs after transfer from primary to secondary school?

Example C

A teacher has become aware of a marked discrepancy between the quality of students' work in class and their homework, which is consistently of poor quality. How can she ensure that students' independent work at home is of a similar quality to that produced in class?

When considering your area for action research it is helpful to take cognisance of Elliott's (1991: 72) caveat. First, you need to ensure that the general idea is related to your field of action, that the situation you intend to change or improve is in need of such action and that the extent to which this can be achieved must not be based on your assumptions but be the result of the action research. You must therefore be prepared for unexpected findings to emerge, which may necessitate the revision of your original general idea.

Formulating the research question

As a teacher you are only too aware of the importance of careful preparation and planning of lessons in your endeavour to assist students in achieving the intended learning outcomes. This situation resonates with Lewin's (1946) notion of 'reconnaissance', which precedes any action research by finding out more about the particular situation you have identified to be in need of improvement. If we return to the three examples given earlier the fact-finding mission may include questions such as the following.

Box 10.2   Formulating the research question

Example A

- What resources (handouts, textbooks) are being used?
- How are these resources being used?
- Are there any alternative materials available within the school? If so, could they be made available?
- Have pupils expressed a preference for other resources? Which?
- Which resources are used in other classes?
- What is the departmental policy on the use of resources?

Example B

- What exactly are the statistical figures indicating a rise in absenteeism?
- What are the official reasons given for pupils' absenteeism?
- Is there a pattern emerging between absenteeism on a certain time of the year, term, week?
- What is the student/parent/carer response when challenged with regard to their absenteeism?
- What is the school policy on absenteeism?

Example C

- What is the school's/department's homework policy?
- How is feedback communicated to the pupils and parents/carers?
- To what extent do pupils and parents/carers take an active role in the monitoring and evaluation of homework?

These questions can inform the formulation of the research questions to be addressed and provide a basic structure around which to plan and conduct the actions. They can also give an indication of possible categories for the collection and analysis of data. By developing a catalogue of questions, initial assumptions may be dispersed in the light of the findings, resulting in a new interpretation of the situation to be investigated. Subsequently, the revised perception can – but need not – lead to a hypothesis, which according to Elliott describes 'the situation', indicates a need for improvement or change and explains the relationship between the two.

Box 10.3   Stating the hypothesis

Example A

A multi-sensory approach to teaching and learning can enhance pupils' learning experience and result in improved learning outcomes.

Example B

The active involvement of pupils and parents/carers is a crucial element in a strategy to combat rising exclusion rates.

Example C

The quality of homework can be improved through a feedback dialogue involving pupils, parents/carers and the teacher.

Such a hypothesis is not to be understood in the strictly scientific/positivistic sense, which is either proved or disproved in the form of measurable quantitative data. Instead, it is to be perceived as a device to frame a critical inquiry into professional practice with the aim of gaining new insights into processes the efficacy of which remained unquestioned previously, and to acquire a more profound understanding of the various, complex factors influencing the teaching and learning process.

The action research process

In their day-to-day practice, theoretical perspectives of teaching and learning may not be at the forefront of teachers' thinking and doing, although occasional reference to pedagogical models can be helpful in justifying or questioning certain practices. Similarly, action research is primarily about 'action', although theoretical perspectives can provide a helpful framework for the research design in terms of the structure of the research process. We will now consider some action research models as presented in the literature.

Kurt Lewin (1952), a social psychologist, conceived the action research process as consisting of a 'spiral of cycles' which start with a general idea, followed by fact-finding (reconnaissance) and subsequent planning of action. After developing and implementing the first action step evaluation takes place, which informs the revision of the original plan. This model was refined further by Kemmis (1980), Elliott (1991) and Carr and Kemmis (1986) and can be translated into a more concrete timetable format, specifying the duration of the action and clearly stating the start and finish and the type of activities employed for data collection and evaluation. As illustrated in Figure 10.1, the insights gained from one cycle will subsequently be used to formulate the new need for change and the planning of the action of the next cycle.

The various models presented in the literature suggest that action research is a neat process made up of logically sequenced stages of activities. However, it can be a 'messy business' (Cook, 1998), which manifests itself in U-turns, cul-de-sacs and offshoots of new, emerging issues, which may also be worth pursuing, but which would detract from the original focus of the inquiry. The model shown in Figure 10.2 provides a possible mapping and sequencing of discrete activities as they may occur in an action research cycle.

Moving from an abstract model to its practical application in the 'real world' is not always straightforward. To help you make the connection, consider Scenarios 9.1 and 9.2 below and the associated questions.

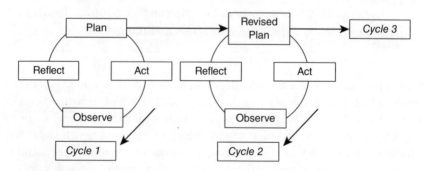

Figure 10.1   Action research model (Carr and Kemmis, 1986)

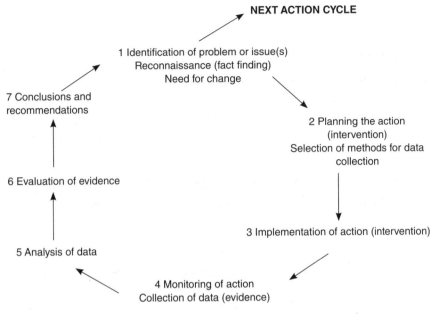

NEXT ACTION CYCLE

1 Identification of problem or issue(s)
Reconnaissance (fact finding)
Need for change

7 Conclusions and
recommendations

2 Planning the action
(intervention)
Selection of methods for data
collection

6 Evaluation of evidence

3 Implementation of action (intervention)

5 Analysis of data

4 Monitoring of action
Collection of data (evidence)

Figure 10.2   Activities inherent in an action cycle

Scenario 9.1   Improving pupil behaviour and learner engagement

As a class teacher of a Year 3 (primary) you would like to administer an intervention to achieve improvements in pupil behaviour and learner engagement. You have identified a number of strategies which you would like to trial:

- Rigorous monitoring of disruptions and identification of causes (e.g. gold/silver/colour stars on a 'Star Chart').
- Introduction of individual and collective reward system for good behaviour, effort and achievement (e.g. a 'Golden' Hour once a month when pupils can choose an activity they would like to do).
- Introduction of an element of pupil ownership by developing a catalogue of classroom rules (to be agreed with pupils and displayed on the classroom wall).

(Continued)

(Continued)

Questions

1. How many action cycles would you include?
2. What would be the duration of each cycle?
3. What would be the start and finish of each cycle?

Scenario 9.2   Facilitating opportunities for continuing professional development through a mentoring/ coaching framework

You are the assistant head of a secondary school with responsibility for staff development and performance management. In order to develop greater coherence between these two aspects, the senior management team has decided to introduce a mentoring/coaching framework for all teaching and support staff within the school. You are unsure as to what extent this new framework will provide opportunities for teachers' professional learning and development in a structured/unstructured, formal/informal environment. You have therefore decided to run a pilot over a 12-month period.

Questions

1. How many action cycles would you include?
2. What would be the duration of each cycle?
3. What would be the start and finish of each cycle?
4. What activities would you select for the collection of data and who would be your participants? Please give reasons for your decision.
5. How would you sequence the activities? Please give reasons for your decision.

Planning your action research project

Although not immediately apparent, on closer examination of teachers' practice and action research a number of parallel processes and activities can be identified. What they have in common is the systematic and coherent way in which they are constructed around a focus of the inquiry. Table 10.1 serves to make the links between teaching and action research more explicit.

Table 10.1   Links between teaching and action research

Teaching	Action research
Topic of teaching unit or scheme of work	Focus of action enquiry (the issue, the problem)
Number of specific lessons	Number of action cycles
Resources required to teach the unit	Resources required to gather evidence
Identification of teacher and learner activities	Identification of researcher and participant activities
Nature of relationship between teacher and learner and how this affects the learning process	Positionality of the research and how this affects the behaviour of other research participants
Ethical considerations: • confidentiality of information • balancing need for information and pupils' right to privacy	Ethical considerations: • balance of power and control • anonymity of participants • confidentiality of information • gaining informed consent
Selection of appropriate teaching/learning/assessment approach and strategies	Selection of appropriate research approach and strategies (quantitative/qualitative/mixed methods)
Validity and reliability of assessment Multi-method approach in the generation of evidence for assessment	Validity and trustworthiness of research findings 'Multi-technique' (Elliott, 1991: 77), triangulation by method, data, perspective, site
Awareness of structural, social, cultural factors inherent in the teaching/learning environment and their impact on the teaching/learning process	Identification of potential methodological, epistemological, ethical issues and their impact on the quality of the research
Monitoring of learner behaviour, attitude and critical incidents Gathering of evidence of learning: • formal and informal • formative and summative	Data collection (quantitative and qualitative), including use of 'analytic memos' (Elliott, 1991) to assist in the interpretation of data and to inform the next cycle
Evidence of learning outcomes (marks and narrative report)	Research evidence (quantitative and qualitative data)
Analysis and interpretation of assessment data	Analysis and interpretation of research data
Conclusions and recommendations with regard to informing teaching and learning strategies with the aim of improving learning outcomes	Conclusions and recommendations with regard to informing professional practice with the aim of enhancing its effectiveness

Action research – a constructivist approach to knowledge creation

According to Capobianco and Feldman it is through the construction of knowledge and understanding that quality in action research is achieved (2006: 499), particularly so as this process takes place within teachers' practice setting and is informed by the personal and professional perspectives of participants in a social constructivist manner. From my own experience as a project leader of collaborative research projects I share this belief, but would also like to emphasise the need for a set of conditions that have to be met. First, collaborative action research in particular must reflect the principles underpinning Wenger's (1998) concept of a community of practice and those informing the practices of a knowledge-producing, epistemic community (Creplet et al., 2003). Accordingly the members of an action research team must share a common goal, demonstrate a mutual commitment to the critical inquiry of a particular issue, problem or situation and share a repertoire of ideas and conceptualisations. Practitioner researchers therefore need to possess a thorough grounding in the nature of action research as well as knowledge of appropriate research methods (Capobianco and Feldman, 2006: 502). As I have learnt from my own experience as an action research project leader, achieving a high level of coherence in terms of shared understandings across all members of an action research team can be problematic, particularly where aspects of multi-disciplinary and multi-agency work is concerned. For example, action research located within the Every Child Matters agenda, which involves stakeholders from diverse professional practice contexts, will have to provide a 'communicative space' (Kemmis, 2006) where all voices can be heard, 'a space in which emergent agreements and disagreements, understandings and decisions can be problematised and explored openly' (Capobianco and Feldman, 2006: 472). For example, this would involve the perspectives of teachers and teaching assistants, as well as contributions from other professional disciplines, such as social services, the police, health, psychology and counselling. In order to identify potential challenges involved in multi-disciplinary research consider Scenario 9.3 and the associated question.

Scenario 9.3

You are the head of a primary school, where the issue of child obesity has been identified as a problem that needs addressing. You intend to implement an intervention programme and evaluate its effectiveness via an action research approach. The outcome of the research will be used to inform curriculum development and school–parent partnerships with the aim of educating children towards a healthier lifestyle.

Question

Whose professional knowledge, experience and expertise could you draw upon in the implementation of an intervention, its evaluation and subsequent curriculum development? Devise a multi-disciplinary team and explain the reasons for your decision.

While diversity of perspectives and professional expertise is a prerequisite for devising a well-informed programme, it can pose enormous challenges for the research coordinator to maintain a certain degree of coherence and consensus among all participants. Troyna highlighted this issue when he stated that 'all research, from its conception through to the production of data, its interpretation and dissemination of findings reflects a partisanship which derives from the social identity and values of the researcher' (1995: 403). In addition participants will have vested interests and work within agendas which are not always compatible.

Reporting your action research

One of the definitions of research includes the requirement that it is made public (Stenhouse, 1975). Within this remit the dissemination of action research outcomes can serve a range of purposes and may be presented in different ways. A teacher's findings may be used within a small circle of colleagues who have agreed to share their experiences and evaluations of particular aspects of their professional practice. A wider audience may be involved if the outcome of an action research project relates to whole-school improvement (head teacher, governors) or is of interest to other, external agencies, such as Ofsted or the local authority. Even if the report is to be disseminated in the public domain by means of a conference presentation or publication of a journal article, the goal of action research would ultimately be to have an impact on professional practice, be it within a teacher's classroom, across departments or across several schools, in the way in which it is reviewed in order to bring about improvement.

Caveats

In this chapter we have attempted to gain an understanding of action research as a strategy of practice-based inquiry with the aim of improving practice. We considered the theoretical perspectives underpinning action research and investigated some of the potential methodological and ethical issues as they can arise in practice-based settings. It has become apparent that the processes involved in action research are not too dissimilar to those inherent in teaching and should therefore come naturally to any education practitioner who is committed to critical investigation and improvement of practice. However, while as a teacher you exercise a certain degree of control over the teaching, learning and assessment process, action research may not present itself as the neatly prescribed route you outlined in your project plan. It does not always progress in a linear fashion but, as high-lighted by Dickens and Watkins (1999), can disperse in different directions, including reverse. It would therefore be foolish to suggest that such an undertaking is devoid of risks and pitfalls. To help you navigate your way through your action research project we would encourage you to take cognisance of the following caveats.

1. Be realistic in terms of the scope of your project and what can be achieved in a given amount of time in a particular practice setting.
2. In collaborative ventures, be aware of individuals' vested interests and different agendas.
3. Maintain positive relationships with all participants at all times.
4. Ensure transparency of the research process through effective communication with all parties involved.
5. Keep a detailed log of the research process.
6. Never apportion blame when things go wrong.
7. Be prepared to consider the views of others.
8. Appreciate the fact that teachers are busy professionals and cannot always give of their time.
9. Be flexible and be prepared for the unexpected.
10. Don't expect to find answers, but be prepared to ask new questions.

Finally, we should take note of the warning sounded by Coghlan and Brannick (2010), which is particularly relevant in school-based action research where, for example, the implementation of policy and curriculum innovation can generate tensions among the various staff affected in terms of internal politics. In such situations action research can be perceived differently by the various stakeholders and even be misconstrued as subversive. It is therefore important to produce regular update reports to ensure that everybody is still in the loop of action.

Further reading

Baumfield, V., Hall, E. and Wall, K. (2008) *Action Research in the Classroom*. London: Sage.

McNiff, J. (2013) *Action Research: Principles and Practice*, 3rd edn. London: RoutledgeFalmer.

Pine, G. (2009) *Teacher Action Research: Building Knowledge Democracies*. London: Sage.

Springer, E. (2004) *Action Research in Education*. Prentice-Hall.

References

Beresford, P. (1999) 'Making participation possible: movements of disabled people and psychiatric system survivors', in T. Jordan and A. Lent (eds), *Storming the Millenium: The New Politics of Change*. London: Lawrence & Wishart, pp. 34–50.

Burton, D. M. and Bartlett, S. (2005) *Practitioner Research for Teachers.* London: Sage.

Campbell, A., McNamara, O. and Gilroy, P. (2004) *Practitioner Research and Professional Development in Education.* London: Sage.

Capobianco, B. M. and Feldman, A. (2006) 'Promoting quality for teacher action research: lessons learned from science teachers' action research', *Educational Action Research*, 14 (4): 497–512.

Carr, W. and Kemmis, S. (1986) *Becoming Critical: Knowing Through Action Research.* Lewes: Falmer Press.

Coghlan, D. and Brannick, T. (2010) *Doing Action Research in Your Own Organisation.* London: Sage.

Cook, T. (1998) 'The importance of mess in action research', *Educational Action Research Journal*, 6 (1): 93–109.

Creplet, F., Dupouet, O. and Vaast, E. (2003) 'Episteme or practice? Differentiated communitarian structures in a biology laboratory', in M. Huysman, E. Wenger and V. Wulf (eds), *Communities and Technologies.* Dordrecht: Kluwer Academic, pp. 43–63.

Dickens, L. and Watkins, K. (1999) 'Action research: rethinking Lewin', *Management Learning*, 30 (2): 127–40.

Elliott, J. (1991) *Action Research for Educational Change.* Buckingham: Open University Press.

Eraut, M. (1984) *Developing Professional Knowledge and Competence.* London: RoutledgeFalmer.

Gray, D. E. (2004) *Doing Research in the Real World.* London: Sage.

Groundwater-Smith, S. and Mockler, N. (2007) 'Ethics in practitioner research: an issue of quality', *Research Papers in Education*, 22: 199–211.

Groundwater-Smith, S., Mitchell, J., Mockler, N., Ponte, P. and Rönnermann, K. (2013) *Facilitating Practitioner Research: Developing Transformational Partnerships.* Abingdon: Routledge.

Kemmis, S. (1980) 'Action research in retrospect and prospect'. Mimeo presented at the Annual General Meeting of the Australian Association for Research in Education, Sydney, November.

Kemmis, S. (2006) 'Participatory action research and the public sphere', *Educational Action Research*, 14 (4): 459–76.

Kemmis, S. and McTaggart, R. (eds) (1982) *The Action Research Planner.* Geelong, Victoria: Deakin University Press.

Kemmis, S. and McTaggart, R. (eds) (1992) *The Action Research Planner*, 3rd edn (1st edn, 1982). Victoria: Deakin University Press.

Lewin, K. (1946) 'Action research and minority problems', *Journal of Social Issues*, 2: 34–46.

Lewin, K. (1952) 'Group decision and social change', in G. W. Sweanson, T. M. Newcomb and T. L. and Hartley (eds), *Readings in Social Psychology.* New York: Henry Holt & Co.; reprinted in S. Kemmis and R. McTaggart (1988) *The Action Research Reader*, 3rd edn (1st edn, 1951). Geelong, Victoria: Deakin University Press, pp. 47–56.

McKernan, J. (1991) *Curriculum Action Research*. London: Kogan Page.

McNiff, J. and Whitehead, J. (2009) *You and Your Action Research Project*, 3rd edn (1st edn, 1996). London: Routledge.

McNiff, J. and Whitehead, J. (2011) *All You Need to Know About Action Research*, 2nd edn (1st edn, 2005). London: Sage.

McNiff, J., Lomaz, P. and Whitehead, J. (1996) *You and Your Action Research Project*. London: Routledge.

Schön, D. (1983) *The Reflective Practitioner*. New York: Basic Books.

Schön, D. (1987) *Educating the Reflective Practitioner*. San Francisco, CA: Jossey-Bass.

Stenhouse, L. (1975) *An Introduction to Curriculum Research and Development*. London: Heinemann.

Troyna, B. (1995) 'Beyond reasonable doubt? Researching "race" in educational settings', *Oxford Review of Education*, 21 (4): 155–65.

Waterson, J. (2000) 'Balancing Research and Action: reflections on an action research project in a social services department; *Social Policy Administration*, 34 (4): 494–508.

Wenger, E. (1998) *Communities of Practice: Learning, Meaning and Identity*. Cambridge: Cambridge University Press.

Winter, R. (1998) 'Finding a voice, thinking with others: a conception of action research', *Educational Action Research*, 6: 53–68.

Winter, R. and Munn-Giddings, C. (2001) *A Handbook for Action Research in Health and Social Care*. London: Routledge.

Zuber-Skerritt, O. (ed.) (1996) *New Directions in Action Research*. London: Falmer.

SECTION 3
MAKING SENSE OF THE OUTCOMES

This final section guides you through the 'post data collection' phase of your study – the drawing of conclusions and action plans as a result of the presentation and analysis of your findings. However, the presentation and analysis of your data is not something that you should start to consider once you have collected your evidence. It needs to be part of the initial research design and influential on the research approach and methodology, so that by the time that you get to this stage the transfer of the evidence into your report or assignment should be as smooth as possible.

As the purpose of completing the research activity is to address the research questions you formulated in the introduction to your study, these should remain the key structural device throughout the report or assignment. However, it may be necessary to structure these elements according to the requirements of the format you are expected to write to. The following chapters have been written to allow for the two formats, 'atomistic' and 'holistic', which are most frequently adopted for the presentation and analysis of research data.

The 'atomistic' approach

Data presentation and analysis are separated.

Presentation

Data from each source are presented separately (often adopting a 'question by question' structure), for example:

- questionnaire responses (from the teaching staff in the school);
- interview responses (from the senior management teachers);
- documentary sources (school policy documents, meeting minutes, etc.).

There is limited opportunity for interaction and comparison between the sources.

Analysis

The initial research questions are used as a structural device with data being reintroduced to support the analytical processes, for example:

First research question: *What are the key issues surrounding the management of behaviour?*

Relevant data from policy documents, teaching staff and managers are compared and then related to past research findings and theoretical perspectives from the literature.

Other research questions are addressed similarly.

The 'holistic' approach

Data presentation and analysis are combined.

Presentation with analysis

The initial research questions are used as a structural device with data being reintroduced to support the analytical processes, for example:

First research question: *What are the key issues surrounding the management of behaviour?*

Relevant data from policy documents, teaching staff and managers are presented and compared and then related to past research findings and theoretical perspectives from the literature.
Subsequent research questions are addressed in the same way.

The way in which the data are brought to bear on the initial research questions will be crucial in the success of the study (see Figure 6.1).

Given that evidence from different sources needs to be presented to address each initial research question it is important that:

1. You have asked and collected the evidence in the first place!
2. You have identified which evidence from each source will be used to address each of the initial research questions.
3. You present the evidence in a coherent and explicit format which will allow for a clear analysis.

It may prove difficult, but it is important to recognise that not all of the information that you have collected will be needed for your research. Be selective in what data you choose to include within the text of your report or assignment (your full findings can always be placed in an attached appendix). However, it is equally important that you collect a full range of evidence in the first place – it is always much easier to collect the data then not use it than not collect it and later wish that you had.

CHAPTER 11

COLLATING AND REPORTING QUALITATIVE EVIDENCE

Having accumulated a wealth of information you will need to develop a system for its storage and efficient retrieval in relation to specific questions or substantive issues in order to present and analyse your findings. While quantitative data lend themselves to be presented in the form of charts and diagrams before undergoing analysis, a more integrated approach tends to be used with qualitative data. This means that reporting and analysing often goes hand in hand.

By the end of this chapter you should have developed an understanding of the principles involved in this process and how it forms a bridge between data collection, interpretation and development of theory. Specifically, you should be able to:

(Continued)

(Continued)

- organise your data by developing key categories and codes;
- make use of qualitative data analysis software programs for the storage and retrieval of data;
- appreciate the relationship between presentation and analysis of findings.

Data storage and retrieval

As a teacher you are most likely to have employed similar procedures in compiling student records, either manually or electronically, which closely mirror those processes involved in the analysis of research data. A systematic approach to the collection and inputting of assessment items is key to ensure the efficient storage and retrieval of often highly disparate information. Box 11.1 is an example from a trainee teacher contributing to an online History Teachers Discussion Forum (HTDF) which aptly illustrates this point.

Box 11.1

I use Excel. I think it's great. As a student, I don't have a mark book or register at all so I have it all done on an Excel spreadsheet. One for each class with several worksheets on each one. Each worksheet has a register, a seating plan (one coloured depending on behaviour, one not for printing out and leaving on the desk) and a mark 'book'.

Took me a while to set it all up, but I really do see the benefits when I take books in. I have a standard set of colours and notations:

Red = Not done

Orange = Unfinished

Pink = Work not in book

Blue = Book not seen.

The advantage of the blue is that when I do finally see the book, I know how far back I have to go to make sure it's all marked. I also have a column that tells me how many times I haven't seen their books. So anyone thinking that I won't notice if they just keep 'forgetting' to hand their books in, will get caught out. It has quite a few effects:

1. I can print out a register and have it in the class file which then gets updated once a week on the computer.
2. I can see who's doing really well, and who's taking the p*** as they've got a student.
3. I can hold up a printed out worksheet (names hidden) and show them how it works and how easily I can see what they're doing – they don't like that!!
4. If I'm asking too much of them, that will be clear too, as the whole class will have orange 'unfinished' cells.
5. When I am not there, I can hand it over to the teacher taking the class and all the information they need is there for them.

The main negative side to it is that I haven't yet managed to work out (other than the clearly obviously long-winded way) how to link in absences with the pink 'Not in book' and the red 'Not done' (when relating it to homework).

Overall, I'm really happy with it, and the teachers I've shown have seemed quite impressed. They've even suggested I take it to parents' evening. Not sure it's that good!

While the quantitative data recorded by this teacher can provide factual information about how often a pupil submitted or completed work, they fail to explain in greater depth why a student was/was not able to submit or complete work. It can serve to identify patterns of pupil behaviour and performance (collectively and individually) and can make teachers aware of potential issues/problems that they need to address. But it cannot go beyond the surface of what can be observed, counted or measured in order to provide explanations for underlying reasons. This, however, is vital to enable a teacher to select and employ appropriate strategies in response to learners' needs. The careful construction of research tools (see Chapters 8 and 9 for specific examples) is thus key to ensure you obtain answers to your research questions. It is also central to the efficient and effective storage and retrieval of data. If the research tool is designed to collect the data in a meaningful and systematic way, it should also make their collation and analysis more straightforward. By using the conceptual framework derived from your reading as the basis for your collection tools, your data should smoothly link back to your literature for ease of analysis.

Organising and identifying sources

Qualitative data, by its very nature, is more open to ambiguity and requires the identification of emergent key themes for it to be organised, collated and interpreted. Traditionally, textual data have been the most common source, but more recently, the development of new technologies has increased an interest in the use of alternative qualitative data, such as visual text (e.g. drawings, paintings and still photographs) and multi-modal text (e.g. video clips or web page materials). The potential value of this kind of data lies not only in its capacity to tap into our emotional and intuitive zones of consciousness, it also provides the participants to become active researchers. For example, teachers can explore the effectiveness of certain learning and teaching strategies by involving their students in the collection of evidence. For example, mobile telephones can provide an affordable tool in the collection of data. However, there are a number of caveats that need to be observed. While such a participative approach can provide students with a voice and a certain degree of autonomy, it also places upon them a responsibility to act in an ethically appropriate manner. In their role as co-researchers they need to be made aware and fully understand the need to consider the privacy, confidentiality and anonymity of participants at all stages of the research process, but especially in their presentation of data.

Responses to open questions are likely to be unique to each individual respondent, so the researcher needs to be sensitive to the potential patterns that might exist and be aware of opportunities for categorisation. While quantitative data can be used very effectively to identify such patterns or trends in relation to a specific phenomenon, it has its limitations with regard to providing explanations for the underlying reasons and the way in which it can give voice to those participating in the research and thus represent their perspective.

Due to the linguistic or visual nature of much of what can be construed as qualitative data, the role of the researcher in the selection and interpretation of the evidence is crucial to the success and validity of the research. All potential for bias should have been acknowledged at an earlier stage and the conceptual literature should be used to justify the coding and data organisation.

To a very large extent, at this level, where qualitative data has a benefit over quantitative data is in the depth and exemplification that it is able to offer. Qualitative data can be collated and aggregated to provide numerical responses, but the real strength is in the way that quoting from respondents is able to offer insight and humanity into the analysis. It is concerned with 'meanings and the way people understand things' (Denscombe, 2003: 267). When presented in narrative form, it provides tones and a means of helping the reader to 'connect' with the research that pure numerical data is unable to convey. By using quotations from interviews, observations, diaries or questionnaires depth and greater meaning can be added to quantitative data, but needs to be employed with care to avoid being perceived as 'anecdotal'. So referencing to the respondent(s) is important.

An effective analysis involves:

- a clear exposition of complex arguments and issues;
- identifying causal relationships;
- elucidating and explaining;
- sustaining a logical argument;
- comparing and contrasting;
- identifying and challenging assumptions;
- explaining.

When presenting qualitative evidence, the source should be clearly identified in some appropriately coded way that distinguishes between respondents but does not individually identify them. This is to allow different responses from the same respondent to be acknowledged. The identifiers can be very simple, for example:

- R_1, R_2, . . . for the different respondents; or
- T_1, T_2, . . . for 'teachers' or 'tutors' and S_1, S_2, . . . for students.

The transcripts of the interviews or qualitative elements of questionnaires, observations or documents should be placed in appendices and appropriately referenced in the text of the study.

Data that have been generated via various sources can be presented as part of the narrative relating to a particular theme that has emerged in the course of the research. This can take the form of participants' questionnaire responses, verbatim quotations from interview transcripts, reflective journal entries, drawings, photographs or vignettes. The example in Box 11.2 below, which investigated mentors' experiences of supporting newly qualified teachers in the early stages of their career (Jones et al., 2008, 2009), provides an illustration of how this can be achieved. It combines the presentation of data with the analysis in terms of emergent issues and key themes and references to the relevant literature in support of the arguments presented. A key theme that emerged from this study and was investigated in greater depth by means of face-to-face, recorded interviews was 'Challenges and benefits'.

Box 11.2   Presentation of interview data

Challenges and benefits

The interviews with a small sample of mentors revealed that mentoring novice teachers poses a multitude of challenges. Mentors working with novice teachers found teachers who failed to act upon advice, showed no improvement despite support given, had limited subject knowledge, had class management issues, lacked personal organisation and found commitment to teaching and the school particularly difficult:

> *Sometimes it is difficult for a mentor to find appropriate words not to offend a novice teacher if he wants to be critically friendly with a novice teacher.* (M1)

In addition, mentors deplored the insufficient amount of time available to provide quality support alongside their teaching activities, an issue repeatedly highlighted in the literature (Barrington, 2000; Jones, 2002), and the difficulty of maintaining a high level of cooperation between the novice teacher and other staff involved in the induction process:

> *Having a full teaching load and some administrative commitments it is difficult for a mentor to sit down with a novice teacher and analyse each lesson in detail.* (M2)

> *There is not enough time to apply many of the new, playful forms of teaching in a classroom for which novice teachers are trained at university.* (M3)

These challenges were balanced by rewarding aspects, such as being able to assist newcomers to the profession on their learning journey and seeing them make progress. Another interesting point, which is directly relevant to mentors' own professional development, was the recognition of the reciprocal benefits derived from mentoring (Hurd et al., 2007).

> *Accompanying them on their journeys, seeing them progress, to walk with them is very stimulating.* (M4)

> *Observing lessons of novice teachers we can see application of the newest and very recent methods and forms of work which can enrich and make the lessons of the mentor more interesting.* (M2)

Mentors referred to the informal, often unplanned, incidental aspect of professional learning (Hodkinson and Hodkinson, 2003), such as the introduction to new pedagogical approaches and techniques, new insights gained through observation and evaluation of practice and engagement in critical dialogue with the novice teacher and other colleagues. The teachers also valued the degree of creativity and autonomy that could be accommodated within their mentoring remit.

Another powerful method of presenting qualitative data in an engaging way are pen-portraits or vignettes. By providing an insight into individuals' lived experiences, they are considered a useful device in the construction of authentic inquiries (Connelly and Clandinin, 1999; Goodson and Sykes, 2001). They can be used effectively to focus on a particular theme, highlight a specific aspect or illustrate a relevant issue in greater depth. In developing pen-portraits or vignettes you can draw on the data relating to one participant only or you can use the entire data set for the development of 'fictional pen portraits', resulting in 'an amalgam of major characteristics, personal histories and common experiences' (Campbell and Groundwater-Smith, 2004: 107). Employing this latter technique has a number of advantages. The vast volume of data generated by semi-structured or open interviews can be presented in a focused and succinct way without losing any of its richness, detail or depth. Key themes, significant aspects or issues are identified in preparation of further in-depth analysis. Finally, the participants are given a voice by means of their individual accounts while their identity is protected by the amalgam of characters. There is, however, one caveat of which we need to be aware. In constructing these narrative accounts, you will inevitably draw on your professional knowledge and expertise as well as your life experiences and must therefore acknowledge your personal biases and how they may impact on you as the researcher. The example below of a fictional pen-portrait is taken from a project conducted on behalf of the Teacher Development Agency (TDA) in England in 2008 (Jones et al., 2008). It was concerned with the professional learning and development of mentors supporting beginning teachers. The themes that emerged from the ten schools and that determined the focus of the vignettes are as follows:

- learning collaboratively;
- professional renewal and reorientation;
- whole-school development and cultural enrichment;
- developing a learning community;
- building teaching capacity;

- facilitating beneficial contacts;
- towards a collegiate culture;
- developing critical self-awareness and professional sensitivity;
- driving improvements in teaching and learning;
- experiencing new perspectives.

Box 11.3 below provides an extract from one vignette.

Box 11.3   Driving improvements in teaching and learning

Anne is a professional mentor at a large secondary school that recently has experienced all the upheaval that becoming an academy can entail. During this period of transition, she believes that the school's involvement in ITE partnerships constituted a stable factor and provided a line of continuity for existing staff and a clear focus for newly appointed staff. When a new head teacher appointed her professional mentor seven years ago, there were only two trained mentors among a staff of sixty. Now there are fifty mentors covering the full range of subject areas provided within the school. Anne firmly believes that working with trainee teachers is a process with reciprocal benefits for both mentor and mentee:

The students [trainees] *are getting information and help from the mentors, the mentors are getting all these fresh ideas that are new from university. It's about building relationships and it's also having an impact on teaching and learning in the school . . . The children are learning far more when different people are giving them different ideas and coming from different ways – a fresh pair of eyes, so to say.*

Anne believes that it is now firmly embedded in the culture of the school to have trainee teachers, as the staff has recognised the benefits to teaching and learning that results from being part of an ITE partnership:

I don't think we'd be up-to-date with the latest teaching methods for some of us. I think it's made a lot of people sit up and think, 'Oh, this is really different and I like this.' I think if we didn't have students [trainees] *a lot of people wouldn't be changing their teaching methods. [.. .] having students* [trainees] *is having a massive positive impact.*

Anne also believes that the culture of the school has been positively affected by the school's involvement in ITE, a sentiment that is reiterated by Simon, a curriculum mentor for English. Simon has been teaching for 18 years and has supported Anne in developing ITE partnerships with a variety of providers.

Well, it keeps you on your toes. That's for sure! The new ideas, just bringing in new ideas, new approaches! It's a case of 'we can't stand still'. We can't rely on what I did four or five years ago. These new ideas come from all over the place. They do research, they get them from university sometimes, they meet other students [trainees]. It's just the drive they have and their ambition and the fact that they are not willing to rest on their laurels and the fact that they'll question what we're doing and saying . . . And you know, they have confidence. They have the confidence to turn round and say, 'Well, shouldn't we be doing this? This is what we should be doing.'

Simon points out that there is a danger for experienced and routinised teachers to become complacent. Collaboratively working with trainee teachers is vital in that it constantly forces established practitioners to articulate their practice and to justify the strategies and techniques they employ in their teaching.

Simon is convinced that the discussions taking place within individual departments inevitably have an impact on the school as a whole. He also believes that having trainees promotes a culture of learning within which it is acceptable to request help. Without trainees, he believes, staff would be more defensive. He also acknowledges that 'some students [trainees] can teach you a thing or two.'

I remember one girl we had, called Mary from the Scottish islands. She had the most wonderful lilt, but she was a very softly spoken person and she never raised her voice. But they listened. And you're thinking, 'Why are they listening?' And you suddenly realise that she is making them listen by not raising her voice. We had another student [trainee] who had all sorts of tricks, charts and league tables. He introduced a competitive element into the classroom: 'Let's see where table A is in the league table now? Oh, you're third from the bottom. You are going to have to do a bit better than that. And you think. 'Ah, I like that.'

(Continued)

(Continued)

Overall, Simon believes that the school's involvement in ITE partnerships has certainly changed its culture. His head of department, Bill, who has been a mentor for nine years, values the presence of trainees in the department, as he sees them playing a vital role in promoting improvement in teaching and learning.

> *What we are trying to do, is to encourage students [trainees] to actually contribute ideas while they are here. And, thankfully, they do. For example, all students [trainees] are invited to departmental meetings and encouraged to get involved. So, if there is anything they can pass on, you know, part of the agenda of the department meetings is always teaching and learning. I insisted on that being in there and if they've got something they want to add, then great, let's talk about it.*

Also, in his one-to-one mentoring role Bill is very much aware of how supporting trainee teachers has a positive influence on his practice as a teacher.

> *Now, at this school, they are very, very keen [on] thorough lesson planning. But being an experienced teacher you are able to go into a classroom and deliver a lesson without a major plan. But, students [trainees] need to see how it should be done. If they are not seeing the right practice from you, how are they supposed to learn and so, it's made me reflect a lot. It's made me think, 'Are my lessons up to scratch? Are my IT skills up to scratch? Am I doing all my plenaries and starters and entering all the objectives on the board?' It's made me perhaps a little better as a teacher.*

At the same time as trainees are learning from the mentors the reciprocal benefits of mentoring are fully acknowledged by Bill and his colleagues, who perceive them as a potential source of information on educational initiatives and developments.

While such vignettes or pen portraits can serve to present and disseminate your research, they can also provide a valuable resource for teachers' continuing professional learning and development. For example, they can be used to generate critical reflection and discussion based on a series of questions. For example:

- What are the drivers for improving teaching and learning in your school?
- Can you recall an example of a trainee introducing new ideas, techniques or resources that have been adopted by a department or across the school?
- How are innovative ideas shared with colleagues in your department and the school as a whole?
- Can you identify areas in teaching and learning where you would welcome further input from members of the wider ITE partnership, e.g. from the ITE provider or mentors from other schools?

In addition to those text-based modes of presenting qualitative data, we now have new technologies at our disposal, which allow us to transmit information via the visual and auditory channels rather than through written text. The power of visual images is also apparent in today's classroom, where electronic whiteboards, access to the World Wide Web and computer-assisted learning are considered powerful tools for teaching and learning. For example, the presentation of such multi-mode data could consist of an audio file overlying a picture (e.g. a child talking about a piece of work they had produced) or a video clip of a classroom scene accompanied by a commentary.

While these visual sources can provide detailed examples of educational contexts and thereby facilitate a better understanding of social interaction and pedagogical processes, they harbour risks with regard to protecting participants' privacy, confidentiality and anonymity. While protecting participants' identity is relatively straightforward in the presentation of written text items, it is more problematic when photographic and video recorded evidence of individuals' social interaction or behaviour is involved and may require sophisticated technological expertise (e.g. blurring of faces, shots from behind the shoulder). In their article Davidson et al. (2009) provide helpful examples of how visual sources can be utilised by qualitative researchers in an effective and responsible manner.

Further reading .

Bazeley, C. (2007) *Qualitative Data Analysis with Nvivo*. London: Sage.
Friese, S. (2012) *Qualitative Data Analysis with ATLAS.ti*. London: Sage
White, C., Woodfield, K. and Ritchie, J. (2003) 'Reporting and presenting qualitative research data', in J. Ritchie and J. Lewis (eds), *Qualitative Research Practice: A Guide for Social Science Students and Researchers*. London: Sage, pp. 287–320.

References

Barrington, R. (2000) *An Investigation into the Induction Period Which Considers the Perspectives of NQTs and Their Induction Tutors*. British Educational Research Association Conference, Cardiff University, September.

Campbell, A. and Groundwater-Smith, S. (2004) *An Ethical Approach to Practitioner Research*. Abingdon: Routledge.

Connelly, F. M. and Clandinin, D. J. (1999) *Shaping Professional Identity: Stories of Educational Practice*. New York: Teachers College Press.

Davidson, J., Dottin, J. W., Penna, S. L. and Robertson, S. P. (2009) 'Visual sources and the qualitative research dissertation: ethics, evidence and the politics of academia – moving innovation in higher education from the centre to the margins', *International Journal of Education and the Arts*, 10 (27): 1–40.

Denscombe, M. (2007) *The Good Research Guide for Small-Scale Social Research Projects*, 3rd edn. Maidenhead: Open University Press.

Goodson, I. F. and Sykes, P. (2001) *Life History Research in Educational Settings: Learning from Lives*. Buckingham: Open University Press.

Hodkinson, P. and Hodkinson, H. (2003) 'Individuals, communities of practice and the policy context: school teachers' learning in the workplace', *Studies in Continuing Education*, 25 (1): 3–21.

Hurd, S., Jones, M., McNamara, O. and Craig, B. (2007) 'Initial Teacher Education as a driver for professional learning and school improvement in the primary phase', *Curriculum Journal*, 18 (3): 307–26.

Jones, M. (2002) 'Qualified to become good teachers: a case study of ten newly qualified teachers during their year of induction', *Journal of In-Service Education*, 28 (3): 509–26.

Jones, M. (2009) 'Supporting the supporters of novice teachers: an analysis of mentors' needs from twelve European countries presented from an English perspective', *Research in Comparative and International Education*, 4 (1): 4–21.

Jones, M., Campbell, A., McNamara, O. and Stanley, G. (2008) *The Impact of ITE Partnership on Teachers' Professional Learning and Development: A Selection of Case Stories of Good Practice*. London: Teacher Development Agency (TDA).

Jones, M., Campbell, A., McNamara, O. and Stanley, G. (2009) 'Developing professional learning communities – the hidden curriculum of ITE mentoring', *CPD Update*, May, 116: 6–9.

CHAPTER 12

COLLATING AND PRESENTING QUANTITATIVE EVIDENCE

It is important to read this chapter in conjunction with Chapter 14; while it is possible to separate the presentation and analysis of your findings, it is essential that there is a consistency and internal integrity between them. It is through your selection, presentation and analysis of your findings that you will be able to demonstrate your true academic abilities – and convince your readers/assessors that you have maintained your focus and have the evidence to back up your conclusions and suggested actions. This chapter will consequently focus upon the processes involved in selecting key information from the evidence you have collected and using appropriate forms, including graphical and tabular, to clarify the findings to support the analysis and interpretation of your research outcomes. As a result of this, by the end of the chapter, you should be able:

(Continued)

(Continued)

- to appreciate the need to structure the presentation of the findings to address the initial purpose of the research;
- to determine the most effective means of presenting different forms of quantitative data.

The nature of quantitative data

While quantitative evidence is most often associated with the positive/normative paradigm (Punch, 2009), it is a leap by Johnson and Christensen (2008) to connect the form of the research data to the research paradigm. Even where 'mixed methodologies' are adopted, allowing, seemingly, both quantitative and qualitative data to be collected, the constraints that this places on the research process are not always helpful.

Thomas (2003: 1) distinguishes between qualitative 'describing . . . characteristics of people and events' and quantitative 'measurements and amounts . . . of the characteristics displayed'. So quantitative evidence will provide an indication of the scale or relative importance of an issue (or problem), while qualitative evidence will attempt to offer an interpretation or explanation. Given these differences, combining evidence from these forms can significantly add to the strength and depth of an argument.

Since, as can been seen from Chapter 11, it is quite possible to code and collate qualitative data into a quantitative form, it is quite likely that even where mainly qualitative evidence has been collected, there may still be appropriate opportunities to employ quantitative data presentation techniques.

Research reports that make effective use of both quantitative and qualitative data will often lead with the quantitative evidence to provide an immediate point of impact as a 'headline', and then follow it up and enrich the interpretation and analysis through the introduction of the qualitative sources. The statistics can often be used to 'grab' the attention of the reader ('8 out of 10 cats said their owner preferred . . .'), but it is left to the qualitative evidence to make a connection at a deeper level (the picture of the well-fed cat and purring owner) to give 'life' to the numbers.

Collating quantitative data

In most cases, the best place to collate and organise the quantitative data that you have collected is on a spreadsheet. Each column will be used to record the response from a different question and each row a different respondent. Hopefully you will find, if you have constructed your questionnaire or document/observation recording schedule well, that once you have inputted the data, the organisation, sorting and tabulation of the data can be achieved with relative ease.

There are a number of free-to-use online survey (questionnaire) tools that provide an output in the form of a spreadsheet that can be easily downloaded and imported into most spread sheet packages. For example, both https://drive.google.com and www.surveymonkey.com/ collate questionnaire responses to spreadsheets which contain their own suite of presentation and analysis tools or provide the opportunity to download to various spreadsheets such as Microsoft Excel.

It is at this stage that the well constructed response and recording sheet, designed at the point that the data collection tool was developed, really begins to pay off – or not as the case may be! Even where the response sheet (questionnaire, observation or documentary analysis schedule, etc.) has been completed on paper and requires data inputting to convert it into an electronic format, where the tool has been constructed to pre-code the responses the task is significantly simplified. The time and effort taken to identify the potential different responses that your research population might give to a question (thereby saving them time as well) will make a significant difference at this stage. For example, an open-response question:

> What is the single most important use you make of the interactive whiteboard in your classroom?

is more of a challenge both to respond to and then collate than:

> What is the single most important use you make of the interactive whiteboard in your classroom? (Tick ONE)
> Displaying date/title/learning objectives ☐ Showing videos ☐ Annotating images and text ☐ Teacher writing ☐ Activating embedded functions ☐ Pupil writing ☐ Other..

where the response options are derived from the analysis of your reading of past research findings and the perspectives of writers in the field.

The use of a spreadsheet allows the use of a variety of tools to collate, analyse and present the data that you have collected. In all cases it is important that you choose the most appropriate means of collation, presentation and statistical analysis for the data that you have.

Each line in Table 12.1 represents the responses of a different 'new teacher' on a four-point scale (poor to outstanding) for each of the five

Table 12.1 New teachers' perceptions of mentor support

	How good has the schoolteacher/mentor support been so far in			
modelling a range of teaching strategies and approaches?	providing guidance and support for assessment tasks (including lesson planning and review points)?	providing timely and constructive feedback (including lesson planning, observations of teaching and review points)?	providing guidance and support (including clear targets) to improve your teaching practice?	helping you to identify and plan to address your developmental needs?
outstanding	good	outstanding	outstanding	good
outstanding	outstanding	outstanding	outstanding	outstanding
good	satisfactory	satisfactory	satisfactory	satisfactory
outstanding	outstanding	outstanding	outstanding	outstanding
good	satisfactory	satisfactory	satisfactory	satisfactory
outstanding	outstanding	outstanding	outstanding	outstanding
good	good	good	good	good
good	good	good	good	good
outstanding	outstanding	outstanding	outstanding	outstanding
good	good	good	good	good
outstanding	outstanding	outstanding	outstanding	outstanding
outstanding	good	good	good	good
satisfactory	poor	satisfactory	poor	poor
outstanding	outstanding	good	outstanding	outstanding
good	outstanding	outstanding	outstanding	outstanding
outstanding	good	good	good	good

categories. In Excel, the use of the COUNTIF function would allow the sum of each grade in each column to be calculated and presented in a pie chart, but for further statistical analysis it would be more helpful if the scale were to be converted to a numerical one (which is a relatively straightforward task using FIND/REPLACE).

Once in an electronic format, preferably a spreadsheet which is compatible with the word processing software that you are using, data in tabular or graphical formats can be imported into your written report or assignment with relative ease. To reduce your stress, consider the collation/presentation issues as you design your research tools!

Quantitative data within the text

Quantitative data provides your study with impact – '85% of parents (n = 38) claimed that . . .' does suggest that the claim (whatever it might be) has significant backing and support and is worth taking note of (assuming, of course, that you have followed the guidance in Chapter 6 and used an appropriate sample). Note that where a percentage is used, it should be accompanied by the population size. Even where raw data (actual numbers) are used, such as

Ten students were identified as having special educational needs

this can be misleading, if not useless, unless it is made clear how many this is out of – 10 out of 29 is very different than 10 out of 290! It is also important to source the data where possible and appropriate, so the statement becomes

The school's annual report noted ten out of 290 students as having special educational needs.

Where the data are 'simple' and can be stated clearly then it is usually best to simply insert it into the text of your study rather than disrupting the flow with breaks for graphics or tables. If a particular percentage of the questionnaires have been returned, this can be stated rather than going to the lengths of constructing and including a pie chart. In fact, a graphical presentation to show that 'all of the questionnaires were returned' can have a negative impact on the quality of your presentation.

Use of tables

As well as for organisational purposes, tables should also be considered for the presentation of data, especially where the data is succinct and well contained with the potential for comparative interpretation. Generally it is more usual (and useful) to use tables to present collated data (such as Table 12.2) rather than raw data (as in Table 12.1).

In Table 12.2 all of the data has been converted to percentages in order to make the comparisons more self-evident in terms of the balance between the alternatives rather than the absolute data. Note that the actual number of respondents for each sub-population has been retained to ensure that the scale of the response is not hidden. It is important to provide each of

Table 12.2   Methods of praise which each group feels pupils will value the most

Method of praise	Pupils	Parents	Governors
Verbal	19%	21%	40%
Commendations	8%	21%	10%
Letters home	56%	43%	35%
Certificates	11%	12%	15%
Other	6%	3%	0%
Total responses	205	121	20

your tables not only with a title which clearly explains the content, but also with a reference – the one above, 'Table 12.3', is the third table in the twelfth chapter of this book.

Table 12.3   A comparison of teacher assessments and exam grades (Year 7 history)

Student	Teacher assessment	Exam
A	8	7
B	15	8
C	13	14
D	11	11
E	11	6
F	9	9
G	5	8
H	7	10
I	11	9
J	12	9
K	8	9
L	10	11
M	10	11
N	11	8
O	7	8
P	9	7
Q	7	5
R	6	5
S	6	6
T	13	13

In most cases, such as Table 12.3, tabulated raw data does not often improve the clarity of the presentation of the evidence. In this example, a comparison of teacher assessments of student learning against exam grades would be made more explicit through a graphical presentation (see Figure 12.7 below). The tabulated results still leave 'too much' for the reader to do in terms of visual analysis to extract anything meaningful from the presentation. However, the data that have been used to construct a graphical representation could usefully be placed in and referred to from the text of the assignment or report.

It should also be noted that tables are often a useful means of presenting qualitative information in a structured and coherent form (see Chapter 11).

Use of graphics

The impact of numerical data can often be further enhanced and simplified through the use of tabulated or graphical presentation; however, the data does need to be explained, interpreted and contextualised – do not expect the numbers alone to be sufficient. In terms of graphical representations of data, it is important to ensure that the correct format is employed for the data being used, as the incorrect graphical format can significantly reduce the quality and thus the impact of your data.

Pie charts

Pie charts should be employed where *mutually exclusive categoric data sets*, as in the case of responses to a multiple-choice question, are used:

> *The meeting with the ADHD (attention deficit and hyperactivity disorder) spe-cialist helped me to understand my child's needs: strongly agree (20); agree (12); disagree (7); strongly disagree (2).*

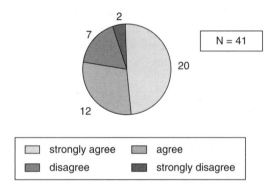

Figure 12.1   Meeting with the ADHD specialist helped me to understand my child's needs
Source: Burton (2007: 156).

It is possible to use a pie chart which has been appropriately titled (making appropriate use of the question that was posed in the questionnaire) to present this data in a very clear and explicit way. Pie charts are frequently presented using percentage data, but should also indicate the total number of responses (n = 41) and include a legend which identifies the content of the segments.

Pie charts can either be presented in absolute or percentage format, but should always sum to '100 per cent'. Where there is no obvious 'order' to the data sets (unlike the example), it should be organised so that, starting at '12 o'clock' and going clockwise there should be a progression from largest to smallest segment. Taking the data from the 'Pupils' column of Table 12.2, the data can be represented in graphical form as in Figure 12.2.

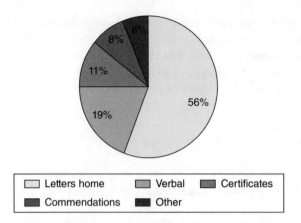

Figure 12.2   Pupils' preferred method of receiving praise

Note that the order of the categories has been changed from the table version to be consistent with the convention of progressing from the largest to the smallest segment. However, if all the data from the table were to be presented in this form, the segments would need to be in the same order in each chart to ensure consistency.

Bar or column charts

Where the comparison is between *mutually inclusive categoric data sets* (i.e. it is possible to respond positively to more than one category) then a bar chart should be used, as the number of responses is likely to exceed the number of respondents. However, this format can also be used as an alternative to pie charts when you are attempting to overlay multiple sets of data for comparative purposes. For a simple bar (horizontal) or column (vertical) chart the categories should be organised in some meaningful way – usually by size or by alphabetical order of the category names. In this example the question posed to students in two Year 10 classes was:

Which languages do you speak?

English O *Polish* O *German* O *Arabic* O *Urdu* O *Other*.................

which could easily result in more than one response from each respondent.

While the number of respondents is 41, the total number of languages spoken is 55. Not only does Figure 12.3 have a title, the axes are also labelled, as are subsequent graphs. By convention the horizontal (x-axis) is the independent variable (the one that you, independently, decide upon the

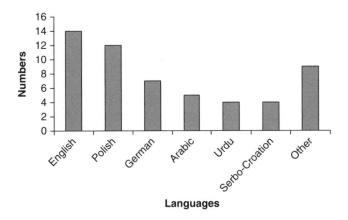

Figure 12.3   Spoken languages in the group

Source: Burton (2007: 157).

content of) and the vertical (y-axis) is the dependent variable (the one that measured).

It is also possible to use bar charts to comparatively present data from different sub-populations (male/female, departments, etc.), but the choice of the actual format does need to be chosen sympathetically for the intended audience. Figure 12.4 compares the duties performed by teachers working in different key stages. To complete such a graphic, the data must already have been aggregated and collated in the form of an average (probably the mean) for the groups.

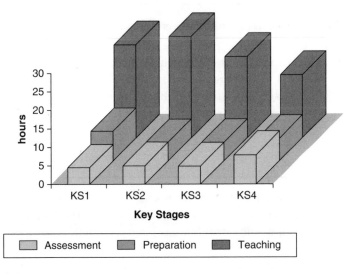

Figure 12.4   Weekly teacher duties (hours)

Figure 12.4 allows the reader to visually compare the relative amounts of time spent of the three different activities by teachers working in different key stages – for example, relatively less teaching and more marking for those working in KS4 and relatively more time spent on preparation by those in KS1.

Data taken from an expanded version of Table 12.1 has been visually presented in Figure 12.5. If a single one of those questions were to be graphically presented, e.g. 'mentor support in modelling a range of teaching strategies and approaches', the obvious format would be a pie chart. By 'stacking' the bars so that each column represents the cumulative responses, then all of the data for several questions can be placed of the same chart with little loss of individual clarity and greatly enhanced comparability.

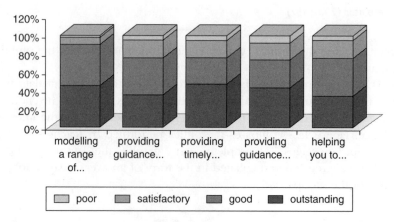

Figure 12.5   How good has the mentor support been so far in . . .

It is possible to represent relationships graphically where both sets of data are presented in numerical form. A table listing reading ages against the chronological age of a group of children may not be particularly easy to assimilate.

Histograms

Histograms look similar to bar charts in some respects, but there should not be any gaps between the individual bars or columns. This format is used to display data which is numerical but has been recorded as grouped interval data, as in Table 12.4.

The 'years of experience' information has been recorded in clusters/intervals of five years (except 26+ years). Unfortunately, Microsoft Excel

Table 12.4   Length of service of teaching staff at a further education college

Years experience	Number of staff
1–5	4
6–10	30
11–15	26
16–20	49
21–25	10
26+	0

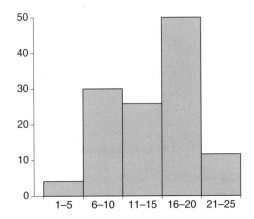

Figure 12.6   Length of service of teaching staff at a further education college

does not include histograms in its standard pack of charts and if using this software you will need to go online to download the 'analysis tool pack' add-in.

Note from Figure 12.6 that histograms use number ranges rather than the categories used in bar charts (see Figure 12.3) and that histograms do not have gaps between the columns.

Scattergraphs

In the scattergraph (see Figure 12.7), each point represents two points of information for an individual offering a visual interpretation of the relationship. In the case of Figure 12.7 this displays the relation between the teacher assessment and exam grade of a group of learners. The shape of the cluster of points provides an indication of the relationship between the two factors. In this particular case, assuming that both assessments are accurate and focuses on the same knowledge/skill base, it would be reasonable to expect that those students with high teacher assessments would also achieve high exam grades – suggesting a cluster of points around a 'line' running from bottom right to top left of the

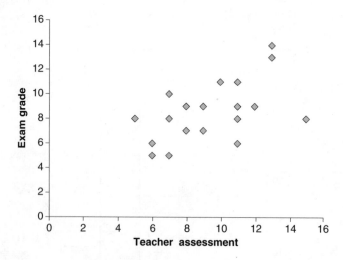

Figure 12.7   Exam grades mapped against teacher assessments

graph – a *positive relationship*. In Figure 12.7 there does appear to be a general indication that there is a positive relationship between the two measures of academic success – refer to Chapter 14 to discover how the strength of this relationship can be statistically measured.

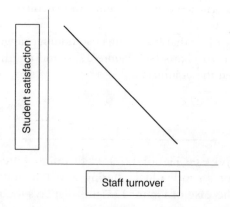

Figure 12.8   Relationship between staff turnover and student satisfaction

This 'positive relationship' between exam grade and teacher assessment in Figure 12.7 can be represented by a 'best fit' line (the line
drawn from bottom left to top right). A negative relationship, for
example one that might be expected between 'staff turnover' and
'student satisfaction' (as staff turnover increases, student satisfaction
falls) might be represented by a best-fit line running from top left to
bottom right (see Figure 12.8).

In general terms, if the plotted points are clustered in a 'circle', or around
a horizontal or vertical line, or randomly over the whole graph, the relationship between the two factors can be regarded as being 'poor' or even
'non-existent'.

Line graphs

Line graphs can be used to display trends over time. A relatively straightforward way to track the impact of an initiative to reduce non-attendance
by pupils in a particular year group over a ten week period (see Figure
12.9) is to plot the unexplained non-attendance for each week.

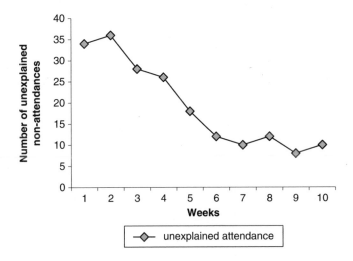

Figure 12.9   Unexplained attendance

In Figure 12.10 the number of days that a school has needed to employ
additional teaching staff has been recorded. However, the graph does need
to be read with care to distinguish between cover for illness (squares), training (triangles) and the total (diamonds), and for presentation purposes
colour printing would need to be considered.

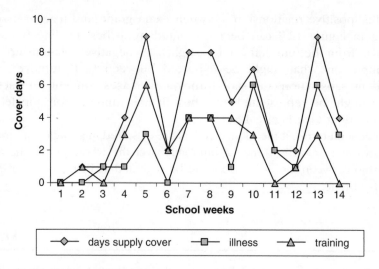

Figure 12.10   Supply cover requirements

Figure 12.10 perhaps provides an example of the limits which graphics should not go beyond. There comes a point at which the attempt to provide clarity through a graphical presentation can become counterproductive when too much information is included in one diagram. Take the example of the graphical representation of the outcomes of an initiative to improve the reading ability of a class of Year 4 children shown in Figure 12.11. Here the mean of the reading age of the children, corrected

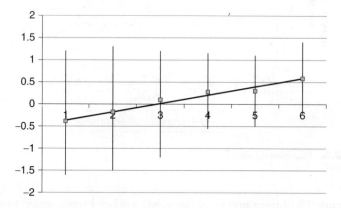

Figure 12.11   Outcomes of an initiative to improve the reading ability of a class of Year 4 children

for their chronological age, has been recorded and calculated at six points during the year. A plotted point at zero on the vertical axis would indicate that the mean reading age was in line with the chronological age – below would be a deficit while above the line the reading age would be better than that expected for children of their age.

The vertical lines at each plotted point represent the standard deviation around the mean (see Chapter 14 for an explanation of the importance of this measure) and the thicker, rising line represents the trend of the mean, from below to above the expected reading age for the group, with a reduced range of abilities (shorter vertical lines – smaller standard deviation).

Positioning of graphical representations of data

It is important to recognise that a balance is required between the data included within the text and the data presented within an appendix. Too much information presented in the text of an assignment or report will reduce the quality of the 'flow' of the argument being presented; too little and the reader will be forced to search for meaningful data to support the analysis being made. Where, due to available space or to ensure that the flow of the assignment is maintained, data is placed within an appendix, it will need to be appropriately referenced to ensure that the reader is able to find it if necessary (the information placed here should be regarded as incidental rather than core). For example, *all* quantitative responses generated in a questionnaire survey could be placed in the appendix (collated – not each individual questionnaire!), while only those scores directly relevant to a particular research question will be incorporated in the text.

Key questions to ask

- Does the inclusion of the table or graphic improve the clarity or impact of the point being made?
- Is the data essential to the flow of the presentation (i.e. should it be included in the text or in the appendix and referred to in the text)?
- Is the data being presented in the most appropriate form?
- Have I adequately explained in the text what the table or graphic shows?

References

Burton, N. (2007) 'The research process', in P. Zwozdiak-Myers (ed.), *Childhood and Youth Studies*. Exeter: Learning Matters, 146–59.

Cohen, L., Manion, L. and Morrison, K. (2011) *Research Methods in Education*, 7th edn. Abingdon: Routledge.

Denscombe, M. (2003) *The Good Research Guide*, 2nd edn. Maidenhead: Open University Press.

Johnson, B. and Christensen, L. (2008) *Educational Research: Quantitative, Qualitative and Mixed Approaches*, 3rd edn. Thousand Oaks, CA: Sage.

Punch, K. (2009) *An Introduction to Research Methods in Education*. London: Sage.

Thomas, R. (2003) *Blending Qualitative and Quantitative Research Methods in Theses and Dissertations*. Thousand Oaks, CA: Corwin Press.

Walliman, N. (2005) *Your Research Project*. London: Sage.

CHAPTER 13

QUALITATIVE DATA ANALYSIS

Once you have coded your data and created main and sub-categories within which they can be stored and easily retrieved, either manually or by means of a qualitative data analysis software program, you can start your analysis. This involves the grouping and re-grouping of codes under broader themes with the aim of reducing the vast amount of data that can be generated to a manageable level from which the data can be distilled further in order to develop your theories.

By the end of this chapter you should have developed an under-standing of the principles involved in this process and how it forms a

(Continued)

(Continued)

bridge between data collection, interpretation and development of theory. Specifically, you should be able to:

- appreciate the relationship between presentation and analysis of findings;
- recognise the need to compare data from different sources;
- understand the importance of comparing the research findings with published research and conceptual frameworks.

Types of evidence

As mentioned earlier, adopting a mixed methodology (quantitative and qualitative data) is an effective strategy of enhancing the validity of research outcomes. While the quantitative data will often provide the immediate 'impact' of your findings ('85 per cent of students (n = 178) agreed that ...'), it is often the qualitative findings, particularly direct quotations or observations that exemplify and give 'depth' to the point the findings make. This leads us to the point of analysis, which must not be equated with the sorting and listing of information, but describes the transition from presenting information to detecting patterns, identifying trends and establishing meaningful linkages between various categories of data. At this stage, many researchers feel overwhelmed by a deluge of data. In their endeavour to move from the presentation of data to analysis and interpretation they often refer to this stage as 'hitting a brick wall'. In this situation it is helpful to return to the original research question and objectives to see whether they can provide an initial impetus in the identification of key categories to restore some order in the data chaos. As highlighted by Robson (2002), 'overload is a constant danger' and 'the main difficulty lies in their analysis' (2002: 456). Computer-assisted/aided qualitative data analysis software (CAQDAS) packages can provide useful tools for the systematic storage and retrieval of data (text and visual recordings) and thus induce the process of analysis in a less painful and more manageable way. Punch (2009) provides a useful description of how these software packages can be used in the development of your conceptual framework and in the construction of your theories. Another way which I have found to be highly therapeutic and helpful in releasing creative energies is through the drawing of diagrams. By allowing your ideas and associations to roam freely outside an existing structure, new, unexpected categories and linkages are generated, which can be incorporated in the conceptual framework underpinning the story you would like to tell.

Maintaining focus and coherence

It goes without saying that the aim of any research project is to seek answers to questions posed. In most cases, at least initially, it is those questions or research objectives that provide some of the key concepts around which data collection will be constructed. However, it is possible that new and unexpected concepts will emerge, which are entirely relevant to the focus of the research and therefore have to be taken into account in the overall analysis and interpretation of data. The most appropriate response to identifying these unexpected concepts is to complete a further search of the literature to see if these findings are either replicated elsewhere or are consistent with conceptual models that you had not previously considered – either way, a revision of your literature review would be the expected outcome.

The organisation of the analysis will tend to be most effective where the initial research questions, posed in the introduction to the study, are employed as the structural device. In this way data from the various sources, both in terms of research populations (and sub-populations) and research tools are combined to address each question in turn. Once the data that you have collected has been comparatively analysed, it then needs to be brought into analytical contact with both the theoretical models and perspectives appropriate to the focus of the study and the outcomes of published research which will already have been analysed in your review of the literature.

It would be simplistic to assume that the process of relating data to the various research questions/objectives is of a linear nature. Some data sets may only be relevant to one research objective, while others may be used to provide answers to several research questions, and others, yet again, may be entirely irrelevant and therefore need to be discarded, however painful this may be to the researcher. First of all, however, you need to code your data in preparation for analysis.

Coding – the breaking down and reassembling of data

Whether in regard to quantitative or qualitative data, coding is generally used as a shorthand to label the data and organise them into a system of categories and subcategories. This can be done manually (using highlighter pens) or by means of computer-assisted software, such as NVivo or Atlas.ti. Coding transcripts of semi-structured interviews, focus group discussions or video recorded evidence of human behaviour and social interaction can be a time-consuming undertaking. This is where computer-assisted analysis software can ease the workload and make the storage and retrieval of data more manageable than a paper-based exercise. Key tasks that can be performed include:

- sorting and categorising the raw data by coding;
- locating, storing and retrieving key phrases, text passages or visual data;
- attaching memos or field notes to relevant data;
- linking of ideas across different data sets;
- recoding and resorting data;
- accessing data at the click of a button.

Basically, coding is the process of reducing and distilling the data into more manageable chunks following three distinct stages:

1. Initial coding, which involves the labelling of data by using pre-existing and emerging codes.
2. Focused or refined coding, which serves the purpose of creating main categories and subcategories and combining, dividing and eliminating codes.
3. Synthesising across the entire data set looking for overarching themes, commonalities and divergencies.

This third stage involves comparing data from different perspectives in relation to a specific aspect or issue to ensure that there is sufficient evidence in support of the researcher's interpretation of the data.

The example shown in Figure 13.1 illustrates how an interview transcript can be coded manually. The key research question is concerned with novice teachers' induction experience and the kind of teacher they aspire to become. There are three key themes that emerg from this extract: the relationship with pupils; the relationship with colleagues; professionalism. Within each theme a number of codes are used. As we can see, some categories for organising the data are already predetermined by the kind of questions that are asked, while others emerge naturally. While this extract focuses on the kind of relationships newly qualified teachers seek to establish with their students and colleagues, it also reveals information about the kind of teacher they aspire to become, namely someone who is fair, objective, inclusive, humane, reliable, friendly and in control.

Newly developed Qualitative Data Analysis Software (QDAS) programs provide useful tools for coding, organising and analysing visual (drawings, photographs, paintings) and multi-modal (video or web page materials) text. Data generated from different sources can be consistently coded, systematically searched and analysed in triangulation with other data.

In this process of labelling text items or other qualitative data, we differentiate between predetermined codes, which can be borrowed from the literature or existing models and frameworks, and open codes, which emerge from the data during the processes of collection, analysis and interpretation. While the former are more akin to a deductive approach, the latter are used inductively. In this sense coding is not to be understood

Interview transcript – recorded conversation with a newly qualified teacher about the kind of teacher she intends to become	Codes
I: What kind of relationship are you trying to establish with your <u>students</u>?	
R: A <u>fair</u> relationship <u>with all of them</u> and with <u>discipline</u> and we <u>all</u> can <u>have a laugh</u> in the lessons. So, I want them to see me as an <u>educator,</u> of course. And I want them to see me <u>not as their friend,</u> (laughs), but as someone they can <u>rely</u> on and as someone they can count on <u>for whatever they need</u>.	Fair, inclusive In control Friendly but not a friend
I want to be <u>professional</u>, and sometimes I go more for the <u>personal</u> way of seeing things. So, I want to be professional, but I also want to say what I feel about everything.	Reliable
I: When you say 'professional', what exactly do you mean?	Professional
R: I used to think that you could only communicate about <u>results</u>, about <u>progression</u>, and that's it. But now I have seen a more <u>human way</u> of addressing problems. And yet, with parents on parents evening, for example, I cannot allow myself to become friends with parents. Then it would be difficult to talk to them about their kids in an <u>objective</u> way.	Personal perspective _____ Outcome focused
I: What about your <u>colleagues</u>? What relationship do you want to establish with them?	Humane
R: Well, I think, with colleagues, I think <u>both sides</u> are very, very important, <u>personal and professional</u>. Sometimes, you have really hard moments and you need to share them with a friend. So, yeah, I want to have these kind of relationship with my colleagues. I want to have a <u>professional relationship</u> where we can <u>help</u> each other with professional issues, but also I want to have a friendship with them where you can talk about anything that worries you, not only <u>from the professional point of view, but also from your feelings</u>.	Objective _____ Relationship with colleagues (collegial, personal, professional) Friendship Mutually supportive Sharing concerns Emotional support

Figure 13.1 Example of manual coding

exclusively as a technical activity, but as an organic, interactive process, which also includes the use of literature, as highlighted by Strauss and Corbin (1998: 49–52). For they believe that concepts emerging from the data can be compared in terms of their properties and dimensions and that reading of the literature can act as a sensitising device, making the researcher aware of subtle nuances in the data. It can also be used to explore, confirm and clarify concepts used in the categorisation of data. In addition, you will draw on your professional practice knowledge (Eraut, 1994) and personal experience to ensure that the codes and categories used in your analysis of data are valid and meaningful.

For example, by listening to interview recordings prior to, during and after coding, and reading of transcripts and interview responses, line by line, word for word, texts can be analysed in a rigorous and systematic manner. Accordingly, 'data are broken down, conceptualised and put together in new ways', a process within which 'one's own and other's assumptions are explored and leading to new discoveries' (Strauss and Corbin, 1990: 57, 62).

Thus categories for analysis can be derived from a variety of sources (e.g. focus group discussion, video recordings, documentary evidence, visual representations), including one's own assumptions, hunches and hypotheses as well as allowing for the emergence of new concepts (Tesch, 1990). While the example in Figure 13.1 illustrates how individual codes can be generated, the example shown in Figure 13.2 shows how codes and sub-codes can be organised under an existing or emergent theme.

Figure 13.2 demonstrates that data analysis is a complex and iterative process, which involves more than simply sorting information items. Instead, it proceeds in a non-linear and unpredictable manner. In this sense it is to be perceived as a continuous dialogue that takes place between the data themselves, predetermined and emergent codes, relevant practical and theoretical perspectives (including government frameworks and the research literature) and, last but not least, the researcher's own professional practice knowledge.

These examples illustrate that in qualitative data analysis the focus is on the meaning, not the measurement, of quantifiable data and that the process of examining the relationship between various data sources requires numerous iterations. One way this complex undertaking can be made more manageable is through the development of a matrix, which can be helpful in detecting emerging patterns, commonalities and divergences and potential linkages between the different concepts. Figure 13.3 shows an example from a study concerned with mentors' professional knowledge base (Jones and Straker, 2006). It is constructed around two axes: a horizontal axis (pre-existing codes) which lists the standards in the statutory induction framework for newly qualified teachers (DfEE, 1998; DfEE, 1999) and a vertical axis (based on emerging codes) which identifies sources on which mentors

An evaluative case study of newly qualified teachers' experience of induction in 1999 (the year of the implementation of the statutory induction framework)

The study followed a predominantly qualitative approach. Data were collected by means of semi-structured questionnaires and face-to-face, recorded interviews with newly qualified teachers prior to, during and on completion of induction and half-way through the year with their induction tutors. Initially, the four cornerstones on which the induction framework rests – namely 'support', 'guidance', 'monitoring' of progress and 'assessment' of competence – provided the key codes for analysis. However, as the process of data collection, coding and analysis unfolded, it became irrevocably clear that additional codes and sub-codes would be required to capture the entirety of newly qualified teachers' experiences and the issues arising from them. Questionnaire responses and interview transcripts were examined systematically, line by line, word for word with the objective of developing an organically growing coding system in relation to the focus of the study. For example, the concept of support manifested itself in various forms and originated from a wide range of sources, as illustrated below.

Support

1.1   NQTs' expectations
1.2   Statutory entitlement
1.3   Support provided by:

      1.3.1   Induction tutor
      1.3.2   Head of department
      1.3.3   Colleagues
      1.3.4   Teaching assistants
      1.3.5   Other school staff
      1.3.6   Peers

1.4   Local authority
1.5   Formal, structured programme

      1.5.1   Internal
      1.5.2   External courses

1.6   Informal support systems
1.7   Examples of support

      1.7.1   Collaborative planning, teaching and assessment
      1.7.2   Lesson observation and constructive feedback
      1.7.3   Observation of good practice

1.7.4 Learning conversations

In addition to the four predetermined (a priori) codes ('support', 'guidance', 'monitoring', 'assessment') new concepts emerged from the data. In selecting appropriate codes the researcher often referred to her own experience as a newly qualified teacher, mentor of trainees and PGCE tutor and her professional practice and theoretical knowledge acquired over the years, bringing various perspectives to bear. For example, 'expectations', 'challenges', 'successes', 'disappointments' and 'coping strategies' were categories considered relevant and emerging from the data. These codes intersected with the respondents' own 'in-vivo' (live) codes, such as 'raring to go', 'finding one's feet' or 'home and dry', which aptly described the three sequential phases commonly associated with induction: initial enthusiasm, tempered by the realisation that in spite of enormous challenges they were beginning to establish themselves as teachers, and finally having their qualified teacher status confirmed.

Further, new and unexpected codes were generated from the data and verified by the literature concerned with the induction of newly qualified teachers, such as the notion of 'professional values' and 'the need for pastoral care', both of which were absent in the statutory framework.

Figure 13.2   Developing a conceptual framework

draw when supporting newly qualified teachers in achieving the induction standards. Although in this study the matrix was used to present the frequency

	Subject knowledge	Planning, teaching, monitoring and assessment	Class management and pupil/ teacher relationships	Professional values and practice	The wider social, cultural and political context
Own experience as a learner					
Own experience as a trainee teacher					
Professional practice					
Roles and/or responsibilities within school					
Roles and/or responsibilities outside school					
Continuing professional development					
Mentor training and development					
Colleagues/ peers/ professional network					
Research/ literature/ educational press					
Other					

Figure 13.3 What informs mentors' knowledge base when working with novice teachers

of citings against the various elements located on each of the axes, it can equally serve as a model for qualitative data generated from interview or focus group transcripts.

The matrix revealed that in supporting novice teachers achieve the Professional Standards for Qualified Teacher Status (QTS) mentors drew predominantly on their personal experience as classroom practitioners, while other sources, such as the research literature or continuing professional development, were cited less frequently.

The intricate process of data analysis

As we have already established earlier, data analysis consists of a number of strategies, which involves the filtering, linking and distilling of a diverse body of information. All three processes serve to identify themes that are related to the focus of the study in response to the research questions/ objectives. These themes may already be inherent in the research questions, but, equally, may emerge from the data. Any new concepts resulting from this process may warrant further investigation by consulting the relevant literature and may lead to new questions to be asked for the purpose of follow-up investigations. Ultimately, they need to be incorporated into the conceptual framework underpinning the research. While the filtering or 'reduction of data' (Gray, 2004: 321) through constant comparison with the research objectives and tentative propositions aims to achieve succinctness and coherence of findings, triangulation is used to enhance the validity of outcomes. It consists of 'the use of a variety of methods or data sources to examine a specific phenomenon either simultaneously or sequentially in order to improve the reliability of data' (Gray, 2004: 406). This can be achieved by combining different methods (quantitative and qualitative), diverse perspectives, research settings and times, and looking for convergent messages, thereby strengthening the validity of a claim. As with every investigation the ultimate goal is to tell a story (Wolcott, 1994). However, this involves more than simply listing a collection of data. This is the point where the creative dimension of the research process comes to the fore. In order to discover what lies beneath the surface of data, we need to engage in critical analysis. By identifying emerging patterns or trends we can explore potential linkages in our endeavour to understand and explain the underlying reasons for certain phenomena. Analysis is thus to be understood as an iterative process that can best be described as a dialogue taking place between the description and interpretation of data as mutually interdependent processes (see Figure 13.4) where analysis informs interpretation and vice versa. As mentioned earlier, the role of literature forms an integral part of this process. This view resonates with Strauss and Corbin who believe that:

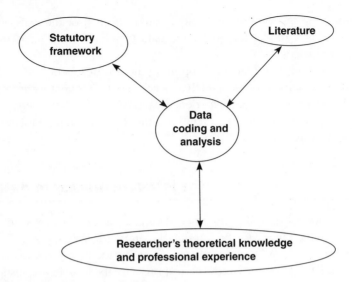

Figure 13.4   The dialogical process of data analysis

> The interplay of reading the literature and doing an analysis of it, then moving
> out into the field to verify it against the reality can yield an integrated picture
> and enhance the conceptual richness of the theory. (1990: 55)

Particularly where the emergence of new codes is concerned, reference to
the research literature can enhance their validity, while further reading can
result in the discovery of new, relevant codes which hitherto have not been
included in the analysis. In addition, it is commonly accepted as good practice to involve more than one researcher in the analysis of data, as it can
provide further perspectives (triangulation) and an element of consistency
with the aim of enhancing the validity of outcomes and trustworthiness of
the research.

Enhancing the validity of research outcomes

In traditional research, validity, reliability and generalisability constitute
the essential quality criteria, the latter two of which are difficult, if not
impossible, to fulfil by qualitative researchers undertaking small-scale
investigations within their own practice setting. While quantitative data
analysis makes use of statistical procedures that lend themselves to
enhancing the validity, reliability and generalisability of research findings in a scientific/positivistic sense, qualitative researchers undertaking

small-scale investigations in their own practice setting frequently employ alternative quality criteria. If a sample is representative, findings can be legitimately generalised to a wider population (Bryman, 1988: 35), but, given the idiosyncratic character of practitioner research, claims for generalisability and reliability beyond the research setting are problematic. Similar problems arise with regard to fulfilling the criterion of reliability, which refers to the degree of consistency with which instances are assigned to the same category by different observers or by the same observer on different occasions. Unlike in a science laboratory, there will never be any two schools or classrooms where conditions for learning and teaching are identical and where these processes can be replicated. We also need to accept that practitioner research is typically provoked through teachers' identification of a problem/issue, which warrants systematic inquiry to bring about improvement of the situation. Consequently, it has to defend itself against claims of subjectivity. In this respect it is helpful to refer to Bassey (1999), whose notions of 'internal validity', 'trustworthiness' and 'transferability' are deemed more appropriate. While the validity value will be largely determined by the extent to which the findings are directly related to the issues or problems identified at the outset of the research and how well they respond to the research questions posed, its 'trustworthiness' is reflected in the selection of appropriate methods and how systematically they have been employed.

Do the data answer the question?

The question whether the data generated answer the research question is central to the process of analysis and relies to a large extent on the appropriate selection of data collection tools. Again, parallels between teaching and research spring to mind in that the methods by which information is compiled must generate valid data. The situation outlined in Figure 13.5 regarding the assessment of modern foreign languages is worth considering in this respect, as it raises issues with regard to the validity of data, i.e. candidates' responses.

As Figure 13.5 demonstrates, the way in which questions are asked can impair the validity of responses, rendering them worthless for analysis. To prevent this from happening rigorous scrutiny and systematic piloting of collection tools, such as questionnaires, is considered a standard requirement with the aim of ensuring that the final version is free from any potential misunderstandings and ambiguities. This is of particular importance where participants with weak literacy skills or low proficiency in English are involved.

The current GCSE and AS/A level examinations in modern foreign languages require candidates to demonstrate competence in understanding and producing the foreign language in speaking and writing.

For example, the listening comprehension requires candidates to respond to questions by extracting relevant information from a text presented to them in the foreign language. While some questions are in English requiring answers in English, others are in the foreign language requiring answers in the foreign language.

What can be said about the validity of the candidates' responses if:

(a)   They do not comprehend the questions in the foreign language, but can understand the text presented to them in the foreign language?
(b)   They are unable to produce the answer in the foreign language, but could give the answer in English?
(c)   The questions are in English and pupils are required to respond in English?

Note! *The objective of the examination is to assess listening skills in the foreign language, not reading* (exam questions) *and writing skills* (written responses).

Questions

1.   What are the issues raised in this example?
2.   In what way can this issue be transferred to practitioner research?

Figure 13.5   Issues of validity in the assessment of MFL

The method of triangulation

One effective strategy employed to enhance the validity of research outcomes is that of triangulation. By bringing together data from different sources by means of different methods and reflecting different perspectives, the validity of findings can be enhanced considerably (Elliott, 1991; Takkashori and Teddlie, 2003; Altrichter et al., 2006) and the trustworthiness of the research process can be strengthened. It plays a key role in the collection and analysis of data and can result in rich, dense data generated from a variety of angles. As in teaching, observation is commonly used to gather information on the teaching and learning process, but other tools, such as questionnaires, interviews, focus group discussion, diaries and logs, audio and video recording, artefacts and supportive documentation are equally acceptable.

To help you understand the principle of triangulation and how it can be incorporated into practitioner research, consider Scenarios 13.1 and 13.2 below and answer the questions provided.

Scenario 13.1   Identification of research participants, data sources and methods

As part of the national strategy to raise achievement in teaching and learning and as a result of Year 10 pupils' underachievement, your school management intends to implement a mentoring programme involving trainee teachers from the HEI with which they are in partnership. The trainee teachers will act as the pupils' mentors with the aim of providing them with academic and personal support via weekly group and one-to-one meetings. You would like to evaluate the effectiveness of this intervention through an action research approach.

Questions

1. Whose perspectives need to be represented in your research team?
2. What kind of data do you intend to collect?
2. What methods/strategies will you employ in the collection of data?
3. Who will be the research participants from whom you will be seeking information?
4. What kind of data sources will you be using for analysis and why?

Please provide reasons for each of your answers.

Scenario 13.2   Triangulation of data, methods and perspectives

You are an assistant head teacher of a secondary school with responsibility for staff development. Against the backdrop of restructuring the children's workforce you would like to devise a training and staff development framework for the teaching assistants in your school. The research you are going to undertake is to provide you with data that can inform the development of a professional training and development programme.

(Continued)

(Continued)

The key research questions to which you are seeking answers are as follows:

1. What are their perceptions of the roles and responsibilities of teaching assistants?
2. What are their professional and personal needs?
3. How well are they integrated into the school community?
4. In what way and to what extent do they enhance the process of teaching and learning?

You have collected the following data:

- quantitative data via structured questionnaires (multiple choice) investigating the perceptions of TAs, teaching and clerical staff of TAs' roles and responsibilities;
- qualitative data via in-depth, face-to-face, unstructured interviews with TAs, exploring their experiences, feelings and opinions regarding their status within the children's workforce in general and their specific role within the school;
- focus group discussion with teaching staff regarding TAs' roles and responsibilities;
- lesson observation;
- informal pupil and parent feedback;
- assessment data;
- pupils' exercise books;
- pupil behaviour and attendance records;
- Ofsted reports;
- school policy;
- staffroom culture and staff relationships;
- national framework for restructuring the workforce.

Question

1. Which data do you consider most relevant in relation to the research focus and the four key questions posed?
2. How would you triangulate the data to enhance the validity of findings?

External validation

Finally, if we accept that practitioner research is about collaboration and sharing, we need to ensure that our claim to knowledge or improved practice can stand the test of scrutiny by other critical audiences. One way of enhancing the validity of your findings is to involve other members of the research team in the coding process and to invite members from your community of practice (colleagues, advisers, head teachers) as well as relevant outsiders (steering group, local authority staff, higher education tutors, children's services) to act as 'critical friends'. By inviting a wider audience the analysis and interpretation of data can be re-examined and, if necessary, moderated, thus enhancing the validity of the inquiry. For example, the coding labels and categories used in the analysis of data should be examined from a range of perspectives to ensure that the meaning attached to it by the researcher is shared and understood by others involved in the research. To illustrate the diversity of meanings assigned to a single word by different people, Strauss and Corbin use the example of the word 'red'. While some will associate it with 'bulls, lipstick and blood' in others it might evoke images of 'a favourite dress, a rose, a glamorous sports car, or none of the above' (1998: 60). Within the context of action research McNiff and Whitehead (2010: 195–7) provide a helpful model, which can be transferred to any research concerned with educational issues in practice settings. It presents five types of validation by a critical audience:

- *Self-validation* – evidence in rigorous approach, e.g. triangulation, piloting of tools.
- *Peer validation* – feedback from practitioners in your field.
- *Up-liner validation* – positive evaluation of your research outcomes by those in authority.
- *Client validation* – improvement of service.
- *Academic validation* – feedback from tutor/mentor in higher education.

Finally, refer to the wider academic community at large, against whose theoretical and practical perspectives you can test the validity of the patterns, trends and linkages that you identified in the process of analysing your data in search of further evidence in support of your claims. Make full and extensive use of the literature you have explored to establish a conceptual and empirical basis for your study – now compare your analysis of your findings against it. How do your findings compare with the outcomes that the theoretical literature and the published research led you to expect?

Further reading

Atkins, L. and Wallace, S. (2012) *Qualitative Research in Education*. London: Sage.

Grbich, C. (2013) *Qualitative Data Analysis*, 2nd edn. London: Sage.

Lichtman, M. (2010) *Qualitative Research in Education: A User's Guide*. London: Sage, Chapters 11 and 13.

References

Altrichter, H., Feldman, A., Posch, P. and Somekh, B. (2006) *Teachers Investigating Their Work: An Introduction to Action Research Across the Professions*. London: Routledge.

Barrington, R. (2000) *An Investigation into the Induction Period which Considers the Perspectives of NQTs and Their Induction Tutors*. British Educational Research Association Conference, Cardiff University, September.

Bassey, M. (1999) *Case Study Research in Educational Settings*. Buckingham: Open University Press.

Bryman, A. (1988) *Quantity and Quality in Social Research*. London: Routledge.

Department for Education and Employment (1998) *Standards for the Award of Qualified Teacher Status: High Status, High Standards*, Circular 4/98. London: Teacher Training Agency.

Department for Education and Employment (1999) *The Induction Period of Newly Qualified Teachers*, Circular 5/99. London: Teacher Training Agency.

Elliott, J. (1991) *Action Research for Educational Change*. Buckingham: Open University Press.

Eraut, M. (1994) *Developing Professional Knowledge and Competence*. London: RoutledgeFalmer.

Gray, D. E. (2004) *Doing Research in the Real World*. London: Sage.

Hodkinson, P. and Hodkinson, H. (2003) 'Individuals, communities of practice and the policy context: school teachers' learning in the workplace', *Studies in Continuing Education*, 25 (1): 3–21.

HTDF (History Teachers Discussion Forum) (2004) Online at: www.schoolhistory.co.uk/forum/index.php?showtopic=3105 (accessed 3 August 2007).

Hurd, S., Jones, M., McNamara, O. and Craig, B. (2007) 'Initial Teacher Education as a driver for professional learning and school improvement in the primary phase', *Curriculum Journal*, 18 (3): 307–26.

Jones, M. (2002) 'Qualified to become good teachers: a case study of ten newly qualified teachers during their year of induction', *Journal of In-Service Education*, 28 (3): 509–26.

Jones, M. (2009) 'Supporting the supporters of novice teachers: an analysis of mentors' needs from twelve European countries presented from an English perspective', *Research in Comparative and International Education*, 4 (1): 4–21.

Jones, M. and Straker, K. (2006) 'What informs mentors' practice when working with trainees and newly qualified teachers? An investigation into mentors' professional knowledge base', *Journal of Education for Teaching*, 32 (2): 165–84.

McNiff, J. and Whitehead, J. (2010) *You and Your Action Research Project*, 3rd edn. Abingdon: Routledge.

Punch, K. F. (2009) *Introduction to Research Methods in Education*. London: Sage.

Robson, C. (2002) *Real World Research*, 2nd edn. Oxford: Blackwell.

Strauss, A. and Corbin, J. (1990) *Basics of Qualitative Research. Grounded Theory Procedures and Techniques*. London: Sage.

Strauss, A. and Corbin, J. (1998) *Basics of Qualitative Research*. London: Sage.

Takkashori, A. and Teddlie, C. (2003) *Handbook of Mixed Methodologies in Social and Behavioural Research*. London: Sage.

Tesch, R. (1990) *Qualitative Research Analysis Types and Software Tools*. New York: Falmer Press.

Wolcott, H. F. (1994) *Transforming Qualitative Data: Description, Analysis and Interpretation*. Thousand Oaks, CA: Sage.

CHAPTER 14

QUANTITATIVE DATA ANALYSIS

Beyond the simple presentation of quantitative data, statistical tests can be applied to further confirm the validity and reliability of the findings. Often this takes the form of testing the extent to which the data represents the population as a whole or the extent to which evidence from different sub-populations or collection tools differ or agree. This chapter will concentrate on the key statistical tools available and how and where they might be applied. It must be remembered that the tests are themselves not an outcome but merely a means of instilling confidence in the statements that you make on the basis of the evidence that you present. By the end of this chapter you should be able to:

- identify the most appropriate form of data analysis based on the nature of the data and your research aims;
- organise your data into a format which will enable you to apply the appropriate test;
- comment on the implications of the data analysis outcomes for your research.

Data validity

Assuming that the evidence has been collected from an appropriately representative respondent base, employing an appropriately constructed research tool (i.e. one that uses language and collection formats appropriate to the understanding of the respondents) there are still a number of ways in which the data collection may be flawed (see Punch, 2009: 244 for further details). However, it is important that you are alive to the possibility of collection and transcription errors.

When completing data entry forms, regardless of the clarity and simplicity of the instructions, there is always the possibility of misinterpretation. In the haste to enter data on to an observation schedule evidence may be mis-coded, especially early in the collection process where you, as the researcher, may not be so familiar with either the categories of observations that you have collected or the accurate recording of what you are observing. In this case it is useful to view the complete set of observation schedules to identify any particular changes in the pattern of the data that, on reflection, appears to be unusual or not easily accounted for by the expected changes. Secondly, where respondents are recording evidence for themselves, such as in the form of a questionnaire, the possibility for misunderstanding is increased. This will often become apparent where you have asked for responses on a scale (strongly agree to strongly disagree or order of preference, for example) and the respondent has inadvertently inverted their responses – indicated by their responses to other questions. Here you will need to make a decision on how you deal with this – there are three basic options:

- reject the questionnaire, thus reducing your response rate (the 'spoilt ballot' approach);
- accept the responses as they stand, with the inherent possibility that you are recording responses given in error;
- assume that the error has been made and 'correct' the responses.

The first two may appear harsh but are defensible. The third may appear a 'common sense' approach but does seriously impinge upon the objectivity and accuracy of the evidence base. If the questionnaire is not entirely anonymised there may be the possibility of checking the responses with the respondent to confirm or alter the original data.

Electronic completion of research tools which feed directly into a spreadsheet does mean, assuming that the transfer process has been correctly constructed, that there should be little opportunity for 'human error' to encroach and lead to errors in transcribing data from one format to another. Setting up such systems may take some considerable time and effort initially but this should be 'paid back' when the evidence does not require further collation following collection. If data is to be transcribed from one format to another, it is vitally important that it is thoroughly checked for possible errors before any analysis takes place – although some forms of graphical presentation may well highlight errors that had not previously been noticed.

Representative data

Rather than presenting all of the data that has been collected a single data point can be chosen or calculated as being 'representative' of the whole population, or at least that part of the population that responded.

- *Median* – reduces the impact of outlining points of data that may skew the results (list the data in order of magnitude and identify the mid-point).
- *Mode* – highlights the most popular response (but there may be more than one of them!).
- *Mean* – incorporates all the data, but can be adversely affected by 'outliers' (data points which are very different from the rest – unusually large or small in comparison).

For example, suppose the reading ages of a group of Year 3 children is as shown in Table 14.1. There are three different 'averages': 7.5 (median), 8.2 (mean) and 8.4 (mode). The median is the 7th out of 13 data points (the middle point).

The mean (μ) is calculated as the sum of all the data (x) divided by the number of data points (n). Algebraically: $\mu = (\Sigma x) / n$.

As the researcher and interpreter of the data, it is your responsibility to justify the choice of the 'average' reading age for the group (see Johnson and Christensen, 2008: 472–80) – which version best represents the abilities of the group as a whole?

The potential value of these three representative 'measures' of the data can be explored in more depth if we consider the way that the data may be spread.

Table 14.1   Reading ages of Year 3 children

Reading age	
6.1	
6.1	
6.7	
7.3	
7.3	
7.4	
7.5	**Median**
8.4	
8.4	**Mode**
8.4	
9.2	
11.5	
12.2	**Mean** 8.2

In Figure 14.1 there is a 'normal' distribution – a large proportion of the responses/results in the middle and a tailing off towards each end. This is perhaps what you might expect from a well constructed test with the bulk of the learners receiving grades within the middle of the scale. In such a case as this all three measures of the average, mean, median and mode would all be (very nearly) the same, on or about the vertical line (AA). However, if the data were to be skewed positively, as in Figure 14.2, then there would be clear differences between the mean, median and mode.

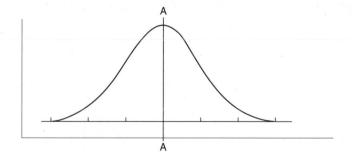

Figure 14.1   'Normal' distribution curve

The mode (AA) would be the lowest of the three measures, followed by the median (BB) and the mean (CC). Typical of this form of data would be the income of staff within a school – with a few highly paid members having a significant impact on the mean pay (CC), whereas, typically, staff

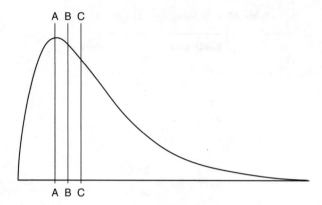

Figure 14.2   Positively skewed normal distribution curve

received a much lower standard of pay (AA). You will need to carefully select the measure which you judge to be most appropriate.

Similarly, with a negatively skewed set of data (Figure 14.3), there are differences between the mean, median and mode, but here they are reversed.

If a school were to have a particularly negative skew to their learners' exam grades, they may wish to use the mode (AA) as the representative grade rather than the mean (CC). However, it must be recognised that 'normal distributions' of data only usually begin to appear with large or very large data sets – more likely with a year group of 200 than a class of 30.

For statistical purposes the mean value for a population is also known as the 'expected' value – in terms of probability, this single figure is taken to be fully representative of the data as a whole.

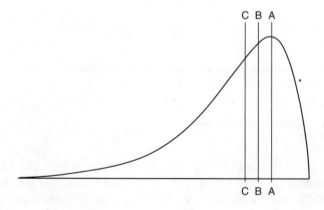

Figure 14.3   Negatively skewed normal distribution curve

Data spread

The spread of the data can be a good indicator of the level of agreement or consistency. For example, for the same 'test', a streamed class (one selected so that all of the learners are of similar ability) is likely to have a much narrower range of marks than a mixed ability class.

- *Range* – simply the largest minus the smallest record (in Table 14.1 this would be 12.2 – 6.1 = a range of 6.1 years). An 'outlier', a point of data far above or below the rest of the data, would have a significant impact on this figure.
- *'Inter-quartile range'* – identifies the range where 50 per cent of the data will lie and is often linked to the median. Whereas the median is the 'middle' data point (with the same number of data points above and below), the upper and lower quartiles are at the ¼ and ¾ points within the data (in the example the inter-quartile range is 7.3 to 8.4 years).
- *Standard deviation* – provides an indication of the spread of the data around the mean, calculated by examining the differences between each data point (x) and the mean (in this case 8.2 years – the mean – plus or minus 1.9 years). For a normally distributed set of data, it would be expected that about 68 per cent of all the data would lie within one standard deviation of the mean. (In this case this would be 9 out of the 13 data points or 69 per cent of the children tested.) The calculation of the standard deviation (σ) is: $\sigma = \sqrt{(\Sigma(x - \mu)^2/n)}$.

In terms of your analysis of the data, the smaller the range, inter-quartile range or the standard deviation of the data, the more the mean or median can be said to accurately reflect the data as a whole. If, for example, you had asked all teaching staff to rate the usefulness of interactive white boards in their classrooms on a 0–10 (poor to good) scale and calculated a mean of 8, then a standard deviation of 1.5 would provided you much greater evidence of consistency of response than a standard deviation of 3. The smaller the measure of the range, the greater the 'clustering' of the data around the mean or median.

A graphic representation of this analysis is the 'box and whiskers', which incorporates the median (vertical line), upper and lower quartiles (box) and the range ('whiskers – horizontal lines) – see Figure 14.4. To complete this diagram, it should lie above a scale which indicates each of these measures.

Figure 14.4   Box and whiskers

Comparative analysis of data

Quantitative data can really begin to have a significant impact on the outcome of a study when opportunities to compare and contrast data from two or more data sets are taken. The five variations below provide an indication of the different forms of comparisons that might be performed.

1. Comparing a sample with a wider population – for example, the test results of a particular group compared with a those of the cohort as a whole as part of a 'snapshot' of performance (see Chapter 1, Figure 1.1).
2. Comparing the same evidence from different groups within the same population – for example, the perceptions of Year 7 and Year 9 pastoral tutors concerning student motivation within a secondary school.
3. Comparing evidence from different sources for the same population – for example, test and teacher assessment grades for a class or their English and maths grades.
4. Comparing evidence from the same source at different points in time – performance or perceptions before and after and intervention as part of an 'impact analysis' (see Chapter 1, Figure 1.2).
5. Comparing empirical evidence with a theoretical 'expectation' – for example, to demonstrate that responses from the population are different from what might be expected randomly.

Comparing data from different population sub-sets

This is a particularly popular use of statistics in educational research. The identification of 'differences' between well defined groups: male and female, different departments, subjects, courses, age groups, and so on. Or, alternatively, between a 'sub-group' and 'the rest of the population', for example those with a particular ethnicity, educational need or position within the educational hierarchy. In the literature on research methodology this is linked to the use of 'null hypotheses' (Cohen et al., 2011; Walliman, 2005) whereby the test will show that there are no 'statistically significant' differences between the evidence from the two sources. By 'statistically significant' we are talking about the differences in the data from the two sources being caused by something more than random chance. Generally, two levels of significance are tested for. A 0.05 level of significance (or 95 per cent level of confidence) means that random chance would only lead to the result 1 in 20 times. The 0.01 level of significance means that it would only have happened by chance 1 in 100 times, i.e. you should be 99 per cent confident that the factor that you had identified has caused the difference. However, for most of these tests there is the inherent assumption that the data is represented by a 'normal distribution' curve (see Figure 14.1) which is not always the case.

The *chi-squared test* compares the extent to which two sub-groups within a population (e.g. male and female) have responded differently to the same questions (e.g. regarding attendance at training sessions – if there are twice as many males as females eligible to attend the session, the expectation would be for there to be twice as many males actually attending if gender is *not* a factor).

The formula for the test is written as:

$$\chi^2 = \sum \frac{(o-e)^2}{e}$$

where:

o = observed result, and
e = expected result

A chi-squared test is used to ask the questions:

1. Is there a relationship in the data between the two variables?
2. How strong is the relationship in the data?
3. What is the direction and shape of the relationship in the data?
4. Is the relationship due to some intervening variable(s) in the data?

For example, consider the question: is the gender balance in the staffing of a secondary school 'fair'? With the generalisation that there will be a greater proportion of men in management roles, is this generalisation reasonable given the data?

To calculate the 'expected' numbers – how many would you expect to be in each category if there was a precisely proportional split, e.g. 21 TAs in total. There are 34 males out of 100 staff (34 per cent); if this same proportion were TAs (34 per cent of 21, the total number of TAs), you would expect to find 7.14 male TAs rather than 3, the actual number. Chi-squared = 9.53 – this means nothing on its own!

Table 14.2   TAs and teacher genders

Gender	TAs	Teachers	Subj. Lead	Fac Head	SMT	Total
Male (obs)	3	17	6	5	3	34
Male (exp)	7.14	16.66	6.12	2.38	1.70	
$(o-e)^2/e$	2.40	0.01	0.00	2.88	0.99	**6.29**
female (obs)	18	32	12	2	2	66
female (exp)	13.86	32.34	11.88	4.62	3.30	
$(o-e)^2/e$	1.24	0.00	0.00	1.49	0.51	**3.24**
Totals	21	49	18	7	5	100
					$\chi^2=$	**9.53**

You need to find the number of 'degrees of freedom' (df) that you are working within. Here we have 5 categories of staff (TAs to SMT) and M/F for each – 10 cells with data in. Putting a line through 1 row and 1 column we are left with 4 cells – 4 df. Using the chi-squared tables (you should be able to find these tables on the Internet – the Wikipedia version is at http://en.wikipedia.org/wiki/Chi-squared_distribution) we can check that the generalisation is only going to be wrong 1 time in 20 (a level of confidence of 0.05). Look down the 0.05 column and across the 4 df row – the figure that you come to is 9.49. The calculated figure is larger than this (just!) so that we can say with 95 per cent confidence that our generalisation is borne out by the data – that there is an 'unfair' balance of males in management positions.

The same approach could be used to test whether there is any significance in the assertion that girls (or any other population sub-group) perform better (or worse!) than the population as a whole, at GCSE, in maths (or any other subject that you have the data for). In mixed-ability teaching groups, do some teachers achieve better results than the rest?

The *Z-test* is used in cases where you wish to compare the evidence from a sub-group of a population to the population as a whole. If you are working in a school with mixed-ability classes, where the performance of all classes, overall, is expected to be the same, the Z-test would provide the opportunity to check this. Using figures for the mean and standard deviation of both the population and the sub-group this test determines the chances of differences between the population and the sub-group being within 'random fluctuations' or actually representing a significant difference.

Box 14.1 Example

If the mean reading age for Year 6 children in a particular town is 11.8 with a standard deviation of 1.2, is a class of 28 children with a mean reading age of 10.9 a simple 'expected random variation' or a significant difference?

The standard error (SE) is calculated as:

(Standard deviation of the population) / (Square root of the sample size) = $1.2 / \sqrt{28} = 0.23$

$Z = $ (Sample mean – Population mean) / SE = $(10.9 - 11.8) / 0.23 = -3.9$

As Z score tables (standard normal table cumulative from the mean) (see http://en.wikipedia.org/wiki/Standard_normal_table) only go to 3.09, we can say with almost certainty that this is a significant difference. However, with the relatively small numbers in the sample, the group could be atypical in the first place!

Comparing data gathered from the same population

Quantitative evidence gathered to explore the performance of a group of learners assessed by different approaches (different tests or different measures), or in different aspects of learning (performance in Maths and English), or changes in performance over time (the same test before and after a learning intervention) is often at the heart of many highly pertinent pieces of teacher research. To ensure that outcomes and recommendations are secure and fully supported by the evidence it is important that the appropriate statistical tests are employed to adequately analyse the data.

Paired student's t-test

A paired student's t-test is the recommended means of analysing the impact of an initiative (see Figure 1.2) through the use of 'before and after' data – test scores, respondent perceptions or other predetermined measures. For each respondent or participant the differences between the pre- and post-initiative scores are recorded and then the mean difference is calculated along with the standard deviation of these differences. These figures, along with the number of respondents, is used to calculate the standard error (SE) (standard deviation / square root of the number of respondents) and t-statistic (mean difference / standard error).

Box 14.2   Example

Table 14.3 indicates the self-perceived motivation levels of 18 students towards PE lessons before and after a self-esteem initiative, with 10 being the highest score possible. Is the improvement significant or just random?

Using the t-distribution table at http://en.wikipedia.org/wiki/Student%27s_t-distribution#Table_of_selected_values to look up 3.96 with 17 degrees of freedom (df) (df = n – 1) shows that you can have 99.9 per cent confidence that the initiative led to an improvement in perceived motivation levels.

While the mean difference is 2.2, what is the true difference likely to be? If we want to be 95 per cent confident of where the true mean lies we need to look up the t-value for 17 df at 95 per cent (2 sided to give the +/– values) which is 2.11.

Table 14.3 Students' perceived level of motivation before and after initiative

Before	After	Difference
4	7	3
3	7	4
4	9	5
7	10	3
4	3	−1
6	9	3
5	9	4
2	8	6
6	6	0
5	8	3
8	6	−2
4	7	3
3	4	1
4	7	3
5	2	−3
4	6	2
6	10	4
6	8	2
	Mean	2.22
	Std Dev	2.39

$$\text{T-statistic} = 2.22 / (2.39 / \sqrt{18}) = 3.96$$

The 'true' mean is the calculated mean +/− t-value multiplied by SE. In this case:

$$2.22 +/- (2.11 * 0.56) = +/-1.2$$

so you can be 95 per cent confident that the true mean difference lies between 1 and 3.4.

Pearson's (product moment) correlation coefficient

Pearson's (product moment) correlation coefficient is a relatively simple and reliable means of analysing your data set for linear relationships. Punch (2009) rightly suggests that it is the 'most important' (p. 270) means of assessing the nature of any correlation between variables. The coefficient can vary between 1 (a perfect positive correlation – an increases in one variable is precisely matched by an increase in the other) to −1 (a perfect negative correlation – an

Table 14.4 Teaching assistant (x) and exam (y)

student	teaching ass'nt (x)	exam (y)	x*y	x^2	y^2
A	8	7	56	64	49
B	15	8	120	225	64
C	13	14	182	169	196
D	11	11	121	121	121
E	11	6	66	121	36
F	9	9	81	81	81
G	5	8	40	25	64
H	7	10	70	49	100
I	11	9	99	121	81
J	12	9	108	144	81
K	8	9	72	64	81
L	10	11	110	100	121
M	10	11	110	100	121
N	11	8	88	121	64
O	7	8	56	49	64
P	9	7	63	81	49
Q	7	5	35	49	25
R	6	5	30	36	25
S	6	6	36	36	36
T	13	13	169	169	169
Totals	189	174	1712	1925	1628

increase in one variable is precisely matched by a decrease in the other). As the coefficient falls towards zero the relationship between the variables becomes less strong to become completely random at 0.

Taking the data first presented in Table 12.2, the basic calculations can be performed as shown in Table 14.4.

Using most versions of Microsoft Excel the whole task is made very easy using the Pearson function (typing '=pearson(' into a cell, selecting the two columns of data (x and y) individually before closing the brackets')' and hitting the return key – for example '=pearson(B2:21,C2:21)' using Table 14.4), but here we will provide the formula to be applied.

$$r = (n(\Sigma xy) - (\Sigma x)(\Sigma y)) / \sqrt{((n\Sigma x^2 - (\Sigma x)^2)(n\Sigma y^2 - (\Sigma y)^2))}$$

where n is the number of pairs of data for x and y.
Inserting the data from Table 14.4:

$$r = (20 * 1712 - 189 * 174) / \sqrt{((20 * 1925 - 189^2)}$$
$$(20 * 1628 - 174^2)) = 0.537$$

which represents a moderately acceptable positive correlation – teacher assessments are confirmed by (or at least consistent with) the exam.

If this test were to be performed for a number of classes, it might be possible to discover which teachers most accurately assessed their learners, i.e. which had the highest Pearson correlation coefficient.

Comparing ranked data

Spearman's rank

Spearman's rank compares the extent to which two sub-groups of a population rank the same list of criteria differently, or the correlation between the rankings of two separate lists by the same population. If the data used above in the example for Pearson's were to be placed in rank order then Spearman could be used instead:

$$\rho = 1 - \frac{6 \sum d_i^2}{n(n^2 - 1)}$$

where:

d_i = the difference between each rank of corresponding values of the two populations, and

n = the number of pairs of values.

Box 14.3   Example

Teachers and students rank the key features of a successful lesson: 1 = most important; 8 = least (see Table 14.5).

The closer to 1 is ρ, the closer the correlation between the rankings of the two groups. The closer ρ is to 0 the less correlation there is and the closer to -1 then the correlation is negative – in the example the teachers and the students would rank the features in the exact opposite order! In Table 14.5,

Table 14.5   Teachers and students difference

Features	Teachers	Students	difference^2		
enthusiasm	5	1	16		
well planned	2	5	9		
good resources	6	6	0		
effective assessment	4	8	16	$\rho=$	0.095238
practical activities	7	2	25		
clear objectives	1	4	9		
good discipline	3	3	0		
linked to other work		$\sum d^2$	76		

$\rho = 0.095$, very close to zero, suggesting that there is little correlation between the lists of the teachers and the students.

Table 14.6 compares rankings following performance in Maths and PE assessments – can KS3 Maths SATs be used to predict KS4 PE performance? There is general agreement, in the 'statistical analysis community', that a correlation coefficient between zero and 0.3 (positive or negative) is an indication that no relationship exists and a very strong relationship between 0.8 and 1 (positive) or –0.8 and –1 (negative). A coefficient of 0.3 would therefore be regarded as very weak, progressing in strength as it nears 0.8. In this particular case the relationship exists and is positive, but is not very strong so that the students' ranking in Maths is unlikely to be a particularly robust indicator or their competence in PE.

Table 14.6 Maths and PE difference

Students	Maths	PE	difference^2	
A	1	1	0	
B	2	5	9	
C	6	6	0	
D	4	8	16	$\rho=0.380952$
E	7	2	25	
F	5	4	1	
G	3	3	0	
H	8	7	1	
		Σd^2	52	

Summary

It is important to note that not all data neatly fits the normal distribution curve which is the foundation of much of the statistical analysis based upon probability and confidence levels. For most of these tests a significant amount of data is required in the first place and then you need to check the shape of the distribution before you can confidently begin to apply z- and t-tests. There is a range of tests for other distributions but this would be needlessly detailed for your purposes at this level of research with a relatively small-scale study. In most cases of comparative data analysis Pearson and chi-squared should provide what you need:

- Pearson – same population, different data;
- chi-squared – different sub-groups, same data.

Even with all of these tests for significance, you must remember that the data needs to be interpreted, explained and placed into context. Simply stating that the test shows that the relationship is unlikely to be the result of pure chance is really only a rather minor part of the process – do not become too obsessed by the statistics to the exclusion of the deeper analysis of the evidence.

More is not always better – ensure that the evidence that you do provide is presented clearly and in sufficient detail, but does not overload the audience with too much information. Succinct is good, dense is not.

References

Cohen, L., Manion, L. and Morrison, K. (2011) *Research Methods in Education*, 7th edn. Abingdon: Routledge.

Johnson, B. and Christensen, L. (2008) *Educational Research: Quantitative, Qualitative and Mixed Approaches*, 3rd edn. Thousand Oaks, CA: Sage.

Punch, K. (2009) *An Introduction to Research Methods in Education*. London: Sage.

Thomas, R. (2003) *Blending Qualitative and Quantitative Research Methods in Theses and Dissertations*. Thousand Oaks, CA: Corwin Press.

Walliman, N. (2005) *Your Research Project*. London: Sage.

CHAPTER 15

DRAWING CONCLUSIONS AND MAKING RECOMMENDATIONS

This chapter will focus on reiterating the ways in which a research topic can be conceptualised, developed and reported in order to ensure a lucid, comprehensible and unambiguous final research outcome and recommendations while differing approaches to structuring research reports, including dissertations and theses, will be explored. Central to this argument will be the concept that researchers should, from the outset of a project, analyse how they intend to develop the overall structure of their investigation. They should develop a simple 'map' of the project that includes overall structure and substructure – ideally discussions with colleagues or supervisor will pay dividends. The chapter will also seek to connect the outputs of research with school development and improvement through

(Continued)

(Continued)

target-setting and strategy enhancement. Specifically, by the end of this chapter you should be able to:

- appreciate the need to maintain consistency between the purposes and the outcomes of the research;
- understand the importance of using the research outcomes and the conceptual literature to determine a future course of action;
- be aware of the strengths and weaknesses of the research that has been performed.

Writing research reports – the importance of structure

Throughout this text we have recommended a rational approach to research which has emphasised the identification of researchable problems, the creation of clear research questions and associated aims, and the construction of a research methodology designed to address the research topic in the most productive way. This rational process extends to the final outputs of the research project since clear problems and carefully crafted aims can, ideally at least, lead in to a seamless research report. The construction of an appropriate structure for a research project is vital from the outset because it facilitates:

- clarity in the research conceptualisation;
- simplicity in the research process;
- ease in analysis of data;
- structural integrity in the final thesis.

With these aspects in mind it is useful to reiterate some of the key points made throughout this text. As has been argued in Chapters 2 and 3, a researcher should try to define, both contextually and conceptually, the research issue, question or overall aim as precisely as possible and in such a way that it cannot be subject to unintended ambiguity. Consequent research sub-questions or research aims should be crafted so as to have equal clarity and be answerable with the resources that are available and through the methods that the researcher intends to adopt. Too many sub-questions may create unforeseen complexity and cause the research to spiral out of control (about four or five is ideal).

Chapters 7 to 10 outlined the best ways to construct research instruments such as questionnaires and interview schedules by emphasising the use of questions that reflect and investigate the research issues stated at the outset of the project. Ideally, these research tools should be structured so that each section of the research tool investigates only one of the research aims (except in the case of certain complex questionnaires where analytical techniques require a complex structure of questions). If employing a blended approach, it is often sensible to use the same order for questions in both surveys and interviews in order to facilitate easy analysis of the data. Chapters 11 to 14 explored in detail some of the many ways of presenting and analysing data, one of the most common of which is the use of a 'stem and branch' analysis that reflects the research aims and the research sub-questions.

This approach will assist in the final writing of the research report since all of the elements of this logical approach will feed into your account of what happened in the process of research, from the defining of the focus, through the justification for the approach to gathering evidence to the analysis and presentation of the outcomes. Such reports can be complex and challenging to write because they contain within them a number of ambiguities and contradictions. A writer needs to tell the 'story' of the research in a way which engages readers but the report must be analytical in nature; the study should help to create new understandings and create new knowledge but it should also synthesise previous research findings and theoretical perspectives. You need to show that you have a mastery not only of the theory but also the practical implications of the findings – the actions you intend to take as a result of your new knowledge and understanding of the situation. However, the paramount challenge is often the necessity to provide a sense of 'narrative flow' while ensuring structural integrity within the work. This may be achieved by following the standard structure of most dissertations, theses and reports in the field of educational research:

- abstract;
- introduction;
- literature review;
- methodology;
- data presentation and analysis of findings;
- conclusion;
- references;
- appendices.

The conclusion can then be appreciated as one of the critical sections of the report in that it should:

- reiterate the overall topic and the reasons for the investigation;
- state the key findings;
- outline practical actions resulting from the study (usually in the form of a prioritised action plan);
- present or represent any 'model' or 'models' that may have been developed;

- suggest any further research that might be pursued;
- outline any inadequacies in the research;
- provide a final statement that may indicate the importance and originality of the research and its potential 'impact' on wider practice.

Drawing conclusions

It is essential that consistency is maintained with the original aims of the research. In effect this means that the initial research questions should be responded to and addressed in terms of the key findings that the analysis of the evidence has revealed linked to relevant references back to the conceptual literature and published research findings.

This section provides an ideal opportunity to highlight the consistencies (and inconsistencies!) between the findings from this study and previous studies within this field. Consistencies can be used to reinforce the position that you take and the recommendations that you make. However, where differences are apparent between these findings and past studies, it is important that while acknowledging these, you should also attempt to seek potential explanations for them. Often the sources of these differences will be found in the context – outcomes from your study can usually be accounted for by differences in educational environment (national school systems, pupil age, school size, nature of the student intake, cultural differences) so that the reliability and validity of your findings can be justified.

As this is the section that a line manager or tutor will often turn to first, it is crucial that the key findings are expressed clearly and the lines of evidence that are being used to justify them are made explicit. Conclusions are not the place for you, the researcher, to express your own opinions independent of the evidence, but the opportunity for you to demonstrate how your thinking has been informed by the study. In the worst cases we do see conclusions that appear to have been plucked out of the air, making the presentation and analysis of evidence and reading that has preceded it absolutely irrelevant – avoid this at all costs! Ideally, it should be possible for the reader of your conclusions to track each of the points that have been highlighted back through the analysis and presentation of the evidence to its collection and, further, to the links to the literature and to the initial research questions and the contextual impetus for the study.

Making recommendations

This is your opportunity to say 'as a result of my study, this is what should happen next'. The key point to focus on is *as a result of my study*. The recommendations must be an appropriate progression emanating from the key findings, justified by both the context and the literature that has been used to support the development of the study. The literature will often supply excellent advice and guidance on potential strategies to progress from where you currently find yourself. Conceptual models that you will have examined in the literature review should provide an indication of the direction that should be taken. Alternatively, or additionally, past research in the field will also provide an indication of how other researchers have responded to similar outcomes.

In an academic context, the recommendations will probably indicate further avenues of study. The main options to consider would be:

- replication of the study in a different context to ascertain how widely applicable the findings are;
- repetition of the study within the same research context to overcome identified flaws in methodology or selection of sources of evidence;
- repetition of the study within the same research context but adopting a different methodology or drawing on alternative sources of evidence in order to reinforce the validity of the findings.

There is an extended discussion of the setting of professional recommendations below.

Professional reports to non-specialist audiences

You, as the practitioner researcher, may wish, or be required, to provide a report to a non-specialist audience such as a school governing body, governors' subcommittee, parents committee, client group, patient organisation or the like. With such an audience the conventions of structure that underpin the more formal method of report writing embodied in a dissertation or thesis may be modified to take account of the level of expertise of the professional discourse of the researcher. Inevitably such reports are likely to be much shorter than a thesis or report to a funding agency and may only contain a few hundred words. Detail may be left out in an attempt to convey key findings, references may be excluded altogether and much of the complex reasoning that goes into a methodology section may be deemed inappropriate. Nonetheless, it is important not to patronise such an audience, and the same essential structure of context, main aims, previous perspective, main approach to the research and main findings can be used to powerful and persuasive effect. One simple method of conveying central messages swiftly is to provide an *executive summary* in the form of a few main bullet points at the start of the report. This approach, often combined with a very clear set of *conclusions and recommendations* can be very effective in leading agreement on changes in practice.

> ## Box 15.1   Ask yourself ...
>
> - What is the audience for my report? Is this a professional audience or a group of stakeholders who may not have specialist knowledge? Have I targeted my report accordingly?
> - Is the structure of my report correct?
> - Have I taken account of the appropriate conventions for report writing for my audience?
> - Is the presentation of my report as clear as it can be?

Using research outcomes to inform practice

Burton and Brundrett (2005) draw on the work of Fullan (1993, 1999, 2003) to argue that the increasingly diverse nature of societies, the revolution in communications technologies, and new attitudes to learning have ensured that complexity and change are an unavoidable part of life in schools. In recent years teachers have become expert at development planning and strategic management can be seen as an attempt to insert a rational model into the frequently disordered and fluctuating circumstances that schools find themselves in (Morrison, 1998: 13). If such change does not lead to sustained improvement that helps pupils and staff, the innovation has not only failed in its targets and goals, it has also cause a great deal of distress for no reason. The best models of change integrate these issues of complexity, moral purpose and the need for sustained and embedded improvement by suggesting that organisational change in schools is based on a number of key factors that echo throughout this text and include engagement of parents and community resources, access to new ideas, professional community, internalising responsibility for change and strategic educational planning (Bryk et al., quoted in Fullan, 1999: 35). Practitioner research can provide a formidable toolkit for analysing the complex social situations that obtain in classrooms in order to influence school strategy and target-setting.

As a general working definition it can be seen as 'the broad overall direction that an organization wishes to move in' (Fidler, 2002: 9). In this sense strategy can been as the *big picture* or the *long-term set of goals* for a school. We must also remember that any good strategy 'involves the whole organization in a holistic way' (Fidler, 2002: 9) and so, quite simply, if a strategy is to be effective, then it must encourage the involvement of as many people as possible so that they have a sense of ownership and will want to take the strategy forward rather than fighting against it or ignoring its most salient points. It has been argued that strategy development can be seen as a 'conveyor belt with short-term plans working their way through and then dropping off the end of priorities or translating themselves into the completion of one element of longer-term planning' (Fidler, 2002: 11). Burton and Brundrett (2005) draw on the work of Davies and Davies (2005: 13) to suggest a four-stage 'ABCD' approach to translating strategy into action:

- *Articulate* Strategy
- *Build* Images, Metaphors, Experience
- *Create* Dialogues (conversations), Cognitive/ mental map, Shared understanding
- *Define* Strategic perspective, Outcome orientation, Formal plans.

(Davies and Davies, 2005: 204)

As Brundrett and Terrell (2004) point out, the key point to keep in mind about this process is that it should *not* simply be a bureaucratic exercise. If it is managed well it is a means of ensuring that the actual process of accountability is systematised and ordered. Development planning is now well established in schools and subject leaders, as the school's middle managers, have a pivotal role to play in its construction and implementation. The key to its success is the extent to which it provides a clear sense of direction which everyone in the subject and senior management team can follow and understand. The standard structure and organisation for what has become known as the planning cycle involves the following key stages: *audit, vision, construction, implementation* and *evaluation*. This cyclical process helps to provide practitioners with answers to several important questions, including:

- Where are we now? (*audit*)
- Where do we want the developing subject/department to be in five years' time? (*vision*)
- What changes to we need to make? (*construction*)
- How shall we manage these changes? (*implementation*)
- How shall we know whether our management of change has been successful? (*evaluation*)

This cycle has close associations with the school improvement model that is outlined below and with the action research model outlined in Chapter 10. The DfES *Guidance for LEAs on Target Setting at Key Stages 2, 3 and 4 for School Attendance* (2004: 2) outlines a number of key principles for school performance targets and suggests that school targets should be:

- based on the prior attainment and expected progress of individual children in each cohort;
- ambitious;
- focused on equity as well as excellence;
- owned.

The notion of benchmarked and ambitious targets accords with the thrust of all the policy on targets in recent years but the focus on equity and ownership is an interesting and new emphasis. The desire for equity came about because improvements in pupil attainment had not been spread evenly across all groups of pupils. This marks an acceptance of the notion that has been prevalent in school effectiveness and improvement circles that in-school differences may actually be more significant than between-school differences. The concept of ownership reflects much of the recent thrust on schools as learning organisations and may be one further indicator of a national acceptance of recent theories of distributed leadership and management. It is notable that this should be:

> A whole-school approach to target-setting, which involves not just head teachers and leadership teams, but also class teachers and, where appropriate, teaching assistants, will ensure that the process is fully informed and rigorous. (DfES, 2004: 3)

This inclusion of teaching assistants no doubt indicates the complex and challenging focus on workforce remodelling. Since such activities operate at the complex level of the individual classroom it is only through the sponsorship of the systematic exploration of personal practice that schools can hope to deliver on such laudable aims.

The DfEE (2001) *Supporting the Target Setting Process* suggests that schools should adopt a policy of target setting within a cycle of school self-improvement as part of a systematic approach to raising standards of pupil achievement. It is suggested that in most schools, Key Stages and expected National Curriculum levels are suitable timescales and measures for use in setting such targets – although these timelines may need to be amended for pupils with special needs. 'Targeting for improvement in this way serves as a focus for action planning, and as a basis for defining success criteria when monitoring and evaluating the effectiveness of the actions that the school has implemented' (DfEE, 2001: 6). The document suggests a five-stage cycle of self-improvement as represented in Box 15.2 below.

Box 15.2   Cycle of self-improvement

Step 1: How well are we doing?

Teachers assess what pupils have achieved in relation to the curriculum taught, where possible and appropriate benchmarked against other, similar groups of pupils from within the school, either in the past or present. In most schools, National Curriculum level descriptions set the standards to use in English, Mathematics and Science, and pupils' performances at the end of a Key Stage are appropriate as measures of the school's overall state of development. Schools may also consider some pupils' achievements in terms of their acquisition of independence skills based on judgements about the frequency of teacher interventions necessary during their learning. The challenge for schools is to identify the kinds of performance information that are available to show what their pupils are achieving and about which such questions can be asked. For those schools concerned about levels of attainment it may be important to first take stock of how pupils' performance is assessed throughout the school and to consider the overall quality of the school's assessment criteria, data collection systems, and record keeping (DfEE, 2001: 7).

Step 2: How do we compare with similar schools?

Teachers consider how well the school is doing, shown by its pupils' achievements, in the wider context of the performances achieved by similar pupils in other schools. Local and national benchmark information should enable like for like comparisons to be made. The performance criteria used in the national benchmark information is the proportion of pupils achieving the expected National Curriculum level, or better, at the end of Key Stages 1, 2 and 3, and GCSE grades and GCSE/GNVQ points scores at the end of Key Stage 4. This information may stimulate key questions such as: 'How do those better performing schools achieve what they do?' and 'What can we learn from those schools to raise the standards of achievement of our own pupils?' (DfEE, 2001: 9).

Step 3: What more should we aim to achieve this year?

Targets are set to drive school improvement and provide impetus and challenge complacency. Statutory targets apply to all schools but all schools can set additional targets that reflect relevant priorities. These additional targets can also be published alongside statutory targets in the school's annual governors' report to parents (DfEE, 2001: 12). To be effective, targets for school improvement, statutory or otherwise, need to be *SMART* targets. This means they should be *Specific, Measurable, Achievable* and *Realistic*, and set against an appropriate *Timescale*. SMART targets will be measurable and reflect the criteria used for measuring pupil performance. Teachers make judgements about translating practice into gains in pupils' performances in the future by deciding what more pupils will achieve when more successful teaching practices are implemented, over and above what they

(Continued)

(Continued)

would be expected to achieve given current teaching practice. These outcomes are the school's measurable targets (DfEE, 2001: 13).

Steps 4 and 5: Taking action

Having analysed the school's performance and set targets for school improvement, schools move from reviewing performance to taking action. Thus the shared and agreed picture of the school's performance and clear targets for improvement turn to action planning. Action plans identify what is needed to achieve the targets, including the important changes that need implementing and how the action plan is to be supported with resources and staff development. Taking action may involve 'process targets', such as improving accommodation or integration opportunities which will contribute to the school's ability to meet its performance targets. It is important to put in place effective strategies to monitor and evaluate gains in pupils' performance as the new teaching practices take effect (DfEE, 2001: 17).

Source: Burton and Brundrett (2005).

Such target-setting is increasingly informed by the use of national data that is progressively becoming accessible to senior managers and teachers. Practitioner research can serve to unpack the issues that may be identified in comparative data, may serve to challenge the presumed causations of perceived school inadequacies, may identify unforeseen issues and may suggest means to remediate and overcome inadequacies in a wide range of areas such a approaches to learning and teaching, leadership and management structures, or relationships with the community of stakeholders. All of this will only be achieved if the research that is carried out meets a perceived need, is rigorous in approach and is persuasive in reporting.

Box 15.3   Ask yourself …

- Who are the key stakeholders that my research needs to be communicated to?
- Have I met the needs of that audience?
- What are the target-setting and strategic implications of my work?
- How can my research findings be fed into the development cycle of my organisation?

Converting recommendations to actions

In the professional context it is always important to ensure that the recommendations that are being made, in additional to being appropriate and applicable, are also within the realms of achievability. This is particularly the case if you are promoting change as a key recommendation of your study. When setting priorities for change within your recommendations the context in which these changes are to be implemented must be considered. Essentially it is a balance between effort, impact and timescale. In an ideal situation you should be able to highlight recommendations which lead to actions which require a minimum of effort to implement but maximise impact within a relatively short timescale. Clearly, this ideal is unlikely to be achieved for all the recommendations that you consider making. Therefore it would be wise to prioritise the recommendations and also to collate them so that those that can be delivered through a combined action or that will at least benefit from being implemented concurrently are able to be identified.

Review the recommendations that you are making and consider how the actions may be prioritised to ensure that early gains can be achieved relatively easily so that more challenging changes can then be approached with greater confidence and enthusiasm. As with all initiatives there will come a point of diminishing returns – where the effort and time that need to be exerted do not appear to be 'worth' the benefits the change brings. Indeed, there is a distinct benefit in drawing up a table in order to compare and contrast, for example, the professional applicability of the various recommendations that have been made.

Using a 0–10 scale for each of the categories in the form suggested in Table 15.1 will result in an 'ideal' recommendation being given a score of 30 (little effort, short timescale and maximum impact). Clearly such a comparison will be purely subjective but it will require you to make a consideration of these important factors.

If an action plan is an expectation of the recommendations then it would be wise to further reinforce the justification for the proposed developments by both identifying the evidence that has been presented in support within the study and also, where possible and appropriate, making reference to other initiatives also being implemented within the context. If it is possible to

Table 15.1 Comparing recommendations for implementation

Recommendation	Effort (10 little; 0 lot)	Timescale (10 short; 0 long)	Impact (10 lots; 0 none)	Total score

demonstrate where complementary links occur with existing initiatives then this will provide further, external, validation for the outcomes of the study.

Conclusion

The influential work of academic commentators such as Hopkins (1985) has established the powerful role of practitioner research in school effectiveness and improvement. It can be argued that government agencies could do more to sponsor research activity in schools and may tend to have a narrow and somewhat positivist view of research but there is strong evidence that there is an increasing willingness to support the notion of teaching as an evidence-based profession (Burton and Brundrett, 2005: 182). Throughout this text we have argued that by establishing the links between the teaching and research processes, practitioners will be able to more effectively develop the skills and attributes that underpin the highest quality teaching and learning.

Many professions have become increasingly technical and technicist in recent decades and there are many who fear a loss of autonomy among practitioners who are progressively more subject to national directives and strategies designed to enhance effectiveness. Practitioner research, if carried out with vigour, confidence, proficiency and skill, can enable the professional to recapture ownership of vital elements of school life. Such research provides a set of analytical tools that can inform, and indeed transform, learning and teaching and enhance school effectiveness so that outcomes are improved and teachers feel more confident about their continued centrality and creativity in the learning process.

This text set out to provide an examination of the need to relate research to personal professional development. The overriding aim that underpins this conception is to engage with new ideas and research findings by testing new practices and evaluating curriculum change through enhanced and formalised reflection. To this end we have attempted to assist the practitioner to understand how research can be used to inform and improve practice, the value of embedding and evaluating initiatives, and an appreciation the value of the processes of educational research to the school practitioner.

Research projects and project reports should be clear, well-structured pieces of work that 'hold together' well. There are, however, several factors that militate against the researcher achieving such structural integrity in their work:

- Practitioner research study is often undertaken in a fractured, interrupted manner.
- The conceptual focus of the study, as presented in the literature review, may be wide-ranging and therefore seem diffuse.

- The methodology may adopt an integrative stance that employs blended approaches to research that may be perceived as evaluative rather than pure research.
- The data derived from different research tools or different cases may seem problematic to assimilate and articulate.
- It can be difficult to integrate the different elements of conceptual statement, review, methodology and analysis.

However, all research activity will have its limitations, but what you will have, as a practitioner, is a deeper, more thorough understanding and appreciation of the issue under study and with that will come the confidence to take control and make (the right and justified) decisions.

References

Brundrett, M. and Terrell, I. (eds) (2004) *Learning to Lead in the Secondary School: Becoming an Effective Head of Department.* London: RoutledgeFalmer.

Burton, N. and Brundrett, M. (2005) *Leading the Curriculum in the Primary School.* London: Sage.

Davies, B. and Davies, B. (2005) 'Strategic leadership', in B. Davies (ed.), *The Essentials of School Leadership.* London: Paul Chapman, pp. 10–30.

Davies, B. and Ellison, L. (2003) *The New Strategic Direction and Development of the School,* 2nd edn. London: RoutledgeFalmer.

DfEE (2001) *Supporting the Target Setting Process.* London: HMSO.

DfES (2004) *Guidance for LEAs on Target Setting at Key Stages 2, 3 and 4 for School Attendance.* London: HMSO.

Fidler, B. (2002) *Strategic Management for School Development: Leading Your School's Improvement Strategy.* London: British Educational Leadership, Management and Administration Society/Paul Chapman.

Fullan, M. (1993) *Change Forces: Probing the Depths of Educational Reform.* London: Falmer Press.

Fullan, M. (1999) *Change Forces: The Sequel.* London: Falmer Press.

Fullan, M. (2001) *The New Meaning of Educational Change.* London: RoutledgeFalmer.

Fullan, M. (2003) *Change Forces with a Vengeance.* London: RoutledgeFalmer.

Hopkins, D. (1985) *A Teacher's Guide to Classroom Research.* Milton Keynes: Open University Press.

Morrison, K. (1998) *Management Theories for Educational Change.* London: Paul Chapman.

INDEX